BOHEMIAN GIRL

· ·

BLANCHE YURKA'S THEATRICAL LIFE

OHIO UNIVERSITY PRESS

ATHENS

Copyright © 1970 by Blanche Yurka
Library of Congress Catalog Card Number: 79–81449
SBN 8214–0071–1
All rights reserved.
Printed in the United States of America.

Text designed by Edgar Frank

To
Mila,
Marchette & Maria

PREFACE

W HEN I BEGAN this book in Hollywood some years ago I had little notion of what was in store for me. I foresaw neither the pain nor the pleasure that reliving my life would bring me.

For over sixty years, since my first appearance in Balfe's *The Bohemian Girl*, until now, having played the title role of *The Madwoman of Chaillot* in London, acting has been my chief passion. As a professional actress I have had my share of false hopes and disappointments: but I have also had moments of great fulfillment such as few other professions are capable of giving. Nor have these moments necessarily come when I was playing a great role on Broadway. Often they have come in the warm response of a small-town audience in some out-of-the-way place where I performed alone, on a bare stage, without props or costumes.

It has been my good fortune to know and work with some of the most distinguished people of the theatre: John Barrymore, Katharine Cornell, Lynn Fontanne and Alfred Lunt, Mrs. Patrick Campbell, Maxine Elliott, and Jane Cowl. I have also known, as beginners, players whose names later became household words: Mary Pickford, Katharine Hepburn, Bette Davis and Fredric March. I have worked with producers whose names are legendary in the American theatre. From all I have learned something.

Apart from the world of the theatre I have also known the world of music, in which my professional training began. The inspiration of working with Leopold Stokowski, then at the beginning of his career, carried through into my work as an actress. My chief hobby has been travel, and in my travels I was privileged to meet some of the great figures of the theatre in other countries: I can never forget my meeting with Constantin Stanislavski in Russia and with George Bernard Shaw in England.

In these pages I have set down my impressions of the persons, places, and events that have made up my life. I have summoned up my family and friends and some of the joyous and tragic moments we shared. To the reader eager for recorded dates, I must confess to a certain vagueness about such matters. But after so many years on Broadway one may perhaps be pardoned for not always having kept track of the exact moment of this or that opening.

Though I have known my share of tragedy and disappointments, I can truly say that I have never known boredom. I hope that the same will be true of the readers of this book.

BLANCHE YURKA

CONTENTS

	Preface	vii
	Illustrations	xi
1.	Sunday's Child	3
2.	My First Audience	10
3.	Farewell to Song	20
4.	Belasco Opens the Door	33
5.	Name in Lights	48
6.	*Daybreak*	61
7.	I Discover Ibsen	78
8.	"My Mildly Incestuous Son"	94
9.	Heartbreak	105
10.	*The Squall*	114
11.	Alhambra by Moonlight	130
12.	Three Highspots	137
13.	Yoga Pays Off	164
14.	A Dip in the Isis	177
15.	A Russian Diary	188
16.	London Interlude	209
17.	Mme. Defarge Arrives in Hollywood	215
18.	"If You Think You're Good, Try Saginaw!"	227
19.	*Electra* Reborn	241
20.	All Czechs Weep	252
21.	Small Beer	261
22.	Playing a Heifer	272
23.	Christmas in Another Athens	284
24.	Wish Me Well	290
	Afterword	301
	Index	303

ILLUSTRATIONS

Facing title page
Blanche Yurka as Gina in *The Wild Duck*

Following page 84
Blanche Yurka's birthplace
"Maminka"
Blanche Yurka, 1889
Tony, Blanche, Mila and Rose Yurka
Charlie Yurka
"Tatinek"
Blanche Yurka in *A Bohemian Girl*
Blanche Yurka in *A Bohemian Girl*
Blanche Yurka as a flower maiden in the first production of *Parsifal* at the Metropolitan Opera House
Rudolph Schirmer
Mila Yurka
Leopold Stokowski, choirmaster at St. Bartholomew's Church, New York
David Belasco
Mary Pickford as Betty in Belasco's production of *The Warrens of Virginia*
Blanche Yurka in her plum-colored duvetyn suit and broad beaver hat. This outfit became her "job-hunting" uniform
Blanche Yurka in *Lord Dundreary,* in the original cos-

tume worn by Laura Keene at the Ford Theatre the night Lincoln was shot

Blanche Yurka in *Daybreak*

Jane Cowl

During a pensive moment

Blanche Yurka as The Woman in *Man and the Masses*

Blanche Yurka as Gina and Helen Chandler as Hedvig in the Actors' Theatre production of *The Wild Duck*

Following page 212

Blanche Yurka in *The Lawmakers*

Ian Keith

Blanche Yurka at the time of her marriage

Reproduction of John Singer Sargent's drawing of John Barrymore as Hamlet inscribed to Blanche Yurka, "To my mother with much love from her wildly incestuous son—John Barrymore—"

Blanche Yurka as Gertrude and John Barrymore as Hamlet

Alfred Lunt

Lynne Fontanne

Blanche Yurka in the Theatre Guild's production of *Goat Song*

Blanche Yurka as Dolores in *The Squall*

Blanche Yurka in her Paris dress: "The prettiest dress I've ever owned."

Robert Loraine and Blanche Yurka as the narrators in *Lucrece*

Blanche Yurka after visiting Elizabeth Arden's Salon

Blanche Yurka as the Nurse in *Romeo and Juliet*

Blanche Yurka as Mme Defarge in the Tribunal scene from the film version of *A Tale of Two Cities*

Mme Defarge/Blanche Yurka—"A Tale of Two Faces"

Blanche Yurka with Frank Lloyd Wright

Edith Hamilton

Blanche Yurka as Mrs. Wendel in the New York revival of *Dinner at Eight*

Blanche Yurka

BOHEMIAN GIRL

CHAPTER 1

SUNDAY'S CHILD

I WAS BORN IN a great hurry one bright Sunday morning in June, 1887, in St. Paul, Minnesota, arriving so precipitously that there was not even time to send for the midwife who usually presided on these occasions in modest households such as ours. Being born on Sunday is said to be lucky!

Both my father and mother had originally come from Czechoslovakia, which in those days was called Bohemia. Mother (we called her Maminka) was eight when her family brought their thirteen children to America and settled in Chicago, where there was a large Czech colony. Willa Cather has drawn a loving portrait of such Czech settlers in *My Ántonia,* and whenever I reread that book I can almost smell the familiar fragrance of baking that permeated our home in St. Paul, Minnesota, on Saturday afternoons.

As soon as they were settled, mother entered public school. Learning English is never easy for a Czech, and when (after she had been struggling with the language for four years) some classmates shouted Bohunk at her once too often, the proud, sensitive little girl closed her books, walked home, and announced that she was never going back, she was going to work.

There were no child-labor laws at that time, and the four or five dollars she would earn would help the family in their struggle to survive in this strange new country, so apparently no effort was made to stop her. She found a job in a fur shop.

When I was an adolescent and already imbued with a great passion for words, I was troubled by my mother's lack of educa-

3

tion in English. She would accept my efforts to correct her with gentle grace, but she never did master this verbal devil, English.

Yet, she was well-read in her own culture. Bohemia was then part of the Austro-Hungarian Empire, and mother knew both German and Czech. She had read Schiller and Goethe in the original and was familiar with most of the best Czech authors. I am constantly surprised at the interest shown in fine literature by Czechs of quite simple origin. Many years later, when I acted in *The Wild Duck,* our general houseworker, a charwoman really, startled me when I gave her tickets for the play. "I will tell you the story so that you can understand what is happening," I said to her (she spoke no English). "Oh no, Miss Blanche," she replied, "I read a Czech translation in the Czech library when you first began to play it."

My father was also a Bohemian. In their own tongue the area was called Czechic, and the natives were known as Czechs. The son of a baker, he was born in Kralovitse, near Pilsen. Since families with limited means could not afford higher education for all their children, the most promising would be selected to go on with more advanced education. Father was selected for this privilege and was enrolled at the Polytechnic Institute from which he was graduated as a surveyor. For several years he worked as an assistant to a government inspector. Then, eager to escape the politically troubled atmosphere prevailing in this region of the Hapsburg Empire, he emigrated to the United States. He was an attractive, prematurely gray, young man of twenty-eight when he joined the Czech colony in Chicago.

It was not easy for a newcomer to find a job, but since father had a natural gift for writing, he soon obtained a post on a Czech newspaper. After a few years of struggle, he heard of an opening for a Czech teacher in the Jefferson School, a grade school in St. Paul, Minnesota. Among his papers we found the following account of his beginnings in St. Paul:

The St. Paul Board of Education decided to employ at Jefferson School, a Czech teacher to instruct the increasing number of Czech children recently arrived from Bohemia. A class of twenty was formed. Vaclav Jelinek, a St. Paul tailor, was appointed to teach them. After four weeks of teaching, Jelinek evidently decided that tailoring was more remunerative. He resigned. But he used his influence for me. . . . I was appointed in his place. The salary was $450.00 for nine months.

It is a matter of record in the history of education in Minnesota that my father's teaching methods were unique for that day. One of his innovations stemmed from the fact that he was a musician of some ability. He began and ended all of his classroom sessions with music. He would write the words to Czech and English songs on the blackboard. The older pupils would copy the words, then sing them back in English for the benefit of the younger boys and girls. Next, father would play the tunes of unfamiliar songs on his violin; the youngsters would quickly pick up the tunes and would soon be singing the English words that went with the music. They learned by imitation and repetition.

Father was also a great believer in physical exercise. My older sister, Rose, used to tell how, whenever his charges seemed restless, father would stop all other work in the class for a few moments of setting-up exercises. The school principal would take visitors to inspect his "model primary room," known for its gymnastics, singing, good discipline, and harmonious spirit.

Father had genuine affection for his pupils. Forty-five years later, when writing of his experiences in teaching, he was still able to mention a surprising number of them by name. He also gave Saturday, his one free day in the week, to the teaching of the Czech language to second-generation Bohemian children who were all too rapidly forgetting the language of their parents. As children we found his insistence that Czech be spoken in our home a nuisance. I can remember sitting in sulky silence through many a meal, for it was then that the rule "Czech only" was most strictly enforced. However, we continued to call our parents Tatinek and Maminka throughout their lifetime, and as I grew older the affectionate flavor of these words always gave me pleasure. I also came to understand the immigrant Czechs' deep love for their native language.

My father was vitally interested in the theatre. He once told me that as a young man in Bohemia he had wanted to go on the stage. To his family this seemed so frivolous an ambition that he soon gave it up. However, amateur acting continued to be his chief hobby, and during his early years in Chicago he devoted most of his spare time to staging and acting in plays produced by members of the Czech colony there. He occasionally appeared in Czech plays produced by dramatic organizations in other cities, and he spent many of his holidays performing as guest star in response to such invitations.

To this day my father remains in my memory as a man of enthusiasm, of great personal charm, with a zest for intellectual pursuits. His enjoyment of these never left him, even in his later years when his sight and hearing began to fail.

After their arrival in America, my mother's family had taken root in Chicago. My grandfather had established his own little hardware store, and almost all of the children had managed to get jobs of some sort with miniscule pay which, nevertheless, contributed to the family bank account.

The social life of the Czech community revolved around the local Sokol—an affiliate of an international Czech organization whose major purpose was to cultivate physical fitness among its members through a series of gymnastic disciplines. But Sokol activities also included cultural programs of music, dancing, and amateur theatricals.

My parents first met at various social affairs at the Sokolovna (the clubhouse) before my father went to St. Paul to teach. He had been immediately attracted to the tall, beautiful girl with her apple-blossom skin and luxuriant hair. But as a struggling journalist on the Czech paper he was in no position to marry. Several years were to elapse before he returned to Chicago from St. Paul to propose to her. (In the years between, my mother had suffered a great deal of unhappiness, but it was to be many years before we, their children, were to learn that story.) They were married quietly, and father brought his bride to the cottage where all their children were born.

When I returned to that house, years later, I wondered where mother had found space to put us all. I had found my spot on the roof of a red woodshed in the back yard shaded by an overhanging apple tree. An inveterate reader, I found that by lying flat on my stomach, I could remain concealed, safely ignoring any voice calling me from below.

I was never conscious of being poor. We children never knew hunger as do millions of children in the world today. To be sure, I never had a *new* dress, made for *me*, until I was twelve years old. The daughter of our rich uncle in Chicago was just my size, so her clothes were passed on to me. But they were beautiful clothes, made of fine materials, and I grew up feeling well-dressed.

Tatinek, an artist at heart, was a man of considerable temperament, which expressed itself frequently in unreasonable outbursts over what seemed to us trifles. He had an old-world concept of what a man's authority in his home should be. There was something magnificent about Tatinek in a rage. Unintentionally, I would undermine these performances when I was a little girl by looking up at him and chortling with glee, whereupon his rage would gradually subside.

Maminka was endlessly patient with him, but his insistence on parental authority deprived him of close companionship with all of his children except for Rose, his favorite. He was forty-seven when I was born, and in his later years, when I knew him best, his authoritarianism had begun to yield under the pressure of the new individualism already emerging in my generation.

My sister Rose was quiet and overly shy. She was rather tall for her age, and this, combined with the fact that family finances were at their worst during her high school years, made her social adjustment still more difficult. It was a long time before she overcame the inhibitions engendered by those early circumstances.

Mila, the eldest, lived with our grandmother in Chicago. She was old enough to earn her living as a dressmaker. I saw very little of her during my early years in St. Paul. Only for a few weeks during the summer would she come home to visit us, bringing into the household such interesting clothes, perfumes and beaux that she appeared to me as a distinctly glamorous figure.

Charlie, my older brother, was a chunky, thickset youngster, very pugnacious. His lack of height bothered Maminka. "My daughters are growing so tall," she would wail, "but my boys stay so short. It should be the other way around." But between fifteen and seventeen, Charlie suddenly shot up to his full height and towered over all of us.

During our childhood, I was the little sister whom he alternately protected and bullied. One supper time I was hanging over the back fence, talking to my favorite school chum. Charlie, sent to fetch me, delivered his message. I paid no attention. Again he said, "Maminka wants you to come for supper." Loftily, I continued to ignore him. Suddenly I was seized by my thick, yellow pigtail, dragged across the yard screaming and kicking, and deposited on the doorstep. "There," he said, panting, "I guess that will teach you to come home when I tell you." My furious complaints were soothed by Maminka. "It is good for your hair to be pulled," she laughed. "It will make it grow thick and long."

Little brother Tony had none of Charlie's truculence. I remember the night he was born, although I was very young indeed. Our little cottage was overflowing with busy neighbors running in and out of Maminka's bedroom. Rose and I were shunted out of the way. Finally I was allowed to go in and peek at a little bundle of blankets from the midst of which peeked a pair of enormous, deep blue eyes. Tony emerged from babyhood an affectionate, sensitive child, tagging along with the rest of us, doing his best to keep up with our games.

As for me, I had to be in everything, from the baseball team to performances of "Living Statues," for which admission was paid in pins. But most of all I loved reading. Words had a fascination for me which they have never lost, and I bandied them about with careless ease. On one occasion, I over-reached myself. One of Mila's beaux was waiting for her in the parlor. Supper over, I hurried as usual to the piano to practice, having learned that I could thus get out of wiping the dishes. I was giving a nine-year-old's earnest interpretation of McDowell's "To a Water Lily," when Bob, the beau, said politely, "You play very nicely, Blanche." During a pause, as I turned a page, I replied loftily, "Yes, Robert, I find music a most excellent laxative."

Our life in St. Paul came to an end because of a reorganization of the curriculum at Jefferson School which resulted in the dropping of father's classes. He heard that a Czech Benevolent Society in New York was looking for an executive secretary. It was one of the organizations which provide death benefits for its members, as well as social advantages. Desperately needing work, for there were no teachers' pensions in those days, father overcame his deep reluctance to leave St. Paul and his beloved Czech activities and cronies and went East the following autumn to try the secretaryship for a year. In the meantime, the family remained in St. Paul.

During that year I sensed that Maminka had many qualms

about the projected move to the big city. She seemed worried and frightened; more than once I saw tears in her eyes. All the family had qualms—except for me. I was too young to realize what was going on. I found a dozen reasons to see this new venture as a good move for all of us. Charlie, the chronic debunker, shrewdly put his finger on my chief reason. One night when I was being particularly persuasive, he said, "Aw, we all know why you want to go to New York. It's because all those theatres are there." Of course I denied it vehemently. But it was the truth—a truth which was to mold my entire life.

CHAPTER 2

MY FIRST AUDIENCE

IN THE AUTUMN of 1900 the family joined Tatinek in New York. Our arrival was a bit forlorn, although Tatinek did put us, bundles and all, into a large horse-drawn vehicle which took us to Czech friends—who somehow managed to put us up temporarily until we found a twenty dollar a month apartment near the East River. In those days the neighborhood was anything but fashionable. The apartments were called railroad flats: the rooms ranged one behind the other, like a train of box cars, the dark inside rooms ventilated only by an airshaft.

The flat had one advantage. Being on the ground floor, it had a basement kitchen opening onto a back yard, which I euphemistically referred to as a garden. Our living quarters were cramped. We slept two in a room except Mila, who slept on a couch in the dining room. All the St. Paul furniture had been sold with the little cottage. We built much of our new furnishings ourselves. I remember very clearly a ghastly straw-filled corner seat which I had insisted upon installing, built of planks of wood anchored to the wall. Yet I was never weighed down by any sense of our being poor, although I did sometimes envy my school fellows their more attractive homes.

I had finished grade school in St. Paul but could not enter high school until I was fourteen. For a year I went to the East 68th Street Grammar School, repeating my eighth grade work. It was an easy, pleasant year. I particularly enjoyed my teacher, Miss Perley. One hour a week we studied drawing. Papa had given us a few drawing lessons, so in my first still-life class I had achieved a fairly good representation of a bowl of fruit. As Miss Perley passed down the aisle, she picked up my drawing and exclaimed over it enthusiastically. I was embarrassed, though flattered, too. When I was graduated I toyed with the idea of going to the Art Students' League instead of to high school. I even sent for a catalog, but when I learned that there would be a tuition fee and, moreover, that there would be a class in which I would have to draw from the nude, I renounced that idea of a career in art with alacrity! We were an old-fashioned family.

Almost immediately after my arrival in New York, I began to take singing lessons. It was a very modest beginning; I had only one lesson a week with a man who had once been a tenor at the opera house in Prague. He was now musical director of the Czech Sokol singing society, which gave an amateur performance once a year. He supplemented his income teaching singing —and he must have needed to, for my lessons cost only seventy-five cents!

That year the club decided to do Balfe's *The Bohemian Girl*. After I'd been studying with him a few weeks, he invited me to be the prima donna of the production. The music was well within my range; the rehearsals were fun. The older members of the music club made a great fuss over the long-legged newcomer from the west, and as a consequence of all this activity, the loneliness which had engulfed the rest of the family, left me untouched.

When my family first came to New York from Minnesota, we knew almost no one. The bleak, unfriendly atmosphere of a large city is hard to face, as any newcomer who has experienced it knows. So it was to the Sokolovna that we had quite naturally gravitated. Within its friendly walls we soon made friends.

Maminka, however, was never able to adjust herself to living in New York. She was essentially a small-town person; she hated the pavements, the crowds, the feeling that no one in a big city cared what happened to anyone else. But she had little time for brooding with a family of five children to feed and the housework to be done. She did every sort of household chore. If a ceiling needed to be washed, she washed it. If a new wallpaper could be afforded, she put it up. She scrubbed, sewed, cooked, even later on, when it was no longer necessary for her to do these things.

I can see her now, sitting serenely in the back yard, after doing a day's washing, freshly bathed and dainty in one of her simple muslin dresses, presently coming in to prepare and preside over the dinner which she had cooked for her hungry brood.

But I? In New York, the things I had always dreamed of became realities. There were theatres to go to, even though one did have to walk to and from school to save the carfares with which to buy admission to the topmost galleries. Moreover, I was confident that thrilling things would soon begin to happen to me; I could bide my time. I kept a scrapbook of theatrical data and swapped clippings with a friendly little Jewish boy who lived in the flat above ours.

The Sokol's first performance of *Bohemian Girl* was a huge success. It was repeated three times and made a nice bit of money for the society. After the final performance I was presented with a handsomely inscribed gold watch. The praise I received was heady wine for a school girl. One of my admirers was a most distinguished and kindly Negro singer, Harry Burleigh. He was soloist at St. George's Church and had written some beautiful songs. He said, "You must go further, my child, you have talent."

Actually, there was already an actress in our family, a cousin, Adelaide Nowak. She was very beautiful and had a lovely speaking voice. At this time she was a member of Richard Mansfield's company. Her stories of the temperamental star and of her long tours with him fascinated me; her repeated disappointments and setbacks merely seemed dramatic and well worth enduring.

My year of marking time at the grammar school over, I was sent to Wadleigh High School on 114th Street. Mother wanted me to follow in the footsteps of my father and my sister, Rose, by becoming a schoolteacher. A schoolteacher's job was safe and the pay secure. I did not argue. Nevertheless, I knew I was not going to be a schoolteacher. Always an erratic student, I applied myself only to those subjects which interested me. Languages, history, English literature I loved; mathematics I loathed. After a fairly good average in my freshman year, my marks in algebra dropped woefully.

But the English classes rehabilitated my scholastic standing. The entire school was given an examination paper on Shakespeare's *Julius Caesar*. This gave me a chance to shine. Mansfield had just played it at the New Amsterdam Theatre, with my cousin as his leading lady. Since Adelaide was playing Calpurnia, I had studied every line and footnote of the play before I went to see it, lest I should lose one ounce of its value. So when I turned in my paper on the play, I knew it was good. When it was returned to me, my startled eyes saw the disappointing mark: 98; only 98! How could that be? I looked up the alleged error. The teacher had made a mistake. With blood in my eye I marched up to the examining teacher. To my delight she admitted her mistake, and thanks to Mr. Mansfield and Adelaide, my mark was now 100.

First year French was another class in which I stood fairly high. Languages fascinated me. Our teacher, Mlle. Sesso, an Austrian, was stern and terrifying in her demands for perfection, but in later years I blessed her for it. My second-year French teacher I adored. She had the dark-eyed charm of a true Parisienne; yet it is Mlle. Sesso whose name I remember and whose grounding in French verbs has served me well many times since.

But my high grades in French and English were insufficient to maintain a very high student rating. I began to hate school. My brief experience as a prima donna at the Sokolovna had spoiled me. What I wanted more than anything else was to become a singer, and Wadleigh High School hardly seemed the place to fulfill that ambition.

As soon as we could manage it my sisters and I bought standee's tickets for *Lohengrin*. I was enchanted with the packed opera house, and we were there early enough to find space at dead center behind the rail, on which we could lean and occasionally rest our feet.

As the flowing music of that first act swelled to its climax my emotions swelled too—indeed, Mila later told me that my tears were not merely running down my cheeks but seemed to pop straight out in front of me. Undoubtedly they wet the collar of the gentleman sitting in the last row! Not until years later in Bayreuth, when I heard Gulbranson's Brunhilde, did Wagner's music affect me so deeply again. It was a lovely introduction to the opera house where, in a few years, I was to spend so much time.

One day I saw an announcement in the daily paper that Heinrich Conried, the new impresario at the Metropolitan Opera House, was going to establish a school where potential recruits to the company would be given scholarships. Until then, it had been considered absolutely necessary to go abroad for study and training. He wished to remedy this.

The whole thing seemed miraculous: I knew I should, I *must* be accepted. The absurdity of my pretensions never entered my mind; some inner voice had always assured me that I must keep reaching for the stars. I took the newspaper clipping to Tatinek and begged him to write to Mr. Conried for an appointment. He did, in his beautiful German, and the appointment was made.

On the appointed day I found myself at the opera house in a room filled with waiting aspirants: church soloists, concert singers or very advanced students. The fact that I was none of these did not faze me. One after another they sang: "Caro nome" in high, bright coloratura; "Elsa's Dream" in smooth-flowing phrases; "Mon coeur s'ouvre à ta voix," which seemed the contraltos' favorite show-piece (as was "Prize Song" for the tenors). I rose, handed the accompanist my roll of sheet music, and sang lustily "I dreamt I dwelt in marble halls"—the only time, I suspect, that it has ever been sung for a Met audition!

Presently Mr. Conried called Tatinek into his office. What exchange of polite German took place I never learned, but the upshot was that I was awarded a scholarship; I was to be the only teenager in the school. I cannot recall feeling any considerable surprise. Joy, yes, joy at the confirmation of what I had expected. I was to stay in the opera school for two years; after that they would see.

Father was proud and delighted. We rushed home to tell the family. Mother had misgivings, but I was too excited to listen to them. I do not remember taking any formal leave of high school. All I recall is that I found myself quite suddenly in the midst of a magical world of music—a world peopled by brilliantly gifted men and women with fascinating personalities, a world which might well have excited a far more phlegmatic nature than mine.

Now began two exciting years. No more trudging fifty or sixty blocks to Wadleigh High School for classes in physics and geometry. Instead I flew on winged feet up elevated stairways, down again into bustling Broadway crowds; then, marvel of marvels, I walked unchallenged through the 39th Street door of the great Opera House, through which were passing the greatest singers in the world.

There were about twenty students in the opera school. We were given lessons in singing and in languages and did simple exercises with a ballet master. An important part of the work was attendance at as many rehearsals and performances as possible. Three boxes were reserved for us at the rear of the second tier. This privilege was primarily intended for the advanced students who might be understudying the minor roles, but, greedily, I became a nightly fixture.

The two years were filled with feverish activity, uncontrolled by any vestige of common sense. My voice was a rambling mezzo-soprano, of very wide range but with a bad break as it went into the head register. I was told that the voice must be brought into focus. A strict vocal diet of scales, solfeggio and simple German Lieder was prescribed. As my singing teacher, Frau Jaeger, spoke no English, I had a daily lesson in German with my father. These unpretentious assignments, in contrast to the vocal pyrotechnics of my more mature fellow-students, irked me considerably. No one in my family knew the proper routine of rest and care that a young singer should observe, and I doubt that I would have listened, had anyone tried to restrain me. My morning lessons over, I would slip in to listen to whatever rehearsal was going on.

On one occasion my determination to miss nothing at the opera house inspired me to devise a most ingenious plan. There was to be a benefit matinee one afternoon for the retired actress, Mme. Modjeska. It had been arranged by her Polish compatriot, Paderewski. All lessons were to stop at twelve so that the house staff might take over. The program was to be brilliant, full of *names,* and I was frantically determined to attend the performance. Tickets were $10.00, and even standing room was $3.00. All "courtesy" was suspended, and consequently getting myself through any proper entrance was out of the question. Yet, be there I must!

When lessons ended at noon, I armed myself with a book and disappeared into the ladies' room on the second floor, locking myself into the farthest compartment. There I perched with my feet tucked under me tailor-fashion, lest they be seen by some passing eye. I sat and read for about two hours. When I saw enough feet moving about beyond the door to make it fairly certain I would not be noticed, I made a casual exit, walked downstairs, and found myself a place behind the orchestra rail, where I stood all afternoon.

After taking all that trouble, I remember clearly only one person on that program—a willowy woman in a black velvet sheath gown embroidered in gold *fleurs-de-lis*. A cloud of black hair framed a fascinating pair of great dark eyes, and her voice was unforgettable. It was Mrs. Patrick Campbell. She read a poem, but all I remember is the beauty of her voice and her graceful movements.

In retrospect the whole circumstance of my being part of that opera house picture seems a little fantastic: a high school girl suddenly in daily contact with a galaxy of the world's most famous singers: Caruso, Scotti, Gadski, Ternina, Eames, Fremstad, Plançon, Nordica, Calvé and Sembrich, many of them the last representatives of a golden age of singing. I not only saw the great ones but heard them at rehearsals. I saw Milka Ternina, so plain in her ugly tailored clothes but noble in her artistry. I saw Fremstad blossom into the full flower of her genius, her molten mezzo extending itself note by note through the sheer exercise of her inflexible will to work and to grow, until the stubborn high notes finally became as mellow and lambent as her middle range. Then she achieved an Isolde of such physical and vocal beauty, of such poignant dramatic verity, that I would have been content never to hear anybody else in the role.

Most of my fellow-students were given small parts from time to time, such as the priestess in *Aida* or the bird-voice in *Siegfried*. The artists in the company were gracious to these neophytes. All eyes and ears, I saw the older girls starting flirtations with some of the singers: Caruso, Scotti and Saleza. So when a very tall, dark young coach looked interestedly at me, I flirted a little too, rather naïvely. Kurt Schindler and I held hands all through one *Tristan* matinee. But my little flirtation came to nothing. Like Parsifal, I walked immune in that sex-saturated atmosphere; my mind was in the cloud-world of music.

Excitement became my daily bread. The most publicized

event of the season was the first production of *Parsifal* outside Bayreuth. *"Bühnen-weih-Fest-Spiel"* (a consecrated festival stage-play) was the laborious designation on the title page of the score. Richard Wagner had decreed that the opera was to be performed only in Bayreuth. This wish had been scrupulously observed as long as copyright laws made it possible to control the use of the score. This restriction was lifted when the copyright expired, and now Mr. Conried was free to do it if he pleased. He *did* please, for he was a shrewd and ruthless business man, quite aware of the publicity value of so exciting an undertaking. The management took full advantage of the violent opposition voiced by the Wagner family. Their accusations of desecration, heresy, violation of the Meister's express wishes made the international headlines and helped stimulate public interest to an almost hysterical pitch.

My first real student assignment was to be one of the Flower Maidens in this production. My voice was not sufficiently mature for me to do any of the solo phrases, and much as I enjoyed singing the charming second act music, just being one among so many didn't satisfy me. But there was one part with which I knew I could do something—the Bearer of the Grail. It involved no singing, but it would permit me to emerge from the ensemble. Because of its place in the action, I knew it could be given a value out of proportion to its seeming unimportance.

I learned that this role had already been assigned to one of the salaried members of the chorus. Undaunted, I broached the subject to the famous Munich director, Anton Fuchs, who had been brought over especially to stage this great musical event. "Please, Herr Direktor, could *I* not be allowed the privilege of carrying the sacred vessel in the first and last acts?" My voice was as persuasive as I could make it. Evidently touched by my eagerness, he granted my request. So, in addition to being one of the Flower Maidens, I was to have my moment of solitary glory.

As the Knights of the Grail solemnly march in for the sacrament of the unveiling of the Grail, the young Grail Bearer leads the procession, carrying his sacred burden. Reverently he places it before the suffering Amfortas and steps down. When the insistent cry *"Enthüllet . . . Enthüllet den Gral!"* (Uncover the Grail!) reaches its climax, the boy, with infinite reverence, mounts the steps, lifts the chalice out of its covered case, places it

before the suffering King, and sinks on his knees in worship.
Bathed in the light pouring from the sacred vessel, he is immersed in its sanctity.

I took my responsibility very seriously. On the day of the performance I fasted and kept very much to myself lest my mood be
disturbed. This devotion to a beloved task had a telling effect.
On my arrival at school the morning after my first performance
I found my fellow students buzzing with excitement over a notice in the morning paper which I had not yet seen. The distinguished music critic of the *New York Tribune*, Henry Edward
Krehbiel, after commenting on the Kundry and Parsifal interpretations, had written:

And while pointing out the beauty of the work of the principals, it
it is a pleasant privilege to lay a wreath at the feet of the little lady
who carried the Grail with such reverent and touching consecration
to her sacred duties.

I doubt if any notice I have ever received has given me more
joy.

The whole adventure was a joyous one; I was fully conscious
of my privilege in becoming a part of that great pattern of musical and dramatic expression, of having seen and felt the music
grow from its first rehearsal until it achieved the sweep of religious ecstasy that marked its eventual performance. To live
within such music, to give one's self to it, in service, however
humble, makes it peculiarly one's own.

As Flower Maidens, we wore lovely flowing costumes especially designed for the production. Mine was that of an iris, and
the purple flowers and lavender draperies were very becoming
to my fair coloring. However, it was only as the Grail Bearer
that I actually emerged from my student anonymity. I have
been amused at reading, somewhere, that prior to my stage career, I had been a "Metropolitan Opera singer." Never has a
reputation been so little justified. My status never went beyond
that of student.

There were several Kundrys during the season. In my opinion
Fremstad's was the finest. Her superb acting talents, the opulent
sensuous beauty of her voice and figure made her seduction
scene in the second act something never to be forgotten. This

was a siren in whose powers of enchantment one could believe. The tragic humility of her "Dienen! Dienen!" in the last act brought tears to my eyes.

There was one prima donna whose graciousness was like sunshine. While Fremstad was my favorite *artist* in the company, Nordica was my favorite *person*. She sang only a few times and had passed her vocal zenith, but there was still an irresistible radiance about her.

I caught my first glimpse of her one afternoon when a few of us were leaving after a Flower Maiden rehearsal. As we passed along the upper corridor behind the grand tier of boxes, we heard wonderful sounds from the 39th Street lobby below. Peering down through the small windows overlooking the lobby, we saw a short woman in shirtwaist and skirt, who somehow seemed tall because of her regal carriage. Nordica, just arrived from Europe, was rehearsing the garden scene with Maestro Alfred Hertz. As she raised her head she saw our bewitched faces framed in the little windows. Without losing a beat, she beckoned to us, pointing to the chairs that lined the lobby wall. We scampered down quietly and sat in a solemnly attentive row. As she finished the brilliant second-act climax she gave us a smile full of fun and said, "Now, children, you know just how it's done."

My accolade came during a pause at a later rehearsal on the stage. As the Grail Bearer, I was kneeling beside her, near the altar, in the final scene. She put her hand on my shoulder and said sweetly, "You do this very nicely indeed, my dear."

At one of the Sunday night concerts which they used to give at the Opera House, she sang the "Inflammatus" from Rossini's *Stabat Mater*. As she reached the end, her famous high C rang out like a celestial trumpet call. It was a sound which no one who heard it could ever forget. I was told that in her early days, when she was a church soloist, it had made her famous. Many artists have crossed my path since those exciting days, but the glow of Nordica's personal radiance shines out most clearly.

CHAPTER 3

FAREWELL TO SONG

THE SECOND YEAR of study at the Opera House found me in that turmoil of impatience which has always been my greatest failing. My greed in wanting to assimilate all the experiences and exploit all the opportunities that the school opened up to me was bound to take its toll. Such intensity created tensions dangerous to my health and voice. Maminka, disturbed that I was spending almost all my time downtown, protested that seeing and hearing so much would make me old before my time. But her warning fell on deaf ears.

Even greater pressures were added when my former singing teacher, eager to exploit my success of the previous year in *Bohemian Girl* as well as my scholarship at the Opera School, invited me to sing in a madly ambitious project at the Sokolovna. It was nothing less than the role of Leonora in *Il Trovatore*. It was sheer madness, of course, and I should have sensed danger when my teacher counselled me to say nothing to anyone at the Opera School. "They might disapprove, though of course it can't hurt you," he said. I wanted to believe him.

We rehearsed evenings. Despite a heavy cold, I struggled through rehearsals, tearing at my poor vocal chords, pounding out the high C's. Of course, the performance was a failure. To this day I cannot listen to the music of *Il Trovatore* without a sense of nausea.

My second season at the Opera School progressed, but my voice did not; at the end of the term my puzzled teachers pronounced their verdict. My scholarship was to be discontinued;

my voice did not justify it. Mr. Conried's blunt frankness admitted of no argument. The back-stage doors of the Opera House were closed to me forever.

After two such exciting years, the sudden slump into inactivity made life seem unbearable. I wandered about the little railroad flat in bleak despair, confused, uncertain as to what my next step should be. I would not even consider going back to Wadleigh High School, yet I found it impossible to study anything systematically by myself. I could not relax; I was sure that somehow fate would point the way.

Again, a little paragraph in the daily newspaper became my signpost. It was an announcement of the opening of the Institute of Musical Art. Among its personnel was listed a familiar name, Mme. Lillie Sang-Collins, a charming Frenchwoman, who had been my favorite among the Opera School teachers. At the Opera House she had encountered certain antagonisms and had left. In my spontaneous pleasure over her new affiliation, I wrote her a note of congratulation. Out of what tiny impulses do our opportunities flower! This one bore rich fruit.

Later I learned that on the very day my note reached her, she was lunching with a very important director of the Institute, Rudolph Schirmer, head of the famous music publishing company. He asked her whether there had been anyone in the opera school whom she would judge to have a future. She replied, "Oddly enough, I've just had a note from one of the girls, a youngster whose personality impressed me. I don't recall her voice at all, but she seemed to me to have the other qualities which go to make a career."

His interest was aroused, and I was summoned to meet Mr. Schirmer. He was distinguished, charming, and very kind. Questions were asked. The abuse of my voice and its dire results were discussed, and my foolishness was censured. But I sang one or two very simple songs well enough to convince them both that there was something worth trying to salvage. I was to be given another chance and every possible opportunity to nurse the strained vocal cords back to normal. Meanwhile, I was to study many related subjects in order to achieve a well-rounded musical education.

I was overjoyed! In this unlooked-for reprieve I suddenly found myself blessed not only with a fairy godmother but a fairy godfather as well. Rudolph Schirmer's generosity and intelligent enthusiasm had helped many an aspiring artist. His charm of manner combined with his discerning taste made his wealth and position powerful instruments for good. I can never forget that he made it possible for me to do all the things I loved most —not only did he make available lessons of all kinds, but there were also tickets to musical events and even to an occasional stage play.

Again I plunged into study, but this time quietly, sensibly, without tension. Long hours were spent in piano practice, classes in harmony, and French lessons with the famous Yersin sisters who had coached many of the greatest artists of the French theatre. I heeded their dictum: "Before you open your mouth you must open your ears." In theory, at least, the Yersin *système* if mastered would produce a flawless French accent. "We want you to become not only a good singer," Mr. Schirmer said, "but a cultivated, interesting woman as well."

Once more I was privileged to hear the best. Already steeped in opera, I now became familiar with other forms of music. Pianists, violinists, lieder singers, symphony orchestras—I listened to them all with expanding interest and understanding.

Grateful for this second chance and determined to justify my sponsors' faith in me, I settled into a new, disciplined routine. Gradually my tense throat muscles relaxed. I sang only the music assigned to me for study, resisting the temptation to work on more spectacular things. The end of term examination gave satisfactory proof of my progress, and it was arranged that I continue at the Institute the following year.

The summer holiday brought a most valuable and interesting experience. Through the influence of one of my teachers I was invited to Greenacre, Maine, where, each summer, some impecunious singer or student of music was given a free holiday in exchange for services. The duties were not exacting: I was to sing one solo on Sunday and one at the midweek session. For this I was to receive transportation expenses plus board and lodging.

The Greenacre Fellowship had been founded by Miss Sara Farmer after she had attended the Congress of Religions at the World's Columbian Exposition in Chicago in 1893. Her experiences at the Congress led her to devote her time and fortune to sponsoring an annual summer forum on the religious concepts of the various creeds. For the site of these forums she selected a lovely spot on the border between Maine and New Hampshire. Participants in the program included lecturers, writers, artists and spiritual teachers of diverse beliefs, with each having an opportunity to present and explain his philosophy and beliefs. It was her hope that these gatherings, with their encouragement of a free exchange of views, would contribute to increased tolerance and understanding throughout the world.

I shared a charming little cabin with a Southern girl, Betty Hughes, who was a pianist. Betty accompanied my solos and occasionally performed, herself. The focal point of our daily life was the guest table at the inn where we took our meals. Here we met a constantly changing stream of distinguished and charming visitors. We especially like Mirza Ali Kuli Khan, the delightful gentleman who later came to Washington as Minister from Persia and made many friends for his country. Betty had met him at Greenacre the year before. On the evening of our arrival he recited to us verses of Omar Khayyam in Persian, and very lovely it sounded, too, though we understood not a word.

One morning, as I sat on our little porch, a handsome, white-haired man strolled by and sat down on the steps to chat. This was one of the privileges of Greenacre; merely being there constituted an introduction. I learned that he was Horace Traubel, the friend and disciple of Walt Whitman, to whose fame and philosophy Traubel had dedicated his life. We became friends, and before he left he gave me two letters of introduction, one to Mrs. Fiske and one to Julia Marlowe. "But why?" I asked. "I'm studying singing, not acting."

"Keep them," he replied. "I see you, one day, acting, not singing. These may be useful." I put them away. After all, one expected people at Greenacre to do unexpected, albeit kindly, things. Over most of the visitors Betty and I would giggle in the privacy of our cabin, while preserving respectful and attentive faces on all public occasions.

There was one other habitué of Greenacre of whom we saw a good deal. He was a painfully shy, hawk-faced man with piercing eyes of striking blue. Modestly he spoke of being a painter. Little did I suspect that he was to become one of the outstanding artists of his time. It was Marsden Hartley.

As summer waned, the Greenacre forum ended. Betty and I

returned to our families in New York, healthy, rested and with
vastly extended mental horizons. I was eager to get back to serious study at the Institute. Under the guidance of Lillie Sang-
Collins, I resumed my earnest efforts to recover from the vocal
insanities of two years earlier. But new difficulties arose, this
time at home. Maminka's health had been gravely impaired by
an attack of influenza. She had lost all interest in her household
tasks, was extremely nervous, and above all, dreaded being left
alone. I've since come to know what a nervous breakdown
means, but at the time I did not grasp the gravity of her illness.
She had slowly recovered from the influenza attack, but when
we did succeed in persuading her to leave her bed, she would
either sit inert, or follow us about from room to room like a
frightened child. As the children dispersed to their daily jobs,
she would repeat, "Where are the others? When are they coming
home? Why must you go downtown?" I could not guess what
was going on in her distracted mind, but some months later, I
was to learn, with terrifying suddenness, much of the family history which had never been known to me.

I told Mme. Lillie little of the situation at home other than,
"Mother is not very well." Actually, with the egotism of youth, I
was glad to put it all out of my mind during those engrossing
hours of study and lessons.

Tatinek's encroaching blindness made it difficult for him to
work; the family had to depend on what my two sisters could
earn; Mila was occupied with her dressmaking, Rose with her
teaching; Charlie had an insignificant job in an insurance office.
Someone had to do the endlessly recurrent housework, and so it
fell upon my shoulders.

The quality of my housekeeping was sketchy, the meals I prepared simple indeed. Leftovers were made up into what I always
called "Waldorf Salad," for I liked the elegant sound of the
name. Finally, Charlie remarked acidly, "Waldorf Salad seems
to change a lot, but it always tastes like yesterday's supper." I
never did learn to cook.

It was during this sad period that a visitor from St. Paul announced that he would like to see Coney Island. I offered to
accompany him—for a sixteen-year-old Coney Island still has
charm. We did everything: we went chute-ing on the chutes, we
rode the ferris wheel, and when we passed a fortune-teller's hut,
our friend had his hand read. Then he sent me in.

Behind the curtains I found the usual frowsy, dark-haired gypsy sitting at her table. She looked at my hand, then up at me. "You have no past to speak of, young lady, it's your future I see . . . You will become famous. Yes, quite famous, but not by doing what you think you are going to do."

"That's silly," I said, "I know very well what I'm doing to do, and I'm getting ready to do it. I'm going to be a grand opera singer."

"No, you will not be a grand opera singer. You will not even want to be one before long." Then, turning to my other hand, she continued, "There is something strange here. I see trouble. It was either in your father's or your mother's life, I cannot tell which. Very serious. It changed many things." I was puzzled. "It is here," she said, pointing to certain lines in my hand, "it happened when one of them was about twenty-five."

I left the tent in disgust and said nothing about the whole episode to my family. Yet before long her words were to come back to me! One night some months later, poor Maminka seemed particularly distraught. She wept continuously and mentioned over and over two names that meant nothing to me. Lying on my bed with only paper-thin walls between us, I was puzzled by her distress. Mila, after quieting her, came in and sat down on my bed. Her face was drawn and tired. She was curiously embarrassed.

"Darling," she began, "there is something I've felt for a long time I ought to tell you. You must have been puzzled and worried at things you've heard Maminka saying"—she hesitated—again that embarrassed expression. "For one thing, I'm just your half-sister. I've never wanted to tell you. I've been afraid it might make a difference."

I stared at her as she continued, "Maminka was married once before; your father is Maminka's second husband." "Your father!" How strange it sounded to hear Tatinek referred to like that. Then she told me the story.

Even as a young girl, Maminka had been in love with Tatinek who, having no steady position, had felt he had no right to reveal his feelings for her. Today it is hard to believe in such restraint, but those were the days when a declaration of love was customarily followed by a proposal of marriage, and this Tatinek felt he could not offer. So, when a well-to-do Czech business man asked for Maminka's hand, her whole family impressed upon her how lucky she was to be making such a good match, and she accepted him. She was eighteen. The wedding supper was held, as was customary in those circles, at the local Soko-lovna. Much good beer had been consumed when Tatinek rose to toast the bride.

Looking across the table at her he said, "I am drinking a toast to the only woman I shall ever love!" There sat Maminka, in love with him, and just married to someone else. He must really have been very tipsy to do such a thing to her on her wedding night.

Maminka bore her first husband three children. Two died as babies. Mila was the only one who survived. The marriage had endured for some eight years when one day Maminka, completely unsuspecting, walked into the back storeroom of her husband's hardware shop and stumbled upon him in a hopelessly compromising position with her closest woman friend. The shock was the greater because for several weeks Maminka had been receiving letters from this friend postmarked from a nearby town where she was allegedly visiting, letters obviously intended to put Maminka off the scent. Stricken by the elaborate deceit of the two people who were supposedly closest to her in the world, she made no scene. She went home, packed a few things, took Mila by the hand, and walked out of the house.

She returned to her family and went to work in a fur shop. Her husband tried to persuade her to come back to him, but she refused. Saving every penny she could from her slim earnings, she determined to get a divorce. When she had saved enough for the purpose, she turned it over to one of her brothers who worked in a lawyer's office. Weeks passed, then months, and she became restless at the continual reports of delay in the divorce proceedings. Finally, her brother broke down and confessed that he had not turned the money over to his employer at all, but had squandered it. Poor Maminka! Bit by bit she again scraped together the necessary amount, and this time took it to the lawyer herself. The divorce was finally obtained, and not long after Tatinek arrived from St. Paul and asked her to marry him.

This was the story Mila told me that night. "When did all this happen to Maminka?" I asked. "When she was twenty-five years old," answered Mila.

Modern psychiatry has made clear the belated effects of emotional shock and repression, but at that time I was puzzled that circumstances in which my mother was blameless should have left so deep a wound. If Tatinek had been a more phlegmatic man, the memory would perhaps have had less power to harm. But in the first years of their marriage, jealousy of his predecessor had amounted to an obsession. He took it out on his stepdaughter, Mila, mercilessly exacting from her impossible standards of behavior and scholarship. He would refuse to sign her report cards unless they bore all A's. When she begged for piano lessons, he insisted that they be taken at 7 A.M. so as not to interfere with her school studies. Mila told me of trudging to her music lessons through the freezing dawns of those Minnesota winters. Her fingers would be stiff on the icy keys. Maminka suffered at seeing her child's life made hellish but strove to hold her peace. She was determined that this second marriage should last. Finally, at sixteen, Mila could endure no more and went to Chicago to live with our grandmother.

This was why in my early childhood I had seen her only during the summers on brief visits home. Only after we had moved to New York did she come into our lives to stay. There began our close companionship which was to remain uninterrupted for the rest of her life. To me, Mila became sister, mentor and friend.

I should best describe Mila as a gay saint, a phrase which would have covered her with confusion, for she was the most modest of women. Nevertheless, her most outstanding qualities were her goodness and her gaiety. She took such joy in the little things of life—the freshness of the morning as she walked to work across Central Park, the beauty of the sunset glow behind the skyline as she returned. Frequently I would meet her and we would walk home together. At the supper table she would tell us of the graciousness or kindness of those whom she had encountered during the day. Mila, whose every impulse was thoughtful and considerate, never took the goodness of others as a matter of course. It was something to be savoured and appreciated. Only once did I hear her make a remark that was even slightly tinged with bitterness. When I asked her about those early days in St. Paul, she answered, "If I allowed myself to think too often about what Papa made of my childhood, I should hate him; and I don't want to hate anyone."

It is said that time heals all wounds, and perhaps the reason proverbs endure is because they are true. Tatinek lived long enough to find himself dependent upon Mila and her slender earnings; upon her loving, unselfish devotion to our entire family; for the very food we ate and the roof under which we slept. One day, during the last difficult years before he died, I heard him say very gently, "You've been a good girl, Miladko, much better to me than I deserve." Never in all those years, so far as I know, did she utter one word of reproach to him.

Despite the worry and strain which clouded our home life, those were years of rich development for me. I met people who influenced my life to an immeasurable degree. For one, there was always Lillie Collins to turn to when things looked blackest. There was so much about her for which to be grateful. First of all, for just being herself, for giving to an eager child evidence of an inner grace, of Gallic charm, of a sanity in her appraisal of values. Her realistic honesty was combined with a rare appreciation of beauty which was characteristically French. She remains in my memory as one of the loveliest women I have ever known.

All during my student days, both at the Institute and at the Opera House, I had only the most meager amount of pocket money. Mila gave me what she could spare, and goodness knows my needs were small. Still, I did have to have carfare (ten cents took you anywhere and back in those days) and, now and then, lunch money. Mme. Lillie often invited me to lunch. Then came an unexpected windfall. One day a fellow student at the Institute told me that the choir in which she sang had an opening for a mezzo-soprano. She described the choirmaster as a man of notable talent and a stern disciplinarian. "Write and ask for an audition," she counselled, "and don't let him frighten you."

I was grateful for that injunction, for seldom had I looked into more penetrating blue eyes. The close-cropped blond head held very erect on a whippet-slim body suggested steely strength and dynamic power even in repose. His name, 1 learned, was Leopold Stokowski, which puzzled me a little, for he neither looked nor sounded Polish. My audition had been set for late afternoon. The long, low, dun-colored room of St. Bartholomew's church was quiet and dim. The interview was brief. I sang a few scales, did a bit of sight-reading. Then came a curt nod and a crisp verdict: "Good. You will receive $5.00 a Sunday.

We rehearse Tuesdays and Fridays, promptly at eight. Good afternoon." He strode out.

Singing at St. Bartholomew's under Stokowski opened up a new world of music, music of a purity and loftiness unfamiliar to ears drenched in the romanticism of opera and lieder singing. We followed the routine of the High Episcopal service, and from time to time gave special performances of such works as the *St. Matthew's Passion* and the rare old music of the earliest composers. Bach, as conducted by Stokowski, was a revelation of dramatic intensity. He demanded clean attack, delicate gradation of sound, and achieved brilliant climaxes.

But it was not only the privilege of listening to such music as Stokowski made which—in retrospect—I value so highly; once again it was the experience of being an integral part of the music, a participant in those exciting crescendi, those sudden pauses. There was the great advantage, too, of working so closely at such an impressionable age with an artist whose precision was that of a most delicate instrument, and whose tirelessness in reaching for a high degree of achievement was to be an unending inspiration all through my life.

But at the time, alas, my appreciation was not always apparent in my behavior. Leopold Stokowski was the youngest choirmaster St. Bartholomew's had ever had and perhaps because of this, as much as by reason of his temperament, he maintained a stern aloofness which fortified his authority. This was important, since many of the older members of the choir had been there for years. The discipline he maintained was positively Prussian. But I had already encountered a few dynamic personalities at the Opera House, so his curt commands riled rather than terrified me. I think he rather enjoyed the fact that occasionally I stood up to him.

There were two rows of chairs set at right angles to the piano in the center of the long rehearsal room. One of Stokowski's stipulations was that all chairs must be filled at five minutes before eight. The occupant was expected to hold his music in his hand, intent and ready to sing the opening bar when the baton was lifted on the final stroke of eight. It was an excellent ruling and one to which for several weeks I tried to conform. But I am, and always have been, afflicted with a congenital inability to cope with time. Either I stand about in a station for forty-five minutes or I just barely catch the train. In those days I usually walked the forty blocks down to the church. If I took a street car, unforeseeable things would delay it. The first time I sneaked into that room, filled with attentive silence, an aura of guilt hung heavily over my vacant chair. I murmured a vague apology. To my surprise I was not struck dead. Whether this getting away with my dereliction encouraged me, or whether I just couldn't gauge time, my tardiness was repeated more than once. One evening, as I slipped in just as the baton was lifted, it paused in mid-air, was lowered, and the choirmaster's voice said wearily, "I suppose all good rules must have an exception. That's what you shall be. Don't explain. Just sit down and sing."

During Lent there were special services which used only a small choir. Those of us who were selected for these vesper services felt highly privileged. Aside from the extra money, the quiet church (seldom filled), the more intimate rehearsals, made one feel a part of some inner circle of initiates. It was during the period of these Lenten Services that an amusing incident occurred.

One Monday morning, while clearing away the Sunday paper, my eye was caught by something in the rotogravure section. It was a special edition celebrating the centennial of Longfellow's birth. I saw among other pictures a silhouette made of the poet while he was at Bowdoin College. His hair was wavy, and he wore an old-fashioned stock collar. But what startled me was that from the hairline to the tip of the chin it was the profile of Leopold Stokowski! I studied it fascinated. How odd that two such different personalities should resemble one another so strongly! My cleaning chore forgotten, I seized the scissors and carefully cut away the flowing hair; the ruffled stock collar, too, went into the wastebasket, leaving the close-cropped contour with which I was familiar. There in silhouette was our choirmaster!

I mounted the cutting on a card. That evening I took it down to rehearsal. In the dressing room where we asembled I lined up my sister choristers behind me and told them to look in the mirror. I wanted to be sure my imagination had not deceived me. As they saw the reflection of the card which I held up, they almost shrieked, "It's Leopold! Where did you get it?" I smiled knowingly and kept my secret. "I made it."

Next day after vesper service, as the choirmaster was leaving the rehearsal room, I interrupted that swift stride which has become familiar to his concert audiences. "Mr. Stokowski, may I see you for a moment? I have something I want to show you." I held up the little card. "Why, that's me!" His impassive mask slipped, together with his grammar. "No, it's Longfellow," I replied. "But I thought the resemblance might interest you." And for once it was *I* who made the swift and effective exit, my precious handiwork firmly clutched in my hand.

Next day's vespers over, it was he who stopped me. With a show of indifference he began, "Oh, that—er—thing you showed me yesterday . . . could I have it?" But I was not going to relinquish my sense of power so easily. "No, I'm sorry, but I want it myself. I'll try to make you another one." I did, but it was not quite so well done. I showed it to him the next day. "No," he said. "I don't like this one. I want the other one." Then, as I looked obstinate, he put on a very wistful look and said, "I'd like to send it to my mother." Of course I gave it to him. I'm sure his mother never laid eyes on it.

There was nothing routine about those choir rehearsals. Occasionally Stokowski would turn to the vocabulary of the other arts to make his point. One evening he used chalk shadings on a blackboard to indicate the gradations of intensity which would build up to a certain climax, adding that at a certain point we were to "throw on a splash of brilliant red." That kind of imagery has stayed with me ever since. Once he even turned to the language of prize fighting, and we learned that music too has punch, drive, and stamina. In years to come I often found myself using the other arts as sources of inspiration and enrichment in crystallizing my ideas about acting.

My studies at the Institute, combined with my choir activities, made for full days and evenings. My voice fluctuated between good lessons when it floated freely and others when the old habit of tightening seemed ineradicable. I have said that Mme. Lillie could make me do anything—anything, alas, except that with which we were most concerned—make me sing consistently well. God knows she tried, using all her resourcefulness as a teacher in the attempt to gently untie the vocal tangles into which I had tied myself in those previous years of misguided enthusiasm. Her patience was inexhaustible and her musicianship an inspiration.

The term drew toward its close. I had been making progress

steadily; for days at a time my voice would stay balanced well above the danger spots. My final lesson before the term audition lifted us both to joyous optimism. "Now don't sing another note until Friday," she said. "Then sing this aria exactly as you did it today. We've turned the corner."

I walked on air—was still walking on it when I entered the high-ceilinged audition room on the following Friday, nervous, but confident. The aria I had been preparing ended on a high B-flat. All went well enough until I neared the last phrase. Terror began to grip me, my throat tightened, and as my voice mounted toward the climax—crack!—it broke. I turned cold with horror. Silence, and a ghastly sense of failure pervaded the room. I felt I wanted to die!

Everyone was very kind. Mr. Schirmer was comforting and reassuring. "You shall try again next week, or whenever you wish. It was just nerves." I shook my head. I couldn't speak. I wanted only to get away. I knew at that moment that I should never try again; that the sick agony of that fright would always haunt me. The dream of glorious, soaring singing which was part of my very being was dead. It was the end. Somehow I got away and stumbled home. How could I ever go back? Fortunately the school term had ended.

Then, a few days later, I was called into the office of Dr. Frank Damrosch, who was head of the Institute. His manner was kindness itself. He asked me to tell him with utter honesty what kind of singer I hoped to become. "One of the great ones, singing the great roles," was my naïve but unhesitating reply. He was sweet enough not to smile. "No other kind of singing career would do?" "No. Just to be a struggling second-rate singer would be too heartbreaking," I answered. Gently he asked me to face a harsh fact.

"You've tried to make a child's throat do the work of a trained artist. It is a sick voice. With endless patience and years of work you could sing artistically. Freely, spontaneously? I doubt it. But you have a dramatic instinct. It shows in your singing. Why not turn to a career where you would not be starting with a definite handicap? Why not go on the stage?" I simply couldn't talk about it, the taste of defeat was bitter. "I don't want to be an actress," was all I managed to reply.

CHAPTER 4

BELASCO OPENS THE DOOR

I FOUND MYSELF LIVING in a vacuum. The orderly routines of study had ceased. In my bitter disappointment over my singing I could not establish new ones. As the weeks passed, I faced the unavoidable fact that I *must* find some way of making a living. There was, as Mr. Damrosch had pointed out, the theatre, but I knew nothing of how one got started. Nor did I have any real desire to do so. Acting in the theatre seemed to me a poor substitute for a life dream which encompassed the larger scale of great music sung by great singers. Yet common sense told me it was a profession in which I might, with luck, make a living.

I tried to find out how one went about it. I knew no one connected with the theatre. My cousin, Adelaide, had married and given up her career. Besides, she disapproved of a stage career for me. I walked up and down Broadway listening to conversations of people who looked like players, hoping to pick up some clue as to where they were going. I did not even know the names of any but the most prominent managers—all of whom were, of course, inaccessible to an unknown neophyte. I have always found it wryly amusing to read publicity outlines of my career. How simple it all sounds. How crowded with activity! Engagement succeeds engagement. But between those words lie weeks, months, sometimes years of delay, of fruitless seeking, of endless baffled efforts to see managers whose lives seem to be chiefly devoted to evading interviews with aspiring Thespians. If one could recount vividly these frustrating experiences—much is

33

blessedly forgotten—the ranks of young aspirants might well diminish. But perhaps not! Each is sustained by the mirage of hope! Each feels that if he persists a chance will open up somehow. So I set about the business of trying to get on the stage.

Broadway seemed a strangely closed world. I knew only that somewhere down on that strange, tawdry street people *did* obviously "get on the stage." Plays were cast, actors and actresses got jobs which earned them their living. Surely it should be possible to find out how they did it. I wandered into producers' offices and out again. One day, in a moment of honesty, I faced the fact that I was rather relieved not to find them in, for usually my efforts to look and sound professional crumbled before the stony eyes of the office boys.

Someone had given me a letter to a second-rate actors' agent. He was chiefly engaged in casting road shows and stock. I would sit for hours on a bench in his office, a dreary little place plastered with endless rows of small dusty photographs of players of all ages; soulful faces, baleful faces, smiling faces. As I studied them day after day they began to look like grinning idiots. There I'd sit from early morning until the office closed. This went on for several months. Occasionally the secretary would try to ease me out, but I would blandly defeat her efforts with, "Oh, I don't mind staying. I want to be sure to be here if anything should turn up." I had the quaint notion that being in sight at the right moment might eventually lead someone to engage me. I am sure the office staff thought me a harmless lunatic, for after a while they ignored me.

I said very little about all this at home. Mother worried about my prolonged daily absences but could do little about it when I explained what I was trying to do. In retrospect I waste no sympathy on myself and my struggles at this time. Although discouragement dogged my steps, I did have a home and family to which I would return. There were other ambitious youngsters (and some no longer young!) to whom "going home" meant returning heartsick and footsore to some bleak furnished room, there to face the grim fact that even the tiny bedroom, the cheap boarding-house meals, were rapidly becoming a luxury. Such problems are an accepted part of the American actor's lot; if he is wise, he realizes and accepts the fact that uncertainty is the only certainty in his chosen profession. But this precariousness, this insecurity, is a most destructive element in an actor's life. It is one of the reasons we have what is called "show business" instead of a profession into which we can pour our best energies with some prospect of minimal continuity.

Since my early days many channels have opened up, enabling a player to practice his craft while job hunting. There are study classes, showcase groups, Off-Broadway theatres, even Off-Off-Broadway stages, where players may at least be seen, even though the salaries—if any—are scarcely at subsistence level. Conditions began to change following the first visit of the Moscow Art Company in 1906 and the subsequent founding of little theatre groups by some of the Russians who remained here. Michael Tchekov, Richard Boleslavsky, Maria Ouspenskaya as well as American directors who followed their lead all contributed to this movement. The books of Constantin Stanislavski have exerted an enormous influence on our theatre. They have become the bible of many teachers and organized groups, such as the Actors' Studio.

Other opportunities have opened up for young actors in the universities and in the subsidized theatres. People like Tyrone Guthrie, Nina Vance, Mrs. Fichandler, in Washington, D.C., William Ball and others, have founded theatres which offer continuous employment in year-round repertory. This kind of activity, if extended throughout the country, could alter the whole prospect of the American theatre. Television, modeling and occasional film assignments are also available to tide over the aspiring actor between engagements. These opportunities did not exist sixty years ago.

When I was beginning in the theatre, I had neither the means to study, nor the know-how to develop intelligently, studiously, what talents I may have had. Of course, I had the basic training of the Opera School and my singing lessons with Mme. Lillie, but what I eventually learned about acting was acquired through watching the work of players whose performances I admired. I developed a surprising ability to get into matinees without paying. And eventually I came to learn from those most exacting teachers: paying audiences.

Discouraged by my failure to get any kind of response to my attempts to break into the theatre, I decided on a change in strategy. Instead of haunting the dreary offices of the second-rate

managers I would go to the top. I would ask Mr. Conried for an
introduction to David Belasco. Down to the Metropolitan I
trotted again. I marched through the familiar 39th Street entrance to the managerial offices. To my surprise, Mr. Conried
saw me almost immediately. He was a funny, ugly, brusque little
man. I explained that I had decided to be an actress and that I
wanted a letter to Mr. Belasco. He looked at me curiously when
I described my unsuccessful efforts to get started. Looking me
squarely in the eye he said, in his strong Germanic accent, "You
know, don't you, that bad girls get along much faster than good
girls?" A little startled by his bluntness, I countered with, "But
that's not necessarily the only way, is it?" "No, but it's the sur-
est," replied Mr. Conried. Nevertheless, though he told me he
did not know Mr. Belasco personally, he gave me a brief, noncommittal introduction mentioning that I had been a pupil at
the Opera School. I flew home and added the following letter:

Dear Mr. Belasco:

I have been trying ever so hard for months to get into the theatre.
I have had no success whatever. I believe that I have talent. But I
don't know how to prove this. Above all I would feel privileged
to work with you. I enclose Mr. Conried's letter to prove that I am
not just another stage struck girl. May I please have an appointment?

I sent it off with my heart in my throat and waited. Never
shall I forget my first sight of the gray envelope with *Belasco
Theatre* in the corner. I hardly dared to open it, but when I
read the brief note inviting me to come to the office, the ache of
all those dreary disappointing months faded away.

On the appointed morning I once more mounted the stairs,
this time on wings. Now I could say to the faceless receptionist:
"I have an appointment." The little office into which I was
shown was dimly lit. It was almost completely filled by a large
desk behind which sat a thin, gray-haired man. I was motioned
to a chair facing the window. A quiet professorial voice put a
series of questions to me. Mr. Belasco's secretary was giving me
the preliminary once-over. I glibly made the most of my music
studies and of my few appearances as an extra at the Opera
House and, of course, as the Grail Bearer. The upshot was a

promise that one day soon I should receive an appointment to see Mr. Belasco. "We will let you know when."

After many days (and it is phrases like that which blandly gloss over some of one's worst hours) another gray envelope arrived in the mail. Would Miss Yurka come to the theatre after the performance on such and such a night? Would she! I counted the days. Then, one evening I put on my one and only evening dress—plain black with a square-cut neck, and, through a drizzling rain, Mila and I trailed downtown, via elevated trains and crosstown street cars. In the theatre lobby another secretary seemed to be waiting for me, a young man this time, with a soft voice and charming manners, whose concern over having to ask me "to wait a little" made me feel like Duse and Bernhardt combined. After the months of snubbing I had endured in various offices this was like a dream. Later I realized that this warm courtesy which pervaded that entire Belasco management flowed like sunshine from the man who was its head. It was something he required of those who worked for him.

As the theatre emptied, the lobby grew dark. The young man motioned me to follow him and led me down the side aisle of the darkened house to the tiny cubicle behind the boxes. There I stood blindly reading and rereading the program I had picked up on the way as if my life depended on memorizing it. At last the heavy door which led backstage opened. I saw silky white hair, small piercing black eyes, the famous reversed collar, and heard an infinitely gentle voice. All were a part of my first impression of David Belasco.

When I rose to meet him my long legs played their inevitable dirty trick, making him seem very short, me, horribly tall. Quickly I sat down again. He asked questions, led me to talk about myself. What depths of inexperience I must have betrayed I can well imagine, for, after all, I had had no actual theatre training. But my long hours of singing and the French and German lessons had evidently been of some use. "Your diction is clear and pure. Your voice has good timbre. I can sense that you have temperament. We must find out if you can act." He suggested that I prepare one or two scenes for him, that I choose them myself, and when I felt ready for an audition he would hear them.

The interview over, he called to the young secretary who had been hovering about and asked him to send for his car, as it was still raining. Half blind with excitement, I followed Mr. Belasco out through the stage door. Suddenly I remembered Mila. I stopped abruptly, blurting out, "Oh, my sister! She's in the lobby, waiting." His little eyes twinkled, whether at the sudden collapse of my dignity or at my need of a duenna, I never knew. When poor, patient Mila emerged from the stygian darkness of the lobby, she, in turn, received a gentle, understanding smile. The last picture we saw, after being helped into the limousine like two princesses, was of a friendly little man waving to us in the doorway, the rain drizzling down upon his beautiful white hair.

Mila, ready to believe the worst of managers in general, asked nervously, "Where are we going? Why does he send you in his car?" "Shut up," I whispered, lest the chauffeur hear us, "at least until we get out of sight. We can always jump out." But we alighted at our doorstep in pristine purity, our combined virtue intact and we ourselves considerably drier than we had been on previous rainy nights.

Yet the next steps were almost unbearably difficult. I mastered my audition material with the help of Mme. Lillie's husband, George, who was a singer and a very sophisticated theatregoer. He rehearsed my two scenes over and over again. Weeks grew into months. Although I learned later that Mr. Belasco's capacity for ruthlessness was as great as his capacity for kindness, I cannot believe that the slow torture of waiting that I had to endure was deliberate cruelty. It may well have been a test of the sincerity of my ambition to be under his aegis. In any case, as the season wore on, it was never convenient for him to see me. Was I expected to drop out of the picture in discouragement? I wondered. The whole matter became a nightmarish game of persistence on my part. For over eight months I would unfailingly turn up at the appointed hour, usually at midnight, after the play (Mother considered it a very odd time for interviews!). I was undaunted. "Neither snow nor rain nor gloom of night" not to mention freezing cold, could deter me from keeping those appointments. Faithful Mila was always at my side, although her own working hours required her to get up at 7 A.M.

The kindly secretary made a variety of excuses. Mr. B. was in conference with his lawyers; Mr. Belasco was suffering from neuralgia; Mr. Belasco was exhausted after an opening and could see no one. Later I came to know that these last two excuses were valid. The unceasing outpouring of his creative energy exacted its toll. He had genius of a kind, despite the tawdry plays on which he so often expended it. Once in rehearsing a very intricate production he worked for hours with the stage hands—these in their turn retiring when the actors, rested and refreshed, resumed their rehearsing. No wonder he went to bed stricken with neuralgia for weeks after the play was launched.

But I did not permit the recurrent postponement of my appointments to deter me. Always I would ask patiently for another. Only once do I remember saying to his manager, Mr. Will Dean, "You know, I don't want to be a nuisance. If Mr. Belasco really doesn't want to see me? . . ." I was assured that he did. Perhaps my persistence intrigued him.

During these weeks I continued to drift about to other managers' offices, pursuing the elusive opening. Each visit to them strengthened my determination to get my start with the Belasco management, where there was at least an organization that gave a dignity to acting, a continuity of activity that approximated one's dream of what theatre should be. And I was right. Even among his contemporaries Belasco was one of the few managers who planned ahead for his proteges, one who re-engaged from season to season supporting players whose work had satisfied him. (Charles Frohman was another.) Those whom Belasco was grooming for stardom were given opportunities to study and develop their natural gifts; I was never among those favored ones. It is an interesting fact that in most instances after stars left his management, their careers waned. Apparently it needed his touch of magic to make their stardust shine.

At home I continued to prepare myself for the oft-postponed Belasco audition. In my incredible naïveté I had selected two most difficult scenes: Shakespeare of course!—the Milford-Haven scene from *Cymbeline;* and also, a scene from Sudermann's *Magda.* I had no one to advise me; no one warned me to try simpler material, and I was blind to the childishness of my attempt to voice Magda's bitterness toward the lover who had discarded her and who was the father of her illegitimate son. I just knew the scene was "drahmatic."

Again, one night, I plodded down to the Belasco at eleven-thirty, quite prepared to hear the usual message of postponement. But even before I spoke I sensed something different in the atmosphere. The stage manager's eyes sparkled: "Mr. Belasco wants you to come back on the stage. He's ready to hear you."

I nearly fainted. Now that the hour had actually come, abject terror seized me. Mila, still with me, was led to a chair in the corner of the wings. The stage manager turned on a few footlights. "Shall I read the cues for you?" he asked. I nodded, speechless with fright. A soft voice just beyond him said, "This is really just to test out the timbre of your voice. There's no reason to be so frightened." I turned to see Mr. Belasco standing against the proscenium arch, smiling benignly. I began the first scene, half expecting to hear, "That's enough," after the first few lines, as I had so often heard at vocal auditions. My voice was strained, unreal, and seemed utterly unrelated to me.

The *Cymbeline* scene finished, I turned to see another white-haired gentleman standing beside Mr. Belasco. His face was suffused with a wistful sweetness. It was David Warfield who had come out of his dressing room after his performance and, seeing lights on the stage, had drifted in to see what was going on.

"Have you prepared something more?" asked Mr. Belasco. "Yes, a scene from *Magda*," I answered. Not a shade of a smile passed over either of their faces. There I stood spouting about "the whole scale of passions that bring us women to maturity . . . love, hate, revenge, ambition, and need—need—need . . . and the highest, the strongest, the holiest of all . . . mother love . . . *all* I owe to you!" It must have been very funny, but if anyone laughed it was inaudibly and invisibly. It was not until later that I learned to laugh at Mila's description of my pea-green face above the plain black silk dress.

Mr. Belasco spoke encouragingly of the "warmth and richness" of my voice. Mr. Warfield was presented to me and made some gracious remark. My coat was laid about my shoulders. "You mustn't catch cold, you know. This stage is drafty," said Mr. Belasco. Mila and I left, my ears ringing with his promise that I should hear from him before long.

I could not believe that it had finally happened. Of course, it was childishly unimportant compared to the miraculous tales of overnight leaps to fame and fortune to which the fan magazines have accustomed us nowadays. I should love to be able to say that he wrote a play especially for me, coached me in it and made me a star. But he didn't. My first engagement paid what is probably the lowest salary ever earned by any actress in a first-class theatre—$1.00 a week! I received exactly that, a few weeks later, as a walk-on in *Grand Army Man,* a play which Mr. War-field was doing on Saturday nights only. However, this economic ignominy was short-lived. As I was handed my dollar bill on the second Saturday night, the stage manager gave me welcome news. I was to be allowed to join, as an extra, for four weeks only, one of the road companies which was to play a return engagement in the outlying "subway circuit." I would be practically unidentifiable in the mob, but I could practice putting on makeup and get used to facing the footlights. "And it will keep you in contact with us," he added.

But this first four-week stint created a small problem. I had said nothing to anyone in the choir at St. Bartholomew's about my interview with Mr. Belasco, nor indeed about my stage aspirations. Even now I did not allow optimism to blind me to some stern facts: I would have to be absent from the Friday evening choir rehearsals, and the four weeks of "extra" work which I had finally succeeded in securing might easily be the full extent of my stage career for the immediate present. In that case I wanted to be sure I could return to my $5.00-a-Sunday job. So I decided to try to eat my cake and have it too.

The next Friday evening's choir rehearsal over, Stokowski once again found his usual swift exit interrupted. With a certain amount of trepidation I plunged. "Please, Mr. Stokowski, may I speak to you a moment?" "Yes?" "I am going to make a peculiar request. I want to be absent from the choir for four weeks beginning next Sunday." "Why?" Monosyllabics of machine gun precision were a characteristic of his speech.

"Well, that's the peculiar part," I said, "I don't want to give a reason. I just want to stay away for four weeks and then come back." One corner of his mouth twitched. "That *is* a peculiar request. But you've said that you realize that. So—report at rehearsal four weeks from tonight." He resumed his quick stride.

My four-week engagement as an extra in *The Rose of the Rancho* was fairly uneventful. It was a play in which a young actress named Frances Starr had captured Broadway. Her stellar honors were worn with a graciousness that she extended to every member of the company, regardless of his position. I was touched to receive from her, the night I joined the company, a telegram of "good wishes for your career"—a bit of thoughtfulness which I have never forgotten. The play was a concoction of synthetic values, beautifully produced but serving chiefly as a vehicle for its star's charm. In it she had been "made" overnight. After four weeks on the subway circuit the company continued its tour, while I subsided once more into my uneventful private life. But this time with what a difference! Tucked away at home in a bureau drawer was a precious document, a contract for the following season, bearing an important signature which committed David Belasco to pay me, when the new season should open, $25.00 a week as a general understudy. At last it was an accomplished fact—I was on the stage.

My return to the choir after so mysterious an absence created a flurry of curiosity among the girls in the dressing room. Only Ella Hopkins, my classmate at the Institute, had been let into the secret. Rehearsal over, came my routine request. "Mr. Stokowski, may I speak with you, please?" I was aglow with the excitement of my great news. "Now I can tell you *why* I had to be away. I'm going on the stage. I was doing extra work for Mr. Belasco these four weeks, but now I'm engaged for next season." His habitual impersonal expression melted ever so little. "When will you be leaving?" "If you don't mind, I should like to finish out the season. The play I am to be in doesn't start rehearsals until the late summer."

His reply was a bombshell. "Splendid! Then we'll be finishing together; I, too, am leaving. This will be my final term as choirmaster. I shall not return in the autumn." From the corner of my eye I could see the others wondering what this unusually animated confab with the master could signify. "And what are you going to do?" I dared to ask. "I shall go abroad for the summer, do a lot of studying and perhaps some composing. Then, possibly, take up orchestral conducting."

And so my time at St. Bartholomew's drew to an end. It had been a very significant experience for me. My early contact with the dynamic personality of Leopold Stokowski was one of the most far-reaching influences of my adolescence. Even more important than the pleasure I derived from becoming acquainted with some of the great literature of sacred music was what I learned from working with an artist who strove for perfection, who persisted unflaggingly until every ounce of capacity had been applied to a given task. His whole approach to work proved a healthy counterbalance to the over-emotional mood in which I had approached my studies at the Opera School.

Leopold Stokowski had little patience with stupidity or fuzzy thinking. Having severely disciplined his own mind, searching, I believe, into many by-ways as well as highways of thought for keener perception and more extensive knowledge, he would rightly demand that any co-worker give him the best of his capabilities. Years later his wife, Evangeline, told me that she had learned more from him than from any human being she had ever known; that in traversing a city block he would observe a dozen things of which the average person would be unaware. It is the kind of awareness that I once heard Dhan Gopal Mukerji, the Hindu teacher, describe—an ability to sense acutely and to see penetratingly things of which the average mentality gathers no impression.

After leaving the choir, I did not see Stokowski again for a long time. About seven years later, while playing in Philadelphia, I was invited to a Friday afternoon concert of the Philadelphia Orchestra. By then my former choirmaster had become the idol of both the music-loving and personality-worshipping public. Tickets were not easy to secure; it was said in Philadelphia that subscription seats for the Symphony had to be inherited.

When I returned to my hotel after the concert I sent him a note telling him how gratifying it had been to see him in the shining place he so richly deserved to occupy; that he probably would not remember his former choirgirl, but nevertheless I had reveled in the beauty of the music he was making. The next day brought a gracious reply and two tickets for the following Friday concert. He wrote that of course he remembered me, and would I be sure to come back afterwards? I was thrilled.

After the concert, the backstage of the Academy of Music was stacked with strangely shaped boxes and huge instrument cases. A group of women surrounded Stokowski. Seeing me standing in the wings he threaded his way through the clusters of advancing ladies and with a cordial greeting said, "Not remember you?

How could I possibly forget anyone who was so consistently disobedient?"

A year or two after that I happened to be in Philadelphia again when Stokowski was making elaborate preparations for a performance of the Mahler Eighth Symphony with its huge chorus and an enlarged orchestra. Since the company with which I was playing would have left the city by the time of the public performance, I wrote asking permission to slip in to a rehearsal. "Yes," he replied, "provided you hide under a seat and do not breathe, since everyone else has been refused."

In the darkened auditorium I listened, fascinated by the music and by the frequent and interesting corrections and comments the conductor made, but also by the curiously thick Slavic accent in which he made them. Gone was the crisp, clipped English speech of our choir days. Here was a man who, one felt, had *learned* to speak English, perhaps even with difficulty. It was the perfect vocal makeup for a great European conductor.

A little bewildered, I started to slip out through the same side hallway by which I had entered, and ran plumb into the men of the orchestra carrying their instruments into the outer foyer. Through their midst strode Stokowski. Forgetting for a moment that I was supposed to remain invisible, I murmured my thanks and then added, "But one thing puzzles me—the accent. Where *did* you get it?" The ghost of that twinkle of the old days appeared. He put his finger to his lips in mock secrecy. And there we left it.

Several years later, under the aegis of Mary Stewart French, I played in a performance of Sophocles' *Electra* on the stage of the Philadelphia Academy of Music where Stokowski's miracles in music were being wrought each week. I took special satisfaction in playing on his stage one of the masterpieces of my theatre world, and moreover, before an audience which included Leopold Stokowski himself. When he came back to my dressing room afterwards and said, "Brava. Your voice is an orchestra in itself," I felt that the years of striving had been well worthwhile.

That performance had one bit of casting of special interest: a slip of a girl named Katharine Hepburn was the leader of the chorus. She read her lines beautifully. The next day she left for Hollywood to be tested for *A Bill of Divorcement*.

However, the attainment of these vaulting ambitions was hardly a part of my thinking in those early days. The little Belasco contract for the following season gave me an unfamiliar sense of security, even though it was only for $25.00 a week. It seemed to call for a celebration. Typically Thespian was my behavior even at that early stage; I borrowed against my prospective affluence to finance my first trip abroad.

Mme. Lillie was planning a much-needed holiday. Mr. Schirmer's widowed mother, a matriarch of eighty, had for years held court at Bayreuth in Bavaria during the Wagner music festivals there. She was an intimate friend of the Wagner family; to her house in the course of the season came all the great and near-great to pay their respects. Mme. Lillie had been invited to be her guest. Mr. Schirmer saw to it that the invitation was stretched to include me.

Out of my choir vesper money I had saved about $100.00. In a naïve effort to start reimbursing him for the thousands he had spent on my musical education, I had offered this money to Mr. Schirmer as a first payment. Deeply touched (for apparently no one had ever tried to repay him before) he insisted that I use my choir savings toward the trip. Mila lent me another hundred, to be paid back later from the following season's Belasco salaries, and my four weeks of extra work had provided a little more. Somehow enough was scraped together for my round trip passage on a one-class boat, a few clothes and a little spending money besides. In mid-June we sailed.

Since those days trips to Europe have become a commonplace occurrence in many people's lives. But no later crossing can ever quite equal one's first encounter with a strange new world. We landed in Antwerp. My first impression was of chimes, lovely sounds pouring from towers of delicate stone lace. In Bruges I remember chiefly silence, peaceful canals and again, lace—but not of stone—soft, exquisite laces so beautiful that I became quite bewildered trying to select a piece within the limits of my slim little budget to take home to Mila. In Brussels the flower market bloomed in the midst of the square surrounded by beautiful public buildings. Everywhere, even in the smallest restaurants and coffee shops, we were offered the most delicious food. And in all three Belgian cities, Antwerp, Bruges and Brussels, there were galleries of unforgettable paintings.

Then came Paris for the first time, under the guidance of Mme. Lillie, who had grown up there and knew every corner of it. She insisted that I keep my eyes closed until the cab reached the Tuileries Gardens so that my first real view of Paris would be westward across the gardens flanked by the Rue de Rivoli, the whole scene bathed in the glow of sunset. "Paris! Paris! Ville de lumière!" I was breathless at the beauty she revealed to me!

Hectic days followed, myriads of images crowding into my eager young mind. A richly encrusted old civilization was being seen and felt for the first time by a neophyte eager to miss nothing. The mental effort of trying to speak in an unfamiliar tongue was more fatiguing than I should have dreamed possible, yet I begrudged the hours needed for sleep. For a few days we stayed at a modest little hotel. Presently I had a few restful days at a pension in St. Cloud while Mme. Lillie visited relatives living nearby.

I would sit in the garden of the little villa pension, chatting with an elderly French lady who was vastly interested to hear I was *"une artiste du théâtre."* We discussed the plays I had seen in Paris and the actresses appearing in them. She had, of course, many a racy anecdote to recount about them. Eventually she asked point blank, "You have a lover to help you?" When I denied the soft impeachment she looked at me bewildered. "But in the theatre you *must* have a lover; how else could you live in suitable style?"

I did not dare describe my own domestic life—Maminka, Mila, the boys and Rose—lest I lose all interest in her eyes. She went on. "Some of our successful actresses have several lovers; one to take care of her jewels and dresses; one for her ménage . . . and one, of course, to protect her theatre interests." I couldn't help wondering when they found time for the business of acting.

Mr. Conried's blunt words echoed in my memory. I suspected the old lady of having read too many scandal-sheets. I could hardly believe the French theatre made its sisterhood quite so dependent upon extra-curricular activities. But her gossip did add vastly to the interest with which I studied them on the stage from that moment on.

In my own plebeian case I had my pennies to do the work of dollars. There was much one could do in Paris in those days without spending a great deal of money. The river steamer running between St. Cloud and Paris took me down the Seine to spend long afternoons sightseeing or at the Louvre.

Early one dawn we left Paris for Germany, stopping briefly in Heidelberg for a glimpse of its charming mediaeval houses. Then we settled down in Bayreuth for the Festival. Bayreuth was completely dominated by the *Fest-Spiel-Haus*, the theatre built on the hill by King Ludwig for Wagner. Music was in the air one breathed, people talked of little else. In "Mama" Schirmer's villa one met everybody: conductors, singers and visiting celebrities. Their attitude toward "the Master's" works bordered on the religious, and the consecration of the performers resulted in magnificently vivid productions, superbly sung.

The art of one singer stands out clearly in my memory. Ellen Gulbranson was like a character out of a Norse saga, heroic in stature and warmly human. She sang the three Brünnhildes on succeeding days in a voice which grew clearer and more beautiful as the days progressed. The illusion created by seeing Wagner's noble concept of heroic womanhood carried through by the same person was very moving. By the time Gulbranson reached the great Spitze scene in *Götterdämmerung* the effect was overwhelming. When the act was over I was in a state of emotional exhaustion. Only Mme. Lillie's threat to send me packing home snapped me out of having violent hysterics.

A few days later I met Ellen Gulbranson at Mrs. Schirmer's. I learned that she led a unique and romantic life in Norway, with her doctor husband, hunting boar and fishing in joyous and carefree retirement. At the height of her career she had been a notable Mozart singer, but now once a year, and this only for the Bayreuth season, she would return to the stage to sing this one role, Brünnhilde. No other. Small wonder that her voice was fresh and tireless.

Bayreuth was full of notables. Lovely Isadora Duncan was living at the Hermitage a few miles outside of Bayreuth; also to be seen was Dr. Karl Muck—stern and silent. Toto Norman, who had been an actress with Mr. Mansfield, wished me well on my journey into her former world of the theatre and gave me a copy of Maeterlinck's *Monna Vanna* with the injunction that I must justify the gift by acting the part one day.

A decade or so later I did play the part for Stuart Walker. On that occasion, Toto's gift served as my prompt book. I sent her a program. She was thrilled, and so—needless to say—was I!

CHAPTER 5

NAME IN LIGHTS

DURING MY ABSENCE abroad, a great change had taken place in our family living quarters. My older brother, Charlie, realizing that the clerk's job at which he had been earning a pittance held no future, had gone to night school and then to dental college. He had graduated just before I sailed for Europe. Tatinek realized that: first, Charlie had to set up an office, and second, we had to have a home large enough to house our family of seven adults. How he did it I have never understood, but he managed to buy an old brownstone house where the two needs could be met under one roof. It must have been bought with the smallest down payment on record. For over a period of many years, all our combined earnings were pooled to carry it and pay taxes. Luckily Tatinek bought on a wide street, East 72nd Street, which turned out to be a blessing since real estate values in that section of the city eventually increased considerably. We finally sold the house in 1929 for four times what father had paid for it.

Very romantic to me was the fact that it had formerly been the home of the great Jewish star, Bertha Kalich. It seemed a good omen. "Madame" and her husband, Leopold Spachner, had lived there all through the years during which she was the idol of Yiddish theatre audiences as well as afterward, when she had won the favor of the uptown Broadway public. There were evidences of her previous occupancy in the rather ornate scheme of decoration. On the ground floor, set aside for Charlie's office quarters, the sun room, south of the long drawing room, had evidently been Madame's music room; musical instruments were painted in each corner of the ceiling. I don't know how this affected my brother's patients, as they gazed upward with distended jaws, but they were given no choice; the expense of furnishing our new home left us with no funds for redecorating. One upper room was rented by Mr. Spachner, to store books and certain pieces of furniture, and how that sixteen dollars a month helped us during those first years!

Mr. Spachner, as the husband of a star, gave sound advice to the new owner's theatrically ambitious daughter. He explained the drudgery a theatre career could entail. "An actress cannot hope to enjoy the comforts of a normal living . . . she does not actually belong to her family, her husband, her child . . . she belongs only to her art and to its demands," he said. But all that sounded very romantic to me. I was undeterred.

Beginning my career as a "Belasco actress *with a contract*," I slipped inconspicuously into the second year of the run of an unimportant but successful Civil War play, *The Warrens of Virginia*. It was the familiar story of a Southern belle who fell in love with a Yankee soldier. I was general understudy for most of the parts, from the black Mammy to the lovely blond heroine, and I was also cast to play Aunt Mollie, the sixty-year-old maiden sister of General Warren.

As I knew less than nothing about character acting, my performance was pretty dreadful. Some kind soul showed me how to make up and put on a gray wig. Fortunately, Mr. Belasco never saw me, for he was immersed in a new production. As I was a replacement, the asssistant stage manager rehearsed me. On my opening night I experienced genuine stage fright for the first time; as I sat waiting to speak my first lines, a nightmare familiar to my childhood gripped me; my hands as they fumbled the bit of sewing in my lap, seemed to grow larger and larger. I stared at them in terror. Suddenly I heard my cue. The sound of my own voice snapped the illusion—my hands looked normal again.

After a few weeks in New York we began the road tour, my first. To me it was a great adventure. We played mostly major cities, with occasional one-night stands. Although it was a company of seasoned veterans, they were surprisingly patient with my ignorance of acting and of theatre etiquette. Emma Dunn, a gifted character actress who played Mrs. Warren, gave me many helpful hints, and her warm humanity enriched my understanding of many things outside of theatrical matters as well.

My close friend in the company was a girl whose childlike daintiness was an amusing contrast to my own somewhat exaggerated maturity of voice, physique and manner. Hers was one part, General Warren's little daughter, which, for obvious reasons, I did not understudy. She was a tiny golden-haired youngster who at sixteen was already a stage veteran, having started acting when she was four years old. Her name was Mary Pickford.

Mary took charge of my backstage ignorance and handled it and me with a firm hand. Young as she was, I learned a great deal from my little mentor. We enjoyed that special camaraderie which only develops on tour when a company is thrown together in constant association. We shared dressing rooms, occasionally reducing expenses by doubling up in hotels as well. Traveling on $25.00 a week called for economy. To me, though, it seemed like affluence after my Sunday choir stipend. Mary, to be sure, earned a great deal more.

We breakfasted daily on bananas and milk because this dish at Child's was filling and cost only five cents. Mary was the eldest child in her family, and her chief concern was how to provide for her mother, sister and brother back East. Most of her salary went to them, and her unselfishness made a deep impression on me. Because of her assumption of family responsibilities, Mary was understandably money-conscious. One day in the dressing room she told me an extraordinary story.

When she was a very little girl, she said, her mother went to a fortune-teller in Toronto. "You have three children," she was told. "One of them will be so rich some day that you can't even imagine it now." And then came the amazing prophecy—I remember Mary's very words: "Her name and face will be known and loved in countries where she will never set foot." It was quite a prospect for the hard-working child!

I found her a delightful traveling companion. And spunky! One snowy winter night in Cleveland we were walking the few blocks back to the hotel after the performance. About halfway there, two men accosted us, apparently mistaking our "professional" reasons for being out at that hour. We quickened our pace, trying to ignore their remarks, but they followed, continuing their comments. Under her breath Mary whispered, "Don't answer yet; wait till we get to the hotel. I'll tell them what's what." As we reached the marquee she turned on them. The flood of invective that poured from the lips of that golden-haired child would have startled a dock-worker. For a moment the men just stood there frozen in astonishment, then took off and scuttled up the street. Mary grinned at me as we went indoors. I felt a little like a St. Bernard being protected by a barking poodle.

Except for Emma Dunn, no one bothered to tell me much about acting. I think they had little idea how eager and willing I was to learn, and I was too self-conscious to be frank about it. Also, alas, in my ignorance, I did a few things which must have appalled the older members of the company. As in choir days, still a poor judge of time, I made a bad stage wait during that tour. It gave the plot a surprising twist and nearly wrecked the performance. The scene was General Warren's living room at 4 A.M. Behind the door, stage right, the Union soldier with whom the lovely Southern heroine was in love, had been locked in, as a prisoner of war.

During my long waits between scenes I would read in my top floor dressing room. One matinee day, descending at a leisurely pace, I suddenly heard my cue. Gen'l Warren was on stage with his family clustered about his knees. The set was flat against the back wall of the theatre and one had to cross under the stage to reach the other side. I realized that there was no time for me to reach my proper entrance there. Frantic, I dashed on stage through the nearest available door. Old Aunt Molly emerged breathless, in a nightgown and nightcap, at four in the morning, from the Union soldier's bedroom!

Why I did not receive my notice then and there, goodness only knows. A story which reached me afterwards might explain it. The star, Frank Keenan, had wanted his daughter to play my part so that she might travel with him at the management's expense. Mr. Belasco cast me instead. Knowing that this contravention of his star's wishes might make my position in the company uncomfortable, Mr. Belasco had casually circulated the rumor that I was the "daughter of the Vice-President of the Associated Press." The star apparently respected that fact, though not my talents. I was reprimanded but, to my great surprise, was allowed to stay.

Mary Pickford had started her acting career as a child of four or five in the tawdry melodramas of that day of the type of *The Fatal Wedding, Bertha, the Sewing Machine Girl,* etc., and these had been her life until she graduated into the Belasco sphere to the *Warrens of Virginia.* While we were on tour, in Cleveland I believe, one of these melodramas was playing and, more in the spirit of fun and adventure than anything else, Ralph Kellard, Charles Waldron (later the brilliant Mr. Barrett in Katharine Cornell's *Barretts of Wimpole Street*) and I went to the matinee. Mary Pickford accompanied us. I don't recall the name of the play, but Ralph, Charles, and I sat there all afternoon laughing at the extravagant melodramatic situations and, of course, at the actors. We made a kind of Roman Holiday of the whole afternoon, a note of smug superiority in our attitudes, I am sure. When Mary and I returned to our hotel after the matinee, she burst into tears. "You were all just awful," she sobbed. "Those actors were working just as hard to be convincing as any of you snobbish Broadway actors. I think you all behaved dreadfully." And I, feeling very shamefaced, could not have agreed with her more. We never referred to the incident again, but it did teach me a lesson.

The tour ended. We disbanded. Mary, facing a summer of idleness which she could ill afford, found work in a dingy "studio" on West 14th Street, where a hawk-faced man named Griffith paid her $5.00 a day for working at a strange new kind of entertainment called "motion pictures." She was a little shamefaced about it when I went down to watch her work; she felt it a comedown for one who had so recently been under the Belasco management. "But after all," she said, "we all have to eat."

Mary's diminutive size, her curls, above all, her charm and her talent were ideally suited to the new medium. It took only a few years before the face and tiny figure of "America's Sweetheart" were "known and loved" from the Atlantic to the China seas, "in lands on which she would never set foot." And I still don't believe in fortune-tellers!

I saw Mary very rarely during her ascent to glory. Once I lunched at Pickfair, but the old intimacy seemed to have evaporated. When she was staying at the Hotel Pierre in New York, years later, she invited me for cocktails. By then she was famous all over the world, and bore her fame simply and modestly. Inci-

dentally, that afternoon at the Pierre I had the pleasure of meeting Maurice Chevalier, whose charm and graciousness I had always admired so much on the stage and screen. I was surprised to
find him a sombre and rather melancholy person—not at all
what one would expect. His appearances in recent years in his
one-man show have sustained his reputation for the gaiety,
charm and intelligence that make him a fascinating artist.

David Belasco developed the reputation of having a genius for
casting. There was never a bad performance in any of his productions. I once asked T. J. Benrimo, one of his steadily employed actors, how Belasco managed always to get such perfect
performances. He said: "The old man does it by the simple
process of spending a little extra money. He will engage a
$400.00 actor for what would be considered by anyone else a
$40.00 part. He knows that good actors cannot give bad per-
formances no matter how small the parts." Personally, I think
that Benrimo was underrating Belasco's extraordinary power of
direction. He had the ability to draw out an actor's potential
talent and was able to get better than average performances out
of every one of his actors. It became almost routine that a Belasco play would open in the early autumn, run all season and
then tour the following season. For fifteen or twenty years he
had almost no failures.

At the time that I happened to stumble into his establish-
ment, I didn't see him do much of the kind of directing for
which he was famous. But someone described an incident to me
which sheds some light on his methods.

A woman star was rehearsing in one of his plays. Although she
was capable and knew her business she seemed unable to rise to
the emotional climax of this particular play. The end of the play
was, in a sordid way, high tragedy. Playing a small part was a
young character actress who had never been able to get anything
but character parts on Broadway. She was a very successful leading stock woman and knew she could play other parts, but because she was not conventionally pretty, she was never given a
chance to do anything else and always played women twenty to
thirty years older than herself.

Belasco could be very kind but he was absolutely ruthless in
his quest for results. He told this character actress that he was
considering putting *her* in the leading part. She memorized it

and worked frantically on it. One day at rehearsal he told the stellar actress that she was dismissed for the day but that if she wished to, she could hang around and see somebody play the part who was really capable of doing it. He then had the character actress rehearse the big scene. Of course her heart was in it and she played it to the hilt. The star who had been humiliated in front of the company went into screaming hysterics. After a moment or two Belasco turned to her perfectly cold-bloodedly and said, "That's what I've been trying to get out of you all day and that's what you are going to keep in the play." Of course the character actress nearly died; she had been used! She went back to her small part, but later Mr. Belasco starred her in another play that suited her talents perfectly. When it served his purpose he could be cruel, but he also made the reputations of the people with whom he worked.

The tour of the *Warrens of Virginia* ended. When I reported to the Belasco office, I had heartening news. There would be a bit part for me in a farce called *Is Matrimony a Failure,* with which "Mr. B." would start his season: rehearsals began in July, and we opened in August. The play—an adaptation by Leo Dietrichstein from the German—was a farce about the upheaval caused in a small town when its married couples find out that through a legal complication, they are not married at all. At that time the theme had not yet been worn threadbare.

Mr. Belasco had assembled a fine company of farceurs. There were four leading roles. One, a young wife, was played by a girl with extraordinarily beautiful dark eyes named Jane Cowl. She had for several seasons been cast in minor parts by Mr. Belasco. This was to be her first lead. There were several other equally good parts, though none were of stellar prominence. I had only a few lines to speak.

In the long intervals between my brief scenes I would sneak into the little red cubicle behind the boxes where my first interview with Mr. Belasco had taken place. As I peered through the curtains at the rear of the box, the changing face of the audience became a fascinating thing to watch and study. Knowing all the lines of the play, I learned much about the way those clever, experienced comedians timed their points. These impressions were to serve me well the following season, when the play went on tour and I graduated from the rank of understudy to play my first really good part, the character lead. During that long tour I gained immensely in confidence and in the ability to handle myself before an audience.

But the next season there was, alas, no part for me on Mr. Belasco's program. Willy-nilly, I had to venture once more into the theatre world outside his comfortable and genial management.

Endless stories have been told about Mr. Belasco—tales of the almost Oriental lavishness of the parties he would sometimes give; the equally Oriental shrewdness of his business contracts with some of his players; his capacity for towering rages and sadistic practices exercised to develop the emotional intensity which he required from some of his budding stars. All these stories were part of the legend which he had become even during his lifetime. But he was capable of great kindness, too. During the out-of-town tryout at the beginning of my second season, I lost my purse. It was a serious matter for me; I would have to borrow enough money to pay my week's hotel bill. Somehow he heard of my mishap. The gentle-voiced secretary stopped me one day. "The Guv'nor has heard about your purse. He has instructed me to take care of your hotel bill, but he thinks you might need this in the meantime." And he handed me my week's salary.

I once heard him give his stage manager a terrific tongue lashing for the dullness of an ensemble scene which we were rehearsing. The scolding of the stage manager was simply an "act." His remarks were carefully planned to stimulate *us* to new effort. Mr. Belasco admitted this to me later.

Out on my own once more, it was not pleasant to beard the agents and the office boys again, though now I was fortified with the fact that I had played a lead with Belasco even though only in a road company. But I had no luck. Weeks and months slipped by. Finally, in desperation, remembering a tip I had had from an older member of the *Warrens* company, I bribed a well-known agent with the promise of an extra fee if she would get me into something—anything. This somewhat dubious deed, I was told, was frequently resorted to in those days when there was no Actor's Equity. Legitimate or not, the bribe produced results. Soon afterward I was engaged for a trivial opus in which I played a New York society girl, a female stuffed shirt if ever there was one. Nevertheless, the play, *An Old New Yorker,* gave me my first opportunity to appear in a leading "society" part on Broadway and to wear some lovely clothes. It gave me very little else, except a depleted bank account, for in those days actresses provided their own clothes when they wanted a part as badly as I did. The play ran one week. My salary was $100, all of which went to the agent. I had spent many times that amount on my various changes.

But the costumes were not a total loss. A few weeks later I had an offer to play in a summer stock company in Dallas, Texas, where they were put to good use. The actor who steered me to the Texas engagement knew little about the management. I took the chance of being stranded.

As the slow train crawled across the continent, Mila and I began to doubt the existence of the state of Texas, map or no map. Nevertheless, we finally arrived at Dallas, moved out to Oak Cliff where the theatre was located, and began a very happy summer. In a ramshackle, wooden structure in an amusement park called The Oak Cliff Casino I played a great variety of roles in plays that ranged from *Madame X,* through *The Great Divide,* to George M. Cohan's musical comedy, *Forty-five Minutes from Broadway,* in which I had to sing and dance. The study for those roles was exacting, to put it mildly, forty to sixty "sides" (the pages on which lines and cues are typed) were my usual weekly stint. Yet I managed to find time for gay parties. Texan hospitality is not to be resisted, and the men of Texas can be charming. Two devoted beaux made my life outside the theatre one long fête. How I managed to go to midnight picnics and Sunday country club lunches while learning all those "sides" is still a mystery to me.

The leading man, a tired Irishman whose eyes were failing him, viewed my hectic social life with a sympathetic and approving eye. One day he warned me: "Take it all, Honey, but when they start talking marriage, run like Hell. For that's when you begin to pay for all this fun." I took his advice. When I returned to New York in September it was with considerably more social experience.

In spite of all the leading roles I had played that summer, no manager of any importance bothered to notice me in the season that followed, nor for several succeeding seasons. Had it not been for the occasional stock engagements with which I filled in

I should have made sorry progress indeed. Nevertheless, one could not play all those varied parts, even under hectic stock company conditions, without learning a great deal about audiences.

While playing one of these engagements at the Chestnut Street Opera House in Philadelphia, I passed a milestone. On my way to rehearsal the second week my eye was caught by the marquee over the entrance to the theatre. I gasped. There, in electric lights, was my name! Just why? I did not stop to inquire. I dashed across the street to a camera store and asked them to snap a picture of the theatre immediately. I wanted to send it to my family, fearful that the name might not be there by evening. The juvenile lead was a tall, thin young man with a quaint personality. When Melchior Lengyel's play *The Typhoon* was being cast he seemed a better type for the stellar role (that of a Japanese student) than the rather burly leading man. So the latter took a week off and the juvenile took his place. He was very good. So good that the next week, on the other side of the theatre marquee, *his* name went up in electric lights which spelled out EDWARD EVERETT HORTON. Recently in Hollywood we compared notes about it and it developed that he, too, had taken a picture of the theatre to send to his family.

Returning to New York I again tramped the stairs to the agents' offices. The one whom I had overpaid to get a part in *An Old New Yorker* the previous season evidently decided to make it up to me. I was sent to see the most charming of managers, Winthrop Ames, who was organizing a road tour for Rudolph Besier's play, *Don*. It was a modestly told story of middle class English life. There were two heroines, the English fiancée of the hero and a sad lady of lowly station, whom he was befriending. Automatically assuming that I was being considered for the persecuted one, I dressed accordingly in a plain dark suit. In the middle of the interview I realized my mistake. It became clear from Mr. Ames' remarks that I was being considered for the ingenue lead! Hastily I pleaded a forgotten engagement and asked to be allowed to come back in the afternoon. I returned in a girlish frock and a wide straw hat; and was engaged for the part of the fiancée. Years later when I confessed my ruse to Mr. Ames, he smiled. "Don't you suppose I knew what was happening?" he said.

Don toured briefly. The play folded in Mikwaukee, and once more I began making the rounds. I wormed my way into the cast of an allegorical play called *Everywoman* which was then on its final road tour. I was cast, of all things, as Vice, a gaudy wench who did a few simple dance steps as she beckoned several underpaid extras to what was presumably their moral doom. Under a flaming red ostrich feathered headdress, which I invented myself, I rolled my heavily beaded eyes with what I fondly hoped was allure, as I had seen it done in some movie.

Mme. Lillie and Mr. Schirmer came to a matinee. He was horrified. "What is she doing playing such a part as Vice?" he asked. I was hurt. Wasn't it real acting to do a part so different from my personality? I asked Mme. Lillie. "After all, he admires Mary Garden when she plays 'Thais' doesn't he? She's certainly no lady!" Mme. Lillie smiled but made no further comment.

I was also understudying the *title* role of Everywoman and *this* time I had a chance to play it, once in New York and once in Springfield, Massachusetts. I believe I did not disgrace myself; in the latter city at any rate I got a very good notice. At the New York matinee Tatinek sat in the first row and explained to the musicians in the orchestra that the leading lady, that afternoon, was his little girl. The next day I resumed my role of the Scarlet Lady.

From this engagement flowered an enduring friendship with Patricia Collinge who played Youth so charmingly. Soon afterward she went into the "Pollyanna" phase of her career. That a mind so brilliant, so caustic and "debunking" as hers should have been immersed for years in treacly parts was ironic. The ingenue quality of her personality being exploited in those days was something she herself deplored. "I think it sour," she once said, "and it comes out so sweet!" Later, her heartbreaking and beautiful performance in *The Little Foxes* reminded the public and critics of her great talent. Since then her brilliant pen and her occasional appearances before the motion picture camera have increased her public considerably.

That summer, by hounding the office of a stock agent named Wales Winter, I found myself in New Haven, where an Italian business tycoon named Poli was running a year-round two-a-day stock theatre where the prices ranged from 10 cents to 30 cents for the best seats. He had a small chain of similar theatres throughout New England and had made a fortune through them. He gave actors a lot of work! We rehearsed every morning; played a matinee every day! Incredible as it seems, I played stellar roles for nine weeks. It was a ceaseless grind of morning rehearsals, daily matinees, with Thursday mornings free for memorizing. Yet I thrived on it. Again I found time for a couple of beaux. I became the pet of my "10-20-30" Poli public. The newsboys all called me Blanche—a sure proof of success.

There were players in such companies who did this kind of engagement year in, year out, fifty-two weeks in the year. They were known to agents as stock actors. This was dangerous for them: stock could either make or break a player. Occasionally, by some miracle, one of them would escape the destructive effects of hasty study and routine direction. Among the fine actors who emerged from this kind of sweat shop were Laurette Taylor, Fay Bainter (who told me she had once played eighty weeks of stock leads), Marjorie Rambeau—and countless others.

A singular thing occurred just after the season ended. The closing bill at Poli's had been the old Belasco success *The Girl of the Golden West*. The sold-out houses made my farewell week a pleasant one, and my New Haven audience gave me warm evidence of their affection. By an odd coincidence, when I returned to New York on the Monday following, I was taken to the Metropolitan to hear the Puccini opera based on the play. Emmy Destinn, the famous Czech soprano, sang the title role of *La Fanciulla del West*. As the performance progressed, I experienced a curious sense of relief. Not so long ago I had been obsessed by the aching longing to be such a singer as this great artist. Any other career had seemed a cheap substitute. Yet now I was acutely aware of the fact that only forty-eight hours earlier, playing the very same part, I had had the sensation of holding an audience in close embrace in just these same situations; they had laughed when I wished them to laugh, had followed with attentive absorption the scenes in which the old melodrama exerted its power.

Here, in the vast reaches of the Opera House, "the girl," for all her glorious singing, seemed a puppet, in contact with her audiences only by remote control. It came to me clearly, and with a comforting sense of relief, that the old ache which I had subtly felt whenever I listened to an opera was gone. I was no longer a frustrated singer who had turned to stage acting as a compromise. Gradually I had been weaned away from my first love, and the healing of the old wound was complete. Henceforth stage acting was to absorb my enthusiastic and undivided energies.

CHAPTER 6

DAYBREAK

MEANWHILE EVENTS IN the world at large had taken a grim turn. First Europe and then America had been caught up in the tragedy of World War I. Actors soon became involved in playing benefits and performing at recruiting rallies. I took part in my share of these and also supported the magnificently organized Stage Women's War Relief. But looking back at that period I am both amazed and shamed at how little the fact that we were at war affected my personal life. My only explanation is that getting a foothold in the world of the theatre required such intense effort and concentration that I tended to ignore whatever went on outside that world.

It took a great deal of energy and all my emotional resources simply to survive the frequent disappointments. For each time that I thought I had finally surmounted some obstacle it would turn out that I was very far from having "arrived." Thus I had returned from my New Haven engagement with very high hopes; the star parts I had played there had given me new confidence. Moreover, I had tasted the heady wine of a small town's adulation (and how the stock company audiences do feed that need of an actor's soul!). There is great danger in this adulation; an actor is prone to forget how much of it is due to his playing consistently good parts; he forgets, too, that the audiences develop an uncritical affection for the player's personality, not for his artistry. However, if an actor can manage not to lose sight of these facts, the confidence derived from a certain amount of work in stock companies can be very valuable indeed. It by no means permitted the kind of slow development to be found in true repertory, but it did have an important place in the lives of many good actors of those days.

At last I felt I was a real leading lady. Some manager, surely, must have seen or at least heard about the remarkable performances I had been giving only two hours away from Broadway! Were not potential stars always being "discovered" in these outposts of the drama? Besides, was I not returning to New York with the most becoming outfit I had ever owned, bought in New Haven's smartest shop? With my two-a-day earnings of $150.00 a week—out of which I furnished my own weekly wardrobe changes—I had treated myself to a plum-colored duvetyn suit and a broad beaver hat of the same color. In that outfit, I was convinced, no manager could resist engaging me on sight.

They resisted, alas, with unanimity and without the slightest effort. Week after week rolled by. I let myself be seen until the lovely plum-colored ensemble began to feel like a uniform. It lost its freshness and I my optimism. Frantically, I pleaded with one of the agents, "Can't you get me something? Not necessarily a lead. I don't even ask to get into a success. I'd just like to open in a play—any play!"

The little gods, the very little ones, must have heard me, for presently I was rehearsing the French maid in a melodrama of intrigue called *Secret Strings*. I had almost nothing to say. My big scene consisted of bringing on a coffee tray, poking a fire and straightening a chair. It was hardly a situation into which to inject all I had learned playing those leading roles in stock, but evidently I did try to do just that, for one day the director caustically begged me not to hold up the play. His sole stage direction to me was, "For God's sake get on with it!" I was crushed.

My chief remaining impression of the whole silly engagement centers around its star, Lou Tellegen. The handsome Greek actor had been brought to this country by Madame Sarah, as he called Bernhardt. During the rehearsals M. Tellegen had smiled upon me. (It was the plum-colored suit that did it, I was sure.)

Night-clubs were in full swing, and when he invited me to go dancing with him after the play I was flattered and pleased. I did not know that he was one of the world's best dancers. The tango was his specialty, showing to magnificent advantage the long, lean lines of his superb body. My dancing, ordinarily adequate, that evening became worse and worse; I muffed step after step. My cheeks grew hot and my spine grew cold with embarrassment. I wanted to drop dead.

But M. Tellegen was charming about it all and apparently

managed to retain some interest in me despite my awkwardness. As we drove up to my family's respectable-looking brownstone house he asked,

"You leev here?"

"Yes."

"Weeth father, mother, seesters and brothers, you say?"

"Yes, Monsieur Tellegen."

A long pause. Then, thoughtfully, "Too bad, too bad." He kissed my hand, waited for me to open the door and left.

Yet it was not only his continental mind that found my living with my family odd—even unconventional. Any number of professional friends remarked upon it, some critically. But I was not too impressed by the results of their more egocentric patterns of living. We pay a price for everything. And the loving devotion of those dear ones was to cushion many of the blows which life deals to all of us.

Eventually (and oh! the tramping of pavements that word covers!) another, even less impressive job turned up. A stock star from the Bronx decided to crash Broadway with a dramatized version of Reginald Kauffman's *The House of Bondage,* billed as a "sensational exposé of the white slave traffic." (Today it would not cause a ripple.) I was engaged to play Violet, the Cockney inmate of the bordello in which we were all supposedly plying our trade. Violet had one or two quite funny lines, and I wore a really seductive costume in my only scene. I managed to acquire a plausible Cockney accent by trekking up to Pelham, after rehearsals, to work with Emma Dunn, an expert in dialects. The play was foredoomed and was ridiculed as it deserved to be. But even my appearance in this meretricious opus brought me one tiny gleam of encouragement.

I received a note from Arthur Hopkins, a new producer who was just beginning to emerge from the relative obscurity of producing sketches for vaudeville. His note suggested that I come to see him. His little office was filled with that concentrated silence which was part of his aura. He broke it to say, "I saw you in that dreadful play last night. You did a good job. I haven't a thing to offer you now, but when I do you'll hear from me." It was the briefest of interviews.

Although his taciturnity never failed to paralyze me, I have always remembered gratefully the kindly hand he held out to me as a beginner. For a beginner one continues to be until that necessary "break" comes, the mere possibility of which keeps us all going on in the face of black discouragement. A young actress gains valuable experience from playing in failures. They can be useful as well as disheartening. But by now I had begun to wonder whether I should ever play more than a week in anything. Fate finally relented.

Mr. Lee Shubert had seen me in one of my fleeting appearances and offered me the chance to be with E. H. Sothern, who was planning a return to the stage after a period of retirement. It was comforting to put behind me the tawdry junk in which I had been playing and to be associated with a distinguished actor. The care which E. H. lavished upon the smallest detail of production was meticulous. Every laugh was planned with arithmetical precision. He had a devoted following which seemed to be drawn from the old guard. I was impressed by their conservative dignity, their Carnegie Hall look, so unlike the composite face which the average New York theatre audience had come to have. It was as though they had emerged from retirement to see their beloved Eddie Sothern again, only to return to their Gramercy Park environs.

The first of his season of plays was a little teacup comedy by Alfred Sutro called *The Two Virtues.* I played the giggling girl companion to the heroine. That part was played by lovely Charlotte Walker. An English actress, Haidee Wright, did one of her brilliantly caustic portraits as the hero's snobbish sister.

Both Miss Walker and I towered over our star, but he seemed not to mind. It was pleasant not to feel apologetic for one's height. He coached Miss Walker in her every inflection, her every movement. After one such session, as Charlotte joined us out in the darkened auditorium, Miss Wright said to her in her curiously quavering voice, "How can you bear to be told every tiny little thing? I marvel at your patience." To which Charlotte replied in her velvety Southern voice, "Miss Wraht, honey, if you knew the pahts that ah've held on to by lettin' stahs teach me how to act!" We all three grinned.

Julia Marlowe, Mr. Sothern's wife, who for many years had co-starred with him, was no longer acting. Together they had made "Sothern and Marlowe in Shakespeare" a household phrase. She was still beautiful—fine bones triumphed over the years. Just seeing her about was exciting. She always dined with E. H. in his dressing room after the matinee. One afternoon she must have slipped in while we were all still on stage. I had been in my adjacent room only a moment when I heard him complain as he passed into his, that he had struck his foot against a stage brace and hurt himself. A voice uttered only three words: "Did you, dear?" Mila and I stared at each other. "Have you ever heard so lovely a sound?" she whispered. One thought of softest velvet, purple pansies, distant music. It was a voice filled with magic. Mr. Sothern told me that even after her retirement she con-tinued to have her daily voice workout with her teacher. Whether she was reading a poem at a recruiting rally or merely speaking to a salesman in a shop the magic sound was potent.

The Two Virtues did only moderate business, so Mr. Sothern decided to dig out an old relic of his father's repertory—*Lord Dundreary,* earlier known as *Our American Cousin.* It had often been revived successfully, but audiences in the meantime had grown much more sophisticated. The mechanics of comedy which E. H. had used all his life were no longer effective. The play had a brief run. It was never revived again. Mine was the part played by Laura Keene with the elder Sothern at the Ford Theatre on the fatal night when Lincoln was shot. All the cos-tumes (the original ones) were still in perfect condition. I wore a lovely tea-rose brocade. No one came to see the play. After three weeks of dreary business, Mr. Sothern revived another of his former successes, *If I Were King.* This play, too, had lost its appeal and the season at the Booth Theatre came to an end. Several weeks of idleness ensued.

Presently Mr. Hopkins, true to his promise of a year or more before, offered me the part of the Queen in a play called *The Happy Ending.* I accepted with delight. Suddenly I had a call from the Shubert office. They had heard that I was going into another play. "But you can't," they said. "Mr. Sothern has de-cided to take *The Two Virtues* on the road. He insists upon having his original cast. You must go."

I refused. They insisted. I protested. They summoned me to rehearsal. I raged. I shuttled back and forth between the two offices, demanding my right of free choice and muttering some-thing about "mediaeval tyranny." But Mr. Sothern won out; someone else played the Queen. I had reason to be grateful for his obstinacy. *The Happy Ending* ran two weeks; Mr. Sothern's tour lasted all season.

Early photographs show him as a strikingly handsome matinee idol. I knew him as a charming man in his late sixties. He had changed very little except for his white hair. A few years after my season with him I met him walking across Boston Common looking marvelously fit, his step springy, his cheeks ruddy. They were a handsome, distinguished couple. I have always been glad to have known, even slightly, two artists whose careers, singly and together, represented such solid achievement and dignity.

Next came another long hiatus in my activities. It seemed odd that the previous season's work led to no offers, not even from Mr. Shubert. Nothing turned up. I did desultory war work and played a short, unsuccessful stock engagement in Denver. But that brief flurry of good parts only added to my restlessness. In New York no one, seemingly, wanted me even for bad parts. Not for any parts at all.

At home illness pervaded the house. In Tatinek's little top-floor room the sunshine poured in over his empty writing table. Failing eyesight and hearing were gradually immuring him in darkness and silence, away from his beloved writing, away from us all.

To make matters worse, my sister, Rose, was stricken with a badly infected finger and threatened with the loss of her arm. We all shared the strain of nursing, of carrying trays of food up three flights, three times a day. The brownstone house seemed like a prison from which I would emerge every so often to do the rounds.

One little haven of diversion was open to me. Now and then I would drop into Neysa McMein's studio five flights up in a shabby but picturesque old studio building on West 57th Street. She was a beautiful woman, in an odd, rugged Nordic sort of fashion, and had made a name for herself in the magazine world with her lovely cover drawings. She had a gift for friendship and had drawn about her a coterie of exceptionally talented people —most of whom were to become very well known indeed, among them Marc Connelly, Dorothy Parker, and Franklin P. Adams. One afternoon, after a particularly futile day, I voiced my deep discouragement to George Kauffman, one of the five

stand on the bank and watch it sparkle. I crossed through the mid-day 42nd Street traffic to the theatre. The business manager who knew me slightly let me slip in.

A special atmosphere seems to pervade a theatre which houses a success. The plot was a simple story of a young French peasant girl, in love with an English officer billeted on her mother's farm. The play was slight, but the star had a fine moment at the end when the heroine, Jeannine, bereft of her love, stands at the window as his regiment marches away. Waving a tear-drenched handkerchief, she manages to utter in a choking voice "Vive la France!" As Jane did it, it was very moving.

When success eludes an actor he develops an exaggerated inferiority complex. I hesitated but finally sent back a timid note: "If you are free and remember me, I'd love to thank you personally for a lovely performance. If not, my thanks are none the less sincere."

The answer came, radiating that warmth I was to come to know so well. As we chatted in her chintz-curtained dressing room, my deep discouragement betrayed itself in answer to her inquiries about my progress. "Two steps forward and three steps back," was the way I described it.

Instantly she took charge. As the wife of Adolph Klauber, the *Times* drama critic, she had for years accompanied him to opening nights. She had seen what I had done with various small parts, she said, and had always believed that I would amount to something. There was a part in a new play on which she was collaborating with Jane Murfin—a good comedy role which she thought I could do. As soon as the play was ready she would arrange that I be cast in it for the out-of-town tryout. I left her, touched by her desire to cheer me, but not allowing myself to count on the hope she held out.

The Japanese spy opus in which I was involved opened in Chicago and was only moderately successful. The few members of the company whom I knew went in for a good deal of steady drinking. This didn't interest me and, consequently, they found me as dull as I did them. I kept more and more to myself.

One day, I was surprised to receive a telegram from Jane Cowl: "Play finished sooner than expected. Part yours. Can you give notice and return immediately for rehearsals?" I gave my notice that evening.

Arriving in New York, I went straight from the train to the

theatre where the company was already in rehearsal. Miss Cowl came breezing in, an unforgettable picture in a flowing full-length cape of dark blue, topped by an immensely wide hat of white straw. On a leash was Bella Donna, a small mole-colored Italian greyhound that someone had given her. The buoyant gaiety which was a part of her vitality pervaded the darkened theatre; energy radiated from her and infused itself into everyone. After the gloom and depression of the past year I felt lifted into sunshine. A good cast, a first-rate management—this was theatre! Mary Boland was playing the stellar role.

Avidly I watched every scene at rehearsal. The play, *Daybreak,* was not an important one—a society melodrama which Miss Cowl and her collaborator, Jane Murfin, had originally concocted for Jane's own use. The aristocratic heroine, married to a wealthy dipsomaniac, has concealed the existence of his son, lest the child should grow up in the nightmare which her life had become. Her nocturnal visits to the bedside of the hidden child, dangerously ill, quite understandably arouse the husband's suspicions, and he has her watched. He assumes her to be having an affair with the doctor who is taking care of the sick child. Eventually there is a reconciliation between husband and wife, but not before the second act climax gives the actress a fine acting opportunity.

My role, that of the wife's sophisticated, realistic friend, kindly under her cynical exterior, was occasionally quite funny. They all seemed to like me in it. I was gratefully happy. As rehearsals progressed the leading lady began to have difficulty with her long speeches and insisted that they be cut. The authors disagreed. One day, just home from rehearsal, I was startled by a telephone call from Miss Cowl. Would I be willing to do a terribly difficult thing for her? But if it did not come off, would I promise not to feel badly, just continue as I was because everyone loved what I was doing and I would certainly make a success of it. But it had been mutually agreed to make a change in the stellar role, and Miss Cowl was insisting I be given a chance to read it. I nearly fainted. "Will you come right down now and read the big scene for us?" she asked. "Archie Selwyn says he knows you can be funny, but isn't sure you can pack a wallop. I know you can."

I tore downtown in a taxi. Fortunately I had listened attentively at every rehearsal, so I was reasonably familiar with the lines. Once more, on an empty stage, I read for an audition. I had crossed a number of stages since that first reading for Mr. Belasco, but this was the chance I had dreamed about ever since. I plunged into the big scene upon which so much depended. When I finished Jane beamed. Her lovely face had "I told you so" written all over it. Archie's impish grin gave zest to his succinct "Rehearsal at eleven, kid. I guess you've got what it takes."

That was the beginning of a friendship which refutes the notion that generosity and good will cannot exist among women of the theatre. Jane was then on the rising crest of a brilliant career; her name was a synonym for success. Few people have had so much to share. Those who have seldom pour it out in such boundless measure. Once at rehearsal she whispered to me, "I've had some success at this game, and it's fun. I think it's about time you had some too."

As rehearsals progressed she gave us a remarkable exhibition of physical and mental energy. During this rehearsal period she was also in the midst of making a motion picture in a Fort Lee studio in New Jersey. As she lived on Long Island, it meant getting up at daybreak (happy omen!) in order to be ready, made-up and on the movie set many miles away, by eight or nine o'clock. Despite the gruelling day spent under the hot studio lights, she would appear at our evening rehearsal looking fresh and lovely, generously eager to "turn her bag of tricks inside out" for me, as she put it. Night after night she spent with us until well past midnight, her unflagging vitality seemingly inexhaustible. Here was the first real coaching I had ever received. There were bad faults to overcome. I had so often felt myself to be too tall that I had a tendency to lean or drape myself against the furniture whenever possible. This was humorously and gently pointed out to me. "Forget you've ever seen Isadora Duncan" was one of her illuminating comments.

We had only seven or eight days into which to crowd an intensive course in acting before the scheduled opening. As one suggestion after another was quickly assimilated I heard Jane say to the director, "Her brain must be made of blotting paper."

The excitement and turmoil of the next weeks were like nothing I had ever experienced. The part was a long and sustained one, building up to a climactic scene which ended in a great burst of defiance at the end of the second act. Try as I would I could not keep my voice from running away with me. Turning it over in my mind, the memory of Stokowski's mode of building up to a climax came back to me. Suddenly I saw the whole scene as an aria. I saw that the emotional line could be permitted to rise, as it might if the scene were being sung, as high as G or A or even to B-flat, but *never* must it touch high C until the final climax was reached.

Next day I kept this model clearly in mind. As I finished, the director's voice called from the dark auditorium, "Swell. You got it. Now hold on to it. Play it just that way." From then on I had the scene under control.

Then there were costumes to be planned. Jane had an unerring sense of what a character should wear, in this instance lovely conservative dresses of chiffon and velvet, and one exquisite morning dress of soft French-blue crepe. One gown in particular I adored—a gray chiffon with delicate sheaves of wheat embroidered all over it in cut steel beads. Underneath went three layers of chiffon in deepening shades of pink. When I stood the effect was that of a column of gray smoke; when I sat down, the lines of the body emerged in sculpturesque expressiveness. Mme. Frances, who designed and executed the dresses, told me later that this particular dress had brought her a clientele which she had never had before—wealthy, conservative members of the so-called "upper-classes" whom she had been trying to reach for ages.

Because of her good taste, Jane always looked like a vision of loveliness. She had carefully analyzed her good and bad features (and she knew exactly what they were). She knew, too, how to make the best of her assets. She said once, "Remember, you are in the public eye until you shut the door of your bedroom at night. Never feel you can afford to look anything but your best, on or off stage."

I knew that my seediness during rehearsals bothered her. One day, at tea, she said plaintively, "That white fox you're wearing, couldn't you give it to some poor relation?" I grinned as I answered, "I suppose so, only you see, it was given to me because I'm the poor relation."

We opened in Asbury Park during the hottest week I have ever lived through. It was a popular summer tryout resort at the time; one was supposed to be able to gauge a play's chances in New York by its reception there. But the weatherman decided otherwise. The heat was inexorable. By mid-week the power-houses had to be shut down to release the fainting workers, and although we had not fainted (actors can stand anything except not acting) all the lights in the theatre were shut off.

At last the tryout was over. At midnight on Saturday I tumbled into bed and slept for eighteen hours without stirring. I had had to study so frantically, keeping myself going with black coffee, that the brief layoff seemed heaven-sent. Returning home after a week of sunshine and sea bathing, I found that further rewriting had been done. That meant more study. There was also a major change in the cast. Now, with the opening only a week away, rehearsals became strenuous again. But I was buoyed up by the management's approval. My absorption in what I was doing was complete.

Late one afternoon I reached home tired but hopeful, filled with faith in the outcome of all our effort. The house seemed strangely quiet. I went down to the kitchen where muted voices could be heard. Mila met me.

"Darling, papa fell asleep at noon and never woke up. He must have slipped away very quietly. The pillow was not even disturbed. We didn't call you home, knowing you have a big job to do."

I crept up to the plain little room. His handsome white head lay peacefully on his pillow. At the foot of the bed hung a crayon portrait of his mother which he had sketched from a photograph. I am sure she, too, heard the murmured "Maminko, draha Maminko!" (Little Mother! Dear little mother) which I had so often heard him whisper, when I sat with him for a little each day.

It was my first encounter with death. It seemed a beautiful release, and the words of Schubert's lovely song which I had often sung, came back to me: *Bin Freund und komme nicht zu strafen. Sei gutes muths; Ich bin nicht wild. Sollst sanft in meinen armen schlafen.* ("I am not foe but friend. Be of good cheer. Softly shalt thou slumber in my arms.") Tatinek had found his rest.

Opening night in New York in one's first "star" part! What layman whose work follows a routine pattern can conceive of the tension under which an actor approaches such an occasion? Some players, I suppose, take it casually, as perhaps it should be taken: as a game for which you have been in training, or a business in which you have learned to function. But I happen to know few of these. I remember, even now, what a major calamity it seemed that my gray pumps were not ready for the opening —specially ordered gray pumps, trimmed with cut steel to match the dress. The factory had not delivered them. It seemed like wanton treachery on the part of the shoemaker. I had to wear ready-made pumps.

At last the curtain rose. No turning back now! In the dim light, with my back to the audience I crept up a stairway from below the stage level, presumably from the lower hall of the house to which I was surreptitiously returning at daybreak. The suspicious husband watched me from the shadows as I vanished into a bedroom.

The prologue over, the first act proper began with a gay high noon breakfast party. As hostess, I poured coffee. Passing a cup to one of my guests, my hand shook; half of the cup's contents spilled into the lap of my lovely blue frock. It was too much! Blindly I proceeded, convinced that all our hopes of success were blasted. How could anyone's characterization hope to rise above a large brown stain on the front of her gown? But the long, endlessly repetitious rehearsals proved my salvation. So solidly had Jane and I built my performance that the play flowed on smoothly to the second act climax which had caused me so much trouble during rehearsals. I was in a trance of concentration. The big scene went well. After the final curtain a "demonstration" took place. Like an automaton I took my curtain calls. People swarmed backstage. Jane, with tears streaming down her cheeks, hugged me, and whispered, "You've done it! They loved you. Did you hear them cheer you? And they are all asking where on earth you've been all their lives?" Only then did I realize that I had not failed her.

The theatre was finally emptied and dimmed; everyone had departed. I had sent my family home with the flowers. Only a work light was left on the bare stage. At last that goal one always keeps in view had been reached. The actor's achievement is as intangible as air—an evanescent thing, its recognition depending on the verdict of some half-dozen men, the all-powerful critics. These, next morning, were lukewarm about the play, but they agreed, for the most part, that an actress had "arrived."

Daybreak ran for about twelve weeks and then went on tour. I have never forgotten the advice given me by a fine actress, Margaret Wycherly, who said to me one day: "Don't fail to enjoy this achievement now, while it is happening. It can never be your *first* success again. From now on you'll have to prove that you can do it again, and better."

I became engaged to a lieutenant, a young man of great intelligence and charm, but seemingly with no capacity to adjust himself to the need of making a living for himself, much less for a wife and possible children. The prospect of living off his mother did not appeal to me, so eventually, after a prolonged and delightful courtship, we went our separate ways. He had always had great faith in my talent, and he loved fine plays. I think he knew as well as I that the theatre would absorb me completely for some time to come.

One afternoon, while driving to the country, I had the thrill of seeing my name on a huge "3-sheet" billboard for the first time. The announcement seemed strangely detached from myself, but it seemed very wonderful. For the tour, my salary was raised from $150.00 to $250.00. Progress! Mila went on tour with me. I took special pleasure in being given, for the first time in my life, drawing rooms on the trains. Mila did not share in my snobbism; she was too friendly a soul to enjoy being exclusive. She would leave me to my elegant privacy and sit out in the Pullman where she could talk to people.

Alas, a new and unknown star proved to have little drawing power, and we closed after a few weeks. But the management shortly thereafter put me into the road tour of a little comedy called *Losing Eloise,* in which I replaced Lucille Watson. It was a filler-in for me. The play had had a fair New York run and was now playing in Chicago. I was delighted at the chance to do a comedy role. Best of all, Jane was appearing in an adjoining theatre.

Again she helped me to select my dresses. And this opening night was free from strain; I needed only to duplicate values already created by my predecessor. After each act encouraging or amusing messages came from across the alley. The opening over, I settled into the enjoyment of my new position.

Life around Jane was like a perpetual holiday. She had a zest for the good things in life, the best of everything—music, acting, food, celebrated people, and she loved sharing them all. As the wife of an important drama critic, she had met many outstanding theatre people even before she herself had become a celebrity. She had an inexhaustible fund of interesting stories about the great and the near great. Since she never wanted to sleep, she would exert her charm endlessly to keep us all staying awake with her, regaling us with amusing incidents about famous people she had known. So once again a fairy godmother, this time one with particularly gay propensities, opened the door to a sunny world of art and achievement for me.

May, 1913, had marked a milestone in the history of the American theatre when a group of courageous souls organized to remedy some of the injustices that had long plagued the lives of actors. There had always been producers who treated their play-ers with consideration. But others had followed practices that created unbearable situations. A company would rehearse an unrestricted number of weeks with no rehearsal salaries, only to have the production canceled, sometimes leaving the actors penniless. Road companies were frequently stranded in out-of-the-way places, the members having to find their way back to New York as best they could. Most actresses furnished all their own costumes (as I had found to my cost). There was no guar-antee of salary beyond the actual number of performances given, regardless of how few these might be. Stars, of course, could protect themselves against such occurrences, and did. But the supporting player, the bit player was in no position to do so; he seldom had the power to insist that safeguards be put in his contract.

Issuing a call to the acting profession at large, the protesting actors formed what has grown into the most powerful instru-ment ever created for the protection of theatre workers: The Actors' Equity Association. The battle for recognition was a bit-ter one and was waged over several years. Managers joined their forces, forming a rival association called the Actors' Fidelity League into which they lured many distinguished players who disapproved of the labor affiliations which the Equity leaders had found it essential to establish. Without the power of other labor organizations, the actors' fight could not have been won.

The theatre world was torn with conflicting interests. Managers threatened to cease producing. Stars were forced to make difficult decisions. In August, 1919, the first strike in our theatre history was called, and the Broadway stream of entertainment trickled almost to a standstill. Great sacrifices were made in all ranks of players. Frank Bacon, who had striven all his life for his place in the sun, had finally achieved it in a play called *Lightnin'*. It had been a smash hit. Unhesitatingly he closed it and joined the ranks of his militant fellow actors. On his marquee in front of the theatre he had had placed instead of his own name a new sign: *LIGHTNIN'—STRUCK!* Many made similar sacrifices.

Ethel Barrymore marched down Fifth Avenue with the striking companies. Ed Wynn acted as Master of Ceremonies for the benefit performances which were given for and by the striking actors at the Lexington Opera House. He was a sensation and became more beloved than ever by his fellow actors as well as by the public. The whole story has been told in detail by Alfred Harding in his book *Revolt of the Actors*. Few stories can cite such glamorous heroes and heroines. Courage and gaiety were shown by players of all ranks, and their willingness to stand together—stars, bit players, extras and chorus members—was a revelation to managers and public alike.

Eventually the fight was won. Actors' Equity Association became the instrument which remedied the most flagrant injustices from which its members had suffered and, moreover, as· sured to managers an equal consideration of their rights when these might be in question. With the steady growth of this organization, the dignity and self-respect of the player has been recognized as his inalienable right. His days as a "rogue and vagabond" were ended.

CHAPTER 7

I DISCOVER IBSEN

F OLLOWING MY SUCCESS in *Daybreak* I was seized with a feverish desire to go on working steadily and increasingly as though to make up for those many months wasted in frustration and idleness.

Without consulting Jane I accepted a part in a war play, *Allegiance,* sponsored by three distinguished people: its author, Amélie Rives, and its joint producers, William Faversham and Maxine Elliott. The play was a failure, but out of the wasted effort remained a colorful impression of that regal beauty, Maxine Elliott, whom someone had christened "The Venus de Milo with arms."

She had planned to make a comeback in *Allegiance* after a long period of retirement but finally decided instead to participate as its co-producer. After rehearsals we would adjourn for refreshment, and over dish upon dish of chocolate ice cream she would regale us with endless anecdotes.

We were booked to play in the theatre on West 39th Street which bore her name, and one of my favorite stories was her account of the building of the theatre. In the early stages of its construction she returned from Europe to find that her partners had altered the specifications that had been agreed upon before her departure. Indignantly she demanded that the structure be demolished and begun again according to the original plan. Her partners protested vehemently.

"We found your plans were not practical, Miss Elliott. You are, after all, an actress, not a business woman." She refused to budge. "Not practical? Are you forgetting that I am a Down East Yankee? There have been serious doubts that I am an actress, but no one has ever doubted my being a business woman." In the face of her adamant refusal to yield, the partners had no choice. At considerable expense to all, including Maxine Elliott, the structure was torn down and rebuilt. "They never again tried to put anything over me," she crowed. And indeed, the word went out to the brotherhood, "Don't tangle with Elliott, she'll win."

On another occasion she told of her relationship with a certain very prominent member of the British Royal Family. He had sent word that he would arrive at her villa accompanied only by his valet. She promptly replied that he was to come only if he were accompanied by his full entourage. "You do not sneak into my house surreptitiously, sire!" she informed him. "When one is mistress to a king one expects to be treated royally." Maxine knew how to handle men.

The failure of *Allegiance* once again left me unemployed. The season slipped by without any good offers. Then, one day Jane Cowl handed me a scenario of a play about an opera singer. It was the work of Gilda Varesi, an actress who had performed brilliantly in a number of bit parts. The play was a dramatization of the life of Gilda's mother, and she wanted Jane Cowl to play the part of the prima donna. The play was to be called *Enter Madame*. Since Jane had other commitments she suggested that I play the role of Madame. My facility in foreign languages would be an asset, as Madame had many foreign phrases in her dialogue. And Jane thought that it would be good showmanship for me to play a glamorous comedy role after the melodrama of *Daybreak*. She discussed the matter with her manager, Arch Selwyn, who agreed with her.

Jane promised to help Gilda with the writing of the play and asked me to agree not to accept any other commitments. She and Gilda were certain that the play would be ready for a late summer try-out. I agreed to wait. Most of that summer I spent with Jane at her home in Great Neck, a small house with comfortable chintz-covered chairs and interesting books strewn everywhere. A wide, deep screened porch invited one to enjoy perfect quiet. From time to time Gilda would read me a scene or two, but as the summer drew to a close the script was still far from finished. It seemed to need Jane's dynamic energy to bring it to completion. This unhappily was not available. The play she was planning to do had hit snags, and she was busy reading scripts in search of another vehicle. September, October, November slipped by—still no prospect of a completed script of *Enter Madame*. I became more and more worried.

During the preceding spring I had taken a brief flyer in religious pageantry in Columbus, Ohio, in a production called *The Wayfarer*. Originally conceived as an amateur venture to celebrate the Centennial of the Methodist Episcopal Church in America, it had grown into an ambitious production involving hundreds of extras and a professional cast of principals. At the Colosseum in Columbus it broke all attendance records as thousands of people flocked to see it. However, that had merely been a "bread-and-butter" engagement, marking time for *Enter Madame*.

Now, as autumn wore on, my restlessness over the delay of *Enter Madame* became acute. In the midst of this, I was approached by the functionaries of the Inter-Church World Movement which had financed the Columbus production. Encouraged by its success they had decided to present *The Wayfarer* in New York at the old Madison Square Garden on East 24th Street. The plan was to rent the Garden for five weeks, beginning in mid-December. Would I participate in my previous role and also direct the casting? My experience, they felt, would be valuable. They would guarantee me nine weeks' salary: four for the directorial job and five for the acting assignment.

Over a year had elapsed since the brief two-week engagements in *Allegiance* and in Jane's little comedy. Four weeks' salary in fifteen months! I asked Jane's permission to take advantage of this opportunity to replenish my lean purse. She was shocked. "You can't do a religious pageant in New York! And what about *Enter Madame?*" she asked. I pointed out that that opus was far from finished and that even *should* it be ready in four weeks, I would be available for rehearsal the day after the opening at Madison Square Garden. It seemed senseless to turn down a guarantee of several thousand dollars when I had earned nothing for over a year. Jane had a husband to pay her bills; I had not. I was accused of being penny-wise and pound-foolish; that it was a mistake to be identified with an arena and pageantry—that I should "lose face" doing it.

As things turned out she was right. From that moment the Selwyn Management lost interest in both *Enter Madame* and me. Later Jane told me that all had not been going smoothly; that the author had had her own ideas about casting and apparently it was only Jane's super-salesmanship which had kept me in line for the part. At any rate, when the play was finally finished, the author persuaded Brock Pemberton to produce it with herself in the title role. Undoubtedly she had hoped for this all along. Who could blame her? Both she and the play had a brilliant and well-deserved success. It ran for two years. But naturally I could not foresee all this. In the excitement and activity of the ensuing weeks at the Garden, I had little time to brood over the wisdom of my decision.

Producing *The Wayfarer* was like taking on the creation of a mammoth circus. The project grew and grew, until Mr. Laurence Rich, the executive director, and I were handling a Broadway cast plus some two thousand extras and choirs of hundreds of voices recruited from Methodist churches for miles around New York. The responsibilities were stupendous.

The production schedule had to be worked like a time clock. The Madison Square Garden poultry show closed at midnight. At 12:30 A.M. we took over. A crew of workmen was waiting to start clearing the place, after which the men were to lay a sloping floor and to proceed with the construction of a stage the width of the east end of the Garden (a whole city block!). Dressing rooms were built, and lighting equipment four times the size of that used at the Hippodrome (then famous for its spectacular productions) was installed. The walls and ceiling of the entire Garden were covered with fire-proofed monk's cloth. This was to give a religious atmosphere as well as to cover the ugly wooden interior. Scenery was built on a commensurate scale.

So much for the physical problems. Mine, as casting director, were equally complicated. This was before the days of microphones, and in the vast reaches of Madison Square Garden certain voices carried, others did not. It was not a question of volume; a small voice like Ruth Vivian's, reading the lines of the crippled boy, carried like a violin; some of the big, resonant voices came out as a blur of sound.

We persuaded Walter Hampden and several members of his company to become the nucleus of the professional cast during their holiday lay-off. I again did the part I had played in Columbus, the allegorical figure of Understanding which accompanied the Wayfarer on his pilgrimage through the ages. The orchestra was conducted by Henry Hadley, who had written a special score for the production. The huge cast, the camels and sheep in the Bethlehem scene, the massed choirs on each side of the stage, combined to make it an undertaking into which no one but visionaries would have ventured.

Added to all this, we had labor troubles. These Mr. Rich coped with. The whole production was insured at Lloyd's against possible failure to open, for $200,000. But open we did; and on schedule. The public poured in, and the final week showed a sizable intake of $80,000 for that one week alone. Fools rush in where "angels" (those wise men of the theatre) fear to tread! Even Morris Gest (who had brought the Moscow Art Company and Eleanora Duse to America) was impressed.

The next play offered me—months later—had promise. It was Eugène Brieux's play *Les Americains Chez Nous,* called in translation *The Americans in France.* Set in the post-war period, it dealt with the conflict between French and American mores and social values as revealed in the courtship by an American engineer of a Frenchwoman with a conservative and old-fashioned background. Despite the American's genuine love for her, she finds herself unable to accept his new world vitality and ideas and ends up by rejecting him.

Leo Dietrichstein, a brilliant actor as well as adapter of many Continental plays, was the director and producer. My brother Tony came to one or two of the rehearsals with me. Dietrichstein, in demonstrating how some of the scenes should be played, acted them so beautifully that Tony commented, "There's only one thing wrong with this play, Sis. It needs Dietrichstein in all the parts, including yours."

The New York run lasted two weeks. Utterly spent by this succession of abortive efforts, I went to Long Island to stay with a friend and to rest. I rested with a vengeance, for my hostess promptly drove her car into a tree; I was thrown out of the car and lay unconscious with a gashed knee and badly cut face until she came back to pick me up.

It was a shocking condition in which to face the opening of a new season—one failure already and what promised to be a first-class nervous breakdown hanging over me. A gleam of good sense saved me: I knew that if I should really crack up, I would eventually have to crawl back past the spot where I now stood. Someone told me of a wonderful course of exercises which proved surprisingly effective. Stretching, twisting, and breathing rhythmically, I made great progress. Not until the course had been completed did my instructress tell me that the work I had been doing was the preliminary study of Hatha Yoga. Over the years I have found these exercises and the discipline they require a most invaluable means of keeping fit. And the headstand which I learned to do then was to be very handy in a play I did some years later.

About this time a fascinating project was launched by a group of actors. In 1922 a meeting was called which most of the prominent (and affluent) players attended. Its purpose was to organize a producing unit which would be manned by the actors and actresses themselves, to produce plays which seemed worthwhile and in which the founding members agreed to appear.

I was evidently not important enough even to be invited to the meeting, but Jane was and I heard all about it from her. In a two-hour session the meeting raised some $200,000, handsome evidence of faith in the project.

The Actors' Theatre, originally called Equity Players, opened in 1923 with Jane Cowl in *Malvaloca*. Plays of varying success followed until in 1924 Katharine Cornell made a real hit in George Bernard Shaw's *Candida*. Other players who appeared later were Laurette Taylor who played *Pierrot the Prodigal*, entirely in pantomime, with music by Andre Wormser, played by George Copeland on the piano. She also appeared in a revival of *Sweet Nell of Old Drury*. It was in this play, Alfred Lunt told me, that he and Lynn determined to present Lynn Fontanne, "skinny Lynnie," as he called her, as a beauty. He said they spent every penny they could lay their hands on for costumes and jewelry. It was a successful investment. The critics raved about the "beautiful Miss Fontanne"—and have been doing so ever since.

In 1924 the Board decided to present Rachel Crothers' comedy *Expressing Willie*. The playwright was genuinely eager for me to play the second lead, a glamorous part calling for beautiful clothes. I was tempted, but simultaneously I received an offer from the Theatre Guild, still functioning in the Garrick

Theatre on 35th Street. They wanted me to play The Woman in
Man and the Masses, a tragic play by the German Socialist
writer, Ernst Toller. I consulted Jane, who, for once, considered
other than practical commerical values. "In my opinion," she
said, *"Expressing Willie* will run a year. You would be very
good in it. But you must do *Man and the Masses.* It is an important play and it needs you."

Man and the Masses had been written at white heat during
Toller's imprisonment following the failure of the post-war revolutionary uprising in Bavaria. That experience fanned into
flaming ardor his pacifist convictions, which poured forth in this
bitter diatribe against all militarism. The short, stark phrases,
written in poetic form and beautifully translated by the poet,
Louis Untermeyer, presented us with acting problems; they had
a rhythm of their own. Lee Simonson, who designed the settings,
was also the director; a more difficult assignment for his first
effort in that new field would have been hard to find. The choral
speeches took endless hours of rehearsal; voices as well as nerves
grew ragged.

Instead of realistic scenery, steps and platforms were designed
duplicating those used by Leopold Jessener in the original German production. They confined our movements to a terrifyingly
limited area. I was always expecting to topple off the high boxes
on which many of my scenes were staged.

My role, a very demanding one, was that of the Eternal Pacifist. Jacob Ben-Ami played the opposing protagonist, the fiery
revolutionary. His job was to incite the masses with his flow of
demagoguery; mine, to control them with gentle reasoning.

The effect of Toller's play on the public in America was nul-
lified by the fact that at the time it was presented, in the early
twenties, the "masses" in this country were getting very high
wages indeed. Laborers of all sorts were in such demand that it
was very difficult to get anything done. The average American
theatregoer was not especially concerned with the hunger and
privations of workers in post-war Germany, only with how to get
a good plumber. Although the play had had a tremendous impact in Germany, in New York the public stayed away in droves.
While I had been prepared for this, I was depressed, as one inevitably is when a play fails to "click." And there was *Expressing
Willie* packing them in!

16 Douglas Street,
St. Paul, Minnesota,
the house in which
Blanche Yurka was born

Karolina Yurka,
"Maminka"

Blanche Yurka, 1889

BELOW: *Tony, Blanche, Mila and Rose Yurka*

Charlie Yurka

BELOW: *Anton Yurka,
"Tatinek," at the Czech Branch
of the New York Public Library*

Blanche Yurka in Balfe's A Bohemian Girl

OPPOSITE: *Blanche Yurka in Balfe's* A Bohemian Girl

Rudolph Schirmer

BELOW: *Mila Yurka*

OPPOSITE: *Blanche Yurka as one of the flower maidens in the first production of* Parsifal *at the Metropolitan Opera House*

David Belasco

OPPOSITE: *Leopold Stokowski at the time when he was choirmaster at St. Bartholomew's Church*

Blanche Yurka in her plum-colored duvetyn suit and broad beaver hat. This outfit became a job-hunting uniform.

OPPOSITE: *Mary Pickford as Betty Warren in David Belasco's production of* The Warrens of Virginia

Blanche Yurka in E. H. Sothern's production of Lord Dundreary, *wearing the original costume worn by Laura Keene at the Ford Theatre the night Lincoln was shot*

Taken when I was first "starred".

Blanche Yurka when she starred in Daybreak

Jane Cowl

*During a pensive
moment*

Blanche Yurka as The Woman in Ernst Toller's Man and the Masses

Blanche Yurka as Gina and Helen Chandler as Hedvig in the Actors' Theatre production of Ibsen's The Wild Duck

One evening while dining with Dudley Field Malone, the internationally famous lawyer who had been a friend of mine for years, I expressed my disappointment. Feeling particularly sorry for myself because the play was not drawing the public, I made a few self-pitying comments. He had attended the performance the night before and had been deeply stirred. There was a scene toward the end where The Woman speaks, in moving phrases, of mankind's need of tolerance. Dudley Field Malone's words startled me: "Don't you realize that many men in public life strive most of their lives for the opportunity to voice sentiments like those? And you are privileged to do it eight times a week, for six weeks! Forty-eight times! I envy you. Be grateful." It was something to think about! Years later, I was to meet Toller in Moscow. And later still, in New York City, I was to see his handsome head lying in the peaceful repose of his self-inflicted death. The horror of seeing humanity once again plunging toward Armageddon was more than his sensitive spirit could endure. One could only echo Shakespeare: "Rest, rest, perturbed spirit."

The Actors' Theatre functioned with fluctuating success. For several years it presented a number of stars in some distinguished plays. But the American public wants hits and only hits. Actually it seems to me a little like a man who is on a diet of oysters and will eat only the ones in which a pearl is found. "Art Theatres" must produce box office results if they are to survive —unless, of course, they are subsidized. New plays—potential hits—were scarce as hen's teeth as, indeed, they always are. As usual in such cases, the board turned to the idea of a revival for the next production. At least there could be distinction in doing a great play.

There is a curious paradox in our American cultural life. Whereas the music-loving public for many years demanded, for the most part, a steady fare of classic masterpieces, so that Stokowski had to fight to include something new and "modern" on his programs, the theatre-going public always wants something new. If there were a similar demand for the work of playwrights of proven genius, the problems of the American producer would be much simpler. For a time, at least, the Actors' Theatre did find its salvation in the classics. To begin with, in order to attract ambitious actors it had to provide great roles, and these could be found in the great classic plays.

Fortunately, the wisdom of this step was proved by the success of *Candida*. Both Katharine Cornell, as Shaw's heroine, and a brilliant performance as Prossy by Clare Eames, brought not only artistic kudos but box office manna to the organization as well.

By this time I had become a member of the Board of the Actors' Theatre, having been invited by Jane Cowl to take her place. One day a meeting of the Board was called to select a bill to follow *Candida*. Several scripts were under discussion. Clare Eames proposed a revival of Ibsen's *The Wild Duck*. There was little or no enthusiasm on the part of most of the Board, certainly none on my part, for I had never read the play. Dave Wallace, the business manager, was sure it would be a disastrous choice.

"Who'd want to see that gloomy stuff?" was his unanswerable comment. Ibsen was known to be poison at the box office, and it was Dave's job, as business manager, to consider that point. Another voice murmured something about "the kiss of death." Clare Eames' alert mind must have sensed that the majority might vote against it, for she suddenly proposed that we adjourn for a day or two, to give all members a chance to "restudy the play." This we agreed to do. As we rose to disperse, Clare, with one of those swift rapier-like movements which were so characteristic of her slim body, crossed to me and whispered, "One of the reasons I want to see this play done is to see you as Gina."

I stared, said, "Oh?" and hurried home to read the play. My unfamiliarity with it was inexcusable, for some time earlier Tony had said to me, *"The Wild Duck!* Now there, Sis is a play!" Even then I had not troubled to read it, once I learned that it was about a lot of dreary people living in a musty garret. I had never considered myself a high-brow actress; studying Ibsen was no part of my aspirations. Now, however, Clare's hurried whisper whetted my interest. The stuffy Archer translation somewhat obscured the full power and beauty of the play, and I was disappointed to find that Gina seemed a drab, colorless creature, the role completely swamped by at least four much better parts. Why, my silly soul demanded, should I be selected to play an inarticulate drudge who sits around silent, while all the other characters are involved in vital situations? And again my hindsight bewailed: "Oh, for that glamorous divorcee in *Expressing*

Willie, still running! If only I'd had brains enough to have chosen that part!"

But a second and careful rereading of *The Wild Duck* revealed an arresting fact: the inarticulate Gina had three out of five curtain speeches. (We know, in the theatre, that an effective speech at the end of the act leaves an indelible impression on the audience.) She also had other scenes which would make a strong impact on the audience: one fine comedy scene, and also a very moving moment near the end of the play where she learns that her child has shot herself. Perhaps, after all, one wouldn't be swamped in a part like that! I voted "yes" for purely selfish reasons. The majority voted the same way.

Rehearsals were a pure delight. We all worked over the translation, each alteration making the script more fluent and colloquial. I found discrepancies in Gina's speech: sometimes she would use a double negative—other times not. Now, there's one thing about a double negative: either you use one or you don't. (That I learned from my mother.) So I used them throughout, and also substituted, with Dudley Digges' permission, an occasional simple word for one of Archer's "fancy" ones. These changes helped make the part believable.

Clare Eames shared the direction with Dudley Digges, their two minds working in perfect harmony on a labor of love. The fascination of seeing that rich pattern of humanity unfold under their inspired directing remains one of the most treasured experiences of my theatre life. All of us worked eagerly, each as deeply interested in everyone else's part as in his own. Slowly, unhurriedly, the characters began to take shape: the fumbling, pitiful mustiness of Cecil Yapp's Old Ekdal; the tight-lipped fanaticism of Tom Powers' Gregers; the unbelievably touching simplicity and pathos of a little girl named Helen Chandler, born to play Hedvig for Ibsen's pure delight, I am sure; and Tom Chalmers' richly compassionate Dr. Relling.

Rehearsals began at 10 A.M. Even after a long day we would frequently find ourselves wishing that there were some way whereby we could all just close our eyes and wake up with our concentration undisturbed. If only one didn't have to go out into the streets and home and then, next day, have to recapture what had been created up to this moment!

Little incidents stand out clearly in my mind: Clare's remark to Helen Chandler, "If you are cute for one second, I'll kill you." Clare's amusing detachment from her own imminent motherhood: "If this baby dares come before the opening, I'll just send it back marked 'Deliver later,'" she said. (The baby had the good sense to wait.)

Dudley's meticulous directing of the lusty dinner table scene required endless repetition—whole days being spent in perfecting its intricate timing, until my trips back and forth from the kitchen began to seem like a dance marathon and Gina a part calling for physical endurance more than anything else.

No one, including myself, paid much attention to Gina. Like Topsy, she "jes' growed" out of her relation to the other characters. I don't remember ever studying the lines. There was so much of interest taking place around me: Gina and I both listened and forgot ourselves, which is the secret of all the Ginas of this world—("hundreds of them in any city block" as Heywood Broun said in his review of the play). Their selflessness, their dedication to service, doing the thing closest at hand to be done, makes these simple souls the earthy foundation on which humanity rests.

Some instinct kept me from doing any more than sketch in the final scene over Hedvig's dead body. I must have sensed that once immersed in the part up to that point, the outburst of grief would take care of itself. I shuffled about in felt slippers, comfortable physically as well as spiritually. Slowly Gina emerged from the printed page.

My pleasant surprise began at the dress rehearsal. A tall, gawky young man was playing one of the chamberlains, a bit part, in the first act. We had chatted during rehearsal. It was Mischa Auer. He came back after the second act, aglow. "Miss Yurka, dear! Such a surprise! Everyone else talks a lot but we watch *your* face to see what their talk does to you. It's really *your* act and you've almost nothing to say, it's fantastic!"

It was my first realization of the power of attentive silence on the stage.

The quiet beginning gave Gina's outbursts later in the play greater value; the first when, cracking under Hjalmar's cross-examination as to the identity of Hedvig's real father, she bursts forth with, "How should I know?" following with the pitiful, "A creature like me!" . . . and then the agonized shock when **she** realizes that Hedvig is dead.

There was one person whose contribution to the performance was quite unintentional. My simple, queenly mother had created for me so clear an image of these "givers" of the world that my personal imagination was scarcely called on in the creation of the characterization. At the early dress rehearsals I wore my hair in a plain bun at the nape of my neck. Mila came backstage. "Why don't you wear it in a coronet braid as Maminka does?" she suggested. "I see her up there all the time you're on the stage."

Up went the hair into the coronet braid, completing a portrait which I had been building unconsciously out of myriads of tiny impressions of my daily life. For mother, too, was one of those earthy indispensable members of the human race. So completely was Gina my mother that often I would say to her, "Well, Maminka, you gave a good performance tonight." I came to look for these women everywhere with a new appreciation. One saw them on the way home from the theatre at midnight, standing on tired feet in some little delicatessen store preparing for the next day's business. I imagine they all have their "Hjalmars" to cope with—some son or husband or daughter, whose egocentric vitality they sustain through their humorous understanding, above all, through their capacity to love.

Towards the end of our third week of rehearsals Dudley Digges, our director, came up on to the stage, called us all together and said, "Children, the play is in fine shape. You could open tomorrow night. As a matter of fact, perhaps you should. The theatre is available. What do you all say?"

We stared at one another, when Tom Powers voiced what I think we all felt. "If we are that good—and we are allowed another week of rehearsals—let's use that week and become that much better." It was a unanimous vote. Our opening night proved the wisdom of that decision.

The marvelously responsive Sunday night audience was made up of actors who were playing in other theatres. Their warm enjoyment flooded across the proscenium, and their delighted laughter over Hjalmar's egotistical foolishness was like an electric stimulus to the cast. We all glowed in response and consequently gave what Frank Lea Short described in his review as "A performance comparable to the best done by the Moscow Art Company."

Mr. Percy Hammond found in my Gina unexpected values

which, apparently, had not appeared in previous portrayals of the part. His review in the New York *Tribune* was most encouraging, especially his favorable comparison of this production with the previous one in which Nazimova had starred as Hedvig:

The same group which outdid itself on *Candida* has made a splendid job in the revival of Ibsen's *The Wild Duck*. It is probably the first adequate presentation . . . of the piece that has been made in America. Nazimova's performance suffered as always from a sort of St. Vitus dance, which disturbed the contour of the piece. In her role, that of Hedvig, Helen Chandler gives a performance truly remarkable in its pathos and beauty. Also, it may be said with thanksgiving, she looks like a girl of fourteen. . . . But the best performance is probably that of Blanche Yurka as the patient, ageless Gina. It dominates the whole piece, even in the moments when she is not on stage. Tom Powers as the detestable Gregers Werle presents at times the aspect of an American go-getter, yet his performance must be excellent for never was a villain more loathed by an audience. Clare Eames and Dudley Digges made a superb job of staging and direction. It seems these two, so unflaggingly excellent as actors, have a talent as directors which is almost greater.

The critics were very kind, continuing to refer to the play even after the opening. In a follow-up review in the Theatre Section of the *Tribune,* Percy Hammond dwelled upon the "unexpected values" that he had found in my portrayal:

The local wiseacres who have been deriding the Actors' (Equity) Theatre for its several blunders were disposed to regard the announcement of Ibsen's "The Wild Duck" as another foolish maneuver. An old, weird and gloomy masterpiece, full, as its author said, of "crazy tricks," it was considered too melancholy for these jubilant days. All of us were surprised, therefore, when it proved a thrilling play.

Many theatergoers are now having a pleasant time watching the miseries of Ibsen's bewildered Scandinavians amongst the clustered woes. The pathetic imbecility of old Ekdal as he shoots rabbits in his garret; the suicide of little Hedvig; the sufferings of Gina for her innocent sins; the shallow roaring of Hjalmar the pompous photographer and the sepulchral drunkenness of Molvik the parson, all are catering to our enjoyment. We like to see the odious Gregers, as a symbol of the meddlesome "reformer," setting mischief afoot; and Dr. Relling, the disciple of "helpful falsehoods," glorified as an instrument of good. They upset the pious tyrannies and give us the joys of revolt. Mr. Huneker used to complain that the mingling of satire and tragedy in "The Wild Duck" confused him—that he did not know when to laugh and when to cry. But that was in 1905, when play-going was not as perfect an art as now it is. Objection has been made that Mr. Warburton Gamble's Hjalmar Ekdal verges upon the burlesque. But so does Ibsen's—which may or may not be a good excuse for Mr. Gamble's suspected over-doing. I think, with others, that his impersonation is an admirable blending of excess and restraint, a fine and difficult modification of the author's grotesque mood. After all, an actor who plays an ass so conceited as Hjalmar Ekdal must do a little braying, lest he be untrue to type and character.

I was surprised the other day while consulting "The Wild Duck" archives to learn that Miss Blanche Yurka does not picture Gina Ekdal according to traditions. Miss Yurka's endeavors, I had thought, were the most effective of the performance, yet, according to the expert accountants, who knew Ibsen as personally as I do Samuel Shipman, she is all wrong. Bernard Shaw says that Gina is a "waddling housewife." Mr. Gosse estimates her as "vulgar." Max Nordau wrote that she is a "female Sancho Panza," and William Archer, the translator, described her as "stolid and unimaginative." Miss Yurka's characterization fills none of these prescriptions. It presents Gina as a queenly humble person, comely in appearance and often elegant in manner. She is majestic and well-dressed, to a degree, sane, practical, sympathetic and dominant. Like Mr. Gamble's Hjalmar, she is better than Ibsen. After seeing Miss Yurka in "The Wild Duck" I can understand why dramatists cut so little figure in the drama.

Everyone, even the stage-hands, loved the play. It used to delight me to see them edge up to the proscenium opening to watch certain scenes night after night. This is always infallible proof that something vital is taking place, for stage-hands listen only when they are interested.

Such different sorts of people were affected by *The Wild*

Duck. One night Julia Hoyt, then a reigning beauty, came backstage, her face drenched in tears. "Look what you've done to me! How can I go to a party looking like this?" she wailed, pointing to her streaked mascara. Beulah Bondi came back, burst into tears, went out to walk around the block, returned and burst into tears all over again. Vilhjalmur Stefansson, the Arctic explorer, was most enthusiastic. Having seen and loved the play in its original Norwegian, he told me later that he hesitated to see an American production. A friend overcame his reluctance and persuaded him to go. For the balance of the run he came twice a week always bringing friends with him. A most pragmatic enthusiasm!

I have learned so to love this deeply human work, and have spoken of it at times with such warmth, that on the occasion of its revival, four years later, Sam Wren, the business manager, admonished me, "Take care, Blanche. One of these days you're going to think you wrote this play." It ranks highest, in my opinion, in the expression of Ibsen's genius. His masterly craftsmanship joined his sense of humanity in a perfect marriage—the humanity full of wry laughter at its own inadequacies, the craftsmanship polishing each idea with power and precision. The poet, John Weaver, once said, after several visits, "It's full of laughs and every laugh hurts."

Richard Dana Skinner, in his book *Our Changing Theatre,* has this to say:

On one memorable occasion, under the direction of Dudley Digges and the late Clare Eames, the revival by the Actors' Theatre made history as one of the few great events of the American Theatre.

Blanche Yurka, whose "Gina" has rightly become one of the classic characters of the American stage, apparently achieves a rather exceptional balance between thought and feeling in the early creation of her roles. If I may hazard making a distinction, I should say that Miss Yurka's first impulse springs from the idea of the part, from what the part implies in spiritual, moral or mystical significance. This is something quite different from an intellectual appraisal. It strikes directly at the theme, at the question the character must face and answer. It is said that Miss Yurka once suggested to a playwright that there were three possible plays centering around a woman—the woman and man, the woman and her child, and the woman and her God. This sharp feeling for theme, as against plot and personality, is, I feel, quite characteristic of Miss Yurka's entire approach to the theater. The part slowly becomes individualized in her mind, through both feeling and analysis. But first of all comes the idea, which must later realize itself in action.

But no personal contribution of any player could weigh against the marvel of the play itself. In an article in the *Saturday Review,* that most exacting critic, George Bernard Shaw, paid this beautiful tribute to Ibsen's genius:

Where shall I find an epithet magnificent enough for THE WILD DUCK. To sit there getting deeper and deeper into that Ekdal home, and getting deeper and deeper into your own life all the time, until you forget that you are in a theatre; to look on with horror and pity at a profound tragedy, shaking with laughter all the time at an irresistible comedy.

Among the plays in which I have appeared some have been trivial, even meretricious, for, after all, actresses must live. But to have been, on occasion, identified with so rewarding a genius as Ibsen is something for which I am endlessly grateful.

CHAPTER 8

"MY MILDLY INCESTUOUS SON"

THE NEXT PLAY I did was really trounced by the critics. And rightly so. *The Lawbreaker*, by Jules Eckert Goodman, was a routine "society melodrama," and not a good one, but its run was marked by one incident of some importance. For the part of my ne'er-do-well brother, they had engaged a young actor whose sincerity seemed to me to be very appealing. At the second or third day's rehearsal he was absent. I spoke to the director, a tall, lean, rather wistful looking man who seemed a little crushed under the dynamic truculence of his boss, Mr. William A. Brady. He told me that the young man had been "let out."

I was genuinely distressed and protested that it was a mistake, that he was very good and that he should be called back. The director said, "Why don't you go up to the office and tell the old man how you feel about it?" Mr. William A. Brady was a fierce Irishman—and I had a faint qualm of terror at the prospect of bearding him in his den. Nevertheless, up I went to express my hope that the young man might be reinstated. I voiced my enthusiasm for his talent in no uncertain terms. Apparently I made some impression, for Freddie Bickel was back next day and eventually gave an excellent account of himself.

What I did not know until much later was that this engagement was a turning point for him. He had decided that if he lost that job he would give up trying to be an actor and to turn to something else. And that would have been a pity both for him and for an adoring public, since, under the name of Fredric March, he has done very well indeed. As a matter of fact, the slightly depressed director, Mr. John Cromwell, has not done badly either.

It was during this engagement that I met a charming and talented actor whom, fourteen months later, I married. At the time of our meeting, Ian Keith was playing the French Ambassador in *The Czarina* with Doris Keane. Our year of courtship was a gay one; he was great fun. We dined together daily, went to matinees on our free days, and on our long walks home after the theatre made plans for a joint career, à la "Sothern and Marlowe" in Shakespeare's plays. Ian had a passion for the Bard, and I have never known anyone who knew his Shakespeare better. We often played a game in which I would open almost any of the plays, give him a cue, and he would continue the lines verbatim. I was familiar with the best known of Shakespeare's plays, but, I regret to say, was never consumed with the desire to play them.

As my love affair progressed, spring and summer slipped by happily. In September Ian went to Chicago to open in a new play. He persuaded me to join him there to take definite steps toward our future together. There was a reason for marrying quietly, away from New York. He felt that his mother, a nervous, unhappy divorcée, would inevitably carry on a bit over losing her only and adored son. He hoped that she would accept the accomplished fact of our marriage with more grace if she were not present at the actual ceremony. I was more than a little reluctant to relinquish the presence of my own beloved family on so important an occasion. Mila, at least, I wanted to have with me, but in fairness to Ian's mother I could not.

Patricia Collinge was living in Chicago in married retirement at that time. I visited her for a week or so; then one afternoon Ian and I went around to a charming little church nearby and were married, with Pat and her husband, Jim, as witnesses. We spent our honeymoon at the Edgewater Beach, a hotel which looked out over the waters of Lake Michigan. We swam, played golf; Ian taught me to dive; I eventually had the courage to dive from a twenty-foot height—Ian was a magnificent swimmer. We occasionally had delightful chats with George Arliss, the English star, who was stopping at the same hotel while playing in Chicago. That all-too-brief interlude of peaceful joy sometimes seems to me the only one I have ever had. Just being happy and seeing that happiness reflected in another's eyes gave a meaning to life which I had always felt sure I should find, but which had until now eluded me. I remember one sunny afternoon sitting quietly and looking across the sparkling waters of the lake. I was alone, Ian having gone to play his matinee. As I sat there I felt myself in harmony with a kind of universal rhythm. A sense of complete fulfillment possessed me. The sun sparkling on the water, the quiet perfection of the day, seemed to whisper "never forget this hour."

Next morning's mail brought a great shock. A letter of good wishes from a friend casually mentioned Mila's convalescence from a serious operation. The friend, of course, had no idea that I had not been told of the operation. In a hurried long distance call I learned that Mila had insisted that my honeymoon should not be clouded by worry over her.

Ian was aware how much Mila had always meant to me and I to her. As his engagement in Chicago was to be over in two weeks he consented to my returning immediately to my sister's bedside. I found her at home just returned from the hospital, pale and thin but cheery and full of courage. She loved Ian for my sake as well as his own and her gratitude to him for "sharing" me so soon after our marriage was touching.

Among the many messages I found awaiting me was a purely professional one. It had been delivered in Arthur Hopkins' usual laconic fashion. My family informed me that one day a voice over the telephone had asked for me. When told that I was away on my honeymoon the voice simply said, "This is Arthur Hopkins. When she gets back have her call me."

I did. The office interview took about three minutes. A greeting, then, "Would you like to play the Queen to John Barrymore's Hamlet?"

I knew better than to waste words when talking to Arthur Hopkins, a red-faced little man whose extraordinary eyes seemed quite kindly and impersonally to be looking straight through all your mental barricades. I answered, "Maybe." He added, "We want her played rather younger than has been customary. They are having a reading rehearsal down on the stage. Why not go down and see how you feel about it?"

These were more words than I had ever heard Mr. Hopkins

utter at one time. I was quite aware, too, that he was the one who would probably be doing the seeing. I had not been under the Belasco aegis without learning that those darkened theatre balconies made excellent observation posts.

Down I went. The stage of the Plymouth Theatre was bare except for a semi-circle of ordinary wooden chairs on which sat the actors already engaged; a table and a work light completed the picture. Tyrone Power, Sr., had a dark moodiness and a glorious voice—both perfect for the King. Rosalinde Fuller's Tanagra-like figure was lovely for the mad little Ophelia. Only John Barrymore, the Hamlet, was missing; Bill Adams, the stage manager read his lines. Yet *Hamlet,* even without the Prince of Denmark, can be fairly exciting. When the rehearsal ended I went upstairs to the little cubicle which was Mr. Hopkins' office. "If you think I can give it what you want," I said, "I would like to do it." "Good," he said. That was all.

I wired the news of the offer to my husband. To my surprise his answer was a furious protest. On no condition was I to accept it. Barrymore was noted for being difficult to play with . . . the part was the worst in all Shakespeare . . . it would ruin me professionally. Anyhow, what of our plans to act together? He ignored the fact that these plans were distinctly at the dream stage.

I was distracted. I hated to cross Ian, although being dutiful was a new role for me. It did seem desirable to be part of so outstanding a collaboration of talents as Hopkins-Barrymore-Robert Edmond Jones. I consulted Jane Cowl as usual, and she heartily agreed. I stressed all this in letters, wires and midnight telephone calls, as tactfully as I could. Ian finally conceded, grudgingly, that there might be some value in doing it, but he insisted that from now on I was to use my married name on the theatre programs. I had not yet grown accustomed to the sight or sound of Blanche Keith myself. Nevertheless, I broached the subject to Mr. Hopkins. He was quietly adamant. "I engaged Blanche Yurka, not Blanche Keith. If this is your husband's idea, I advise you to get that matter settled at once." I hated to reopen the telegraphic arguments. It seemed a delicate subject for a bride to argue about. I let the matter slide, signed up and broke it to Ian on his return. I don't think he ever quite forgave me.

We had been rehearsing for over a week, still sitting in that semi-circle of wooden chairs, when John Barrymore arrived from the coast. I, of course, was thrilled. My memories of *Peter Ibbetson, Justice,* and his Fedya in *Redemption* were now enriched by a personal contact with the impish, irresistible Barrymore charm. Ethel had always had it for me; Jack's was equally potent. There was an element of apprehension, however, in my interest and my excitement. Those were the days when, wherever two or three people were gathered together, the conversation would eventually get around to Barrymore: his looks, his idiosyncrasies, his genius, or lack of it—depending on the speaker. I had heard strange tales of his bullying of previous leading ladies; one, so the story went, had had one of her ribs cracked! So before signing the contract I requested a two-weeks' notice clause. Mr. Hopkins demurred; when he decided anyone was right for a part, he told me, he desired no changes; he wanted his actors for the run of the play.

"But," I said, "I've heard that Mr. Barrymore can be very difficult to play with. I won't put myself in the position where I can't escape if he makes me unhappy." There was a long pause. Then Mr. Hopkins said, "Will you trust me to see that he doesn't do that? If anything goes wrong, you come to me first." So of course I signed on his terms. What Mr. H. said to Jack I do not know, but it must have been impressive, for no one could have behaved better. People asked me eagerly, "How does he treat you?" I think they were disappointed when I reported: "Charmingly."

Of rehearsing in the usual manner, of experimenting with the scenes, there was almost none. John Barrymore obviously had planned his own performance down to the smallest movement; it soon became apparent that our job was to be found in places where his movements required us to be.

In an early talk, Jack (one soon thought of him as that) had described to me vividly what the stage picture of that first court scene was to be. "A hunt dinner is in progress; it's a drunken orgy . . . tankards roll off the table . . . slabs of meat are thrown to great hunting dogs . . . court ladies loll with their shoulders and bosoms half bare . . . it is to be a sensuous, dissolute court, dominated by a lecherous king. In the midst of it Hamlet sits, a mute black figure, bathed in firelight." (I think

something was said about a roaring fire.) Just how all this was to
be accomplished he didn't say; I expect it was the frustrated
painter in him speaking. It sounded marvelous. It never happened. Certainly Jack's own passionate, bitterly humorous reading of the part, his almost incestuous handling of the closet
scene, bore out what he had told me of his concept of the play.
As for the rest of us, when we stood on the steps of Robert Edmond Jones' austerely beautiful set in which all of us remained
rigidly in our corners, all I could think of was a glorified Penn-
sylvania Station with each of us guarding his own gate. Nevertheless, it was all a wonderful background for Barrymore's performance, which was, after all, what the public paid to see.

One day just before we were to open, word was passed around
that his sister, Ethel, was coming to rehearsal. Jack was excited.
It was to be our first uninterrupted run-through of the play.
The thrill of creativity illuminated everyone's performance; in
my opinion no later performance we gave ever quite equalled it.
All through the closet scene I scarcely moved, so paralyzing was
the intensity of the wild-eyed Hamlet, so compelling his biting
scorn, so poignant his pathos. I could not have moved had I
wished to. As the scene ended he whispered to me, "That was
perfect. Now for Christ's sake don't let anyone change you one
iota."

The opening night approached. The day before we had a sort
of dress parade of costumes. Incredible as it seems, we opened
without ever having actually gone straight through the play in
full dress at any time. My costumes were long flowing ones of
clinging wool jersey in lovely colors. My favorite was the crimson one I wore in the last act. Many people spoke of it—somebody commented, "As you lay there on the steps after drinking
the poison the gown looked like spilled blood." It was at this
point in the play that I once lived through an agonizing quarter
hour. I was struggling with bronchitis. One evening as I lay
"dead" in full view of the audience my throat began to contract.
The more I resisted the urge to cough the more insistent that
urge became. My imagination conjured up Barrymore's face—
and vocabulary—should his "dead" mother suddenly burst into
a paroxysm of coughing. Slowly, in silent agony, I began to
count and to tell myself, "You can swallow once more; now once
more . . ." I grew purple, I'm sure, under my makeup as the

final scene drew toward its end. At last came the blessed line
"the rest is silence." How I thanked God that it still was! The
curtain closed and a cough tore through my throat such as has
seldom been heard in this world. Jack, as he left the stage, observed quietly, "You seem to have a cold."

I minded just a little that I was playing mother to a man older
than myself, so I cheated by wearing my hair in youthful ring-
lets and in general striving to look as much as possible like a
candidate for Ophelia. It was a silly thing to do, and I felt thoroughly ashamed of it on the afternoon the Moscow Art Company came to our matinee. Altogether that was an unfortunate
performance. Jack, apparently very nervous in the presence of
such notable artists, overplayed quite badly. This keyed us all so
high that the whole performance lost its usual values. When the
group of Muscovite artists came backstage, Stanislavski, doubt-
less searching for something he could say quite honestly, gave
me one of my worst notices in the part. "You make her a very
young mother." That was all; it was enough.

The engagement on the whole was not comfortable. The permanent setting was open at the sides and top so that the wings
had to be kept pitch black. Since there was no room to cross
behind the set, and the dressing rooms were some distance away,
one came down for the first scene and then sat for hours awaiting one's next cue. It was, of course, a privilege to listen for a
hundred consecutive performances to the beautiful reading of
those glorious lines. But eventually even that palled a little.

I was interested to note that Jack almost never sustained the
entire performance at his top best. It varied a good deal. It was
as though his reserve of energy was limited, so that he was forced
to save himself. Each night some scenes would be superbly
played, others perfunctorily, and they were never the same
scenes. By the time he reached the "Pelion on Ossa" speech with
Laertes in the graveyard scene, he usually strained a bit, using
volume instead of increasing speed for his mounting climax.
Sometimes I wondered if he would get through.

He grew very fatigued by the almost impossible task of playing Hamlet eight times a week, month after month. No one, in
my opinion, should do it. But such is our American theatre system that actors have to if they are to play it at all. Yet one day,
toward the end of the road tour, overtired, he evidently drew

upon some untapped "second wind" and lashed into his defiance of Laertes with such blazing, scornful frenzy that I stood beside the grave mesmerized, scarcely able to speak the few lines allotted to the queen mother.

The Hamlet season on Broadway lasted 101 performances. Jack (a little childishly, I thought) wished to exceed Edwin Booth's record of 100 performances. He did. Closing a play to sell-out business seemed mad to me. But close we did. However, the following year we played it on the road.

One thing I had to learn, as a part of my marital experience, was never to praise the work of other actors to Ian. He had the basic insecurity of a young actor, even though he had played a few fine parts (the French Ambassador in the *Czarina* with Doris Keane, and the young lead in *Laugh, Clown, Laugh!* under Belasco's direction). And, of course, he considered himself a "natural" in any Shakespearean part. When the termination of Barrymore's Broadway run in *Hamlet* was announced, he conceived the, to me, startling idea of taking over the part after Jack's departure. I dared not say what I wanted to say— knowing his temper to be somewhat volatile. After all, people came to see Barrymore—not Shakespeare's play. So I just looked blank and said nothing, hoping that my lack of concurrence would speak for itself.

However, he went to Barrymore's dressing room one evening before the performance and proposed that he take over the part when Jack left. The reaction was quite in the Barrymore vein. Said Jack: "But you see, Keith, if you proved better than I am, it would be very bad for me. If I proved better than you, it would be bad for you. I don't think it's a good idea, old man."

So often during the run of *Hamlet,* people would ask, in a whisper (why a whisper I don't know!) "What's he really like?" —hoping, I am sure, to hear some terrible tale of temperament gone berserk—or of studied rudeness to a fellow player—or even, on occasion, to an audience. (His insertion of a line about "barking seals" one night when a noisy audience was troubling him went the rounds of the cocktail parties.) I could only reply, in common honesty, that he was unfailingly courteous, even courtly in his manner toward me—and on one occasion, when I was obviously unhappy over Ian's behavior, he went to considerable lengths to be kind.

We had an amusing interchange of greetings at Christmas time. Much has been made in the press and in conversation of his "incestuous" treatment of the closet scene. So I had a card put on his dressing table, with my inscription over MERRY CHRISTMAS, "To my son, from his mildly incestuous mother." The next day, on my dressing table, was a charming reproduction of the drawing of him as Hamlet by John Singer Sargent with the inscription: "To my mother from her wildly incestuous son."

His humor, when he chose to exercise it, was irresistible. During the road tour, the second season, he was growing very restless and perhaps bored by the strain of playing the demanding role eight times a week—and by the disciplines it imposed upon him. In any case, after the closet scene, he would step before the curtain to acknowledge the applause and make a speech. These speeches would begin with a courtly expression of thanks and then he would go on to recount the comments made on his performance by Paul, his Negro dresser—comments which were pungent, frank and infinitely amusing. The whole company would crowd into the front of the wings to listen. The stories were never the same and the audiences responded with laughter and delight to his informal joking. The interval over, he would retire behind the curtain. In three minutes or so, it would rise, he would reappear—perfectly in key, powerful, moving—Hamlet himself, again recapturing his audience completely. It was something to see, something to have experienced.

It was not long after this engagement that I received an invitation from the Theatre Guild to join the cast of Franz Werfel's *Goat Song* which was already in rehearsal with Lynn Fontanne and Alfred Lunt. Playing with these two charming people is among my most pleasant recollections. It was my third appearance with the Theatre Guild. Werfel's powerful and cryptic play was one of the Guild's bravest undertakings, for it required an expensive cast and was on a strange, mystical, tragic theme. Lee Simonson designed vignette settings, on movable platforms, beautifully lighted against a great blue cyclorama. Pictorially it was one of the Guild's finest achievements.

We were all Serbian peasants. Lynn looked marvelous in the colorful costumes, and she and Alfred played the unhappy lovers with poignant power. I played the mother of the strange subhuman creature whose unseen presence dominated the play. It

was a play full of symbolism, a lot of which I never did understand nor, I feel sure, did the audience. This did not prevent it
from being an exciting and deeply moving experience. Appearing briefly as the peddler in the last act, Edward G. Robinson
gave one of those richly colored performances which made him,
at that time, a real asset to the Guild. Losing him for so many
years to the screen was one of the theatre's calamities.

The Lunts were wonderful to work with, and I enjoyed the
opportunity of getting to know Lynn and Alfred better. Their
fresh enthusiasm about their work is infectious, their standards
inspiring. The first time I had ever seen Alfred act was in Booth
Tarkington's *Clarence*. He played a farcical figure, but in one
brief scene, a love scene, he registered such sincerity that I
turned to Jane Cowl, with whom I was seeing the play, and said,
"That man is no saxophone-playing comic. He'll be doing very
serious parts one of these days, you'll see." His beautifully simple rendering of the quiet tragic mood of Robert Sherwood's
play *There Shall Be No Night* was only one of many deeply
moving portrayals, but in my opinion it was the best performance he ever gave.

And all women could take heart at Lynn's flowering from
gangling girlhood into the warm, glowing physical beauty which
delights her audiences even today. Each season she has grown in
loveliness, until, in her Greek costumes in *Amphitryon,* her
beauty reached its peak.

How beautifully the Lunts have built their lives! Personal
affection, enriched by generous appreciation of each other's
gifts, makes as near a perfect life as any theatre pair can hope
for. Their kind of rare co-ordination can only grow out of a continuity of association and a great deal of experimenting. It is
sometimes in the humdrum routine of daily life that the secret
of a scene suddenly reveals itself. To be able instantly to share it
and thus ignite the spark of creative imagination must contribute vastly to their store of acting magic. No matter how gifted
mere individuals may be, this magic can all too rarely be
achieved by the hasty assembling of a cast which has only a few
weeks of preparation, only to have the results scattered again
after the play closes. Stanislavski once said, "It is not surprising
that you in America have so little great acting. It is a miracle
that you ever have any, working under such a system."

The Lunts, through their eager search for plays in which they could alternately or simultaneously score and through their continuous professional association, have overcome many of the evils of this system. Their life is well described in the trite but expressive phrase from La Tosca: "Vissi d'arte—vissi d'amore," for these two people do seem to live for their art and for each other.

In the early spring of that year Maminka died. As we stood for a while in the sunshine of Kensico Cemetery following the service, I noticed the pine tree growing straight and tall behind the newly made grave. It seemed to represent her. Its deep roots, its strong branches, its calm, quiet strength made it a perfect monument.

CHAPTER 9

HEARTBREAK

F OR THE FIRST time in my life, I settled down into a
routine of domesticity. I had found a small three-room apartment on East 72nd Street—a top-floor flat in a remodeled house
only three blocks from what had been my home. I learned to
cook modest meals; I shopped and kept the apartment tidy.
Seemingly, our marriage was going well. But little danger signs
soon began to appear. I had had an engagement; Ian had not.
This situation is never a comfortable one. Egotism creates a
major difficulty in all actors' marriages. I, of course, had had a
head start in my career, although Ian's stunning performances
in *The Czarina* and in *Laugh, Clown, Laugh!* had brought him
a great deal of attention in a remarkably short time. But I was—
no question—a little better known than he and had made some
valuable connections. Ironically enough it was my use of one of
these to his advantage which finally brought about the catastrophe.

Ian had not been offered a really worthwhile engagement
since our wedding. Suddenly, in the early spring, what seemed
like an ideal opportunity for him opened up. A group of representative managers decided to pool their interests in an effort to
produce an annual spring theatre festival. They would start
with Shakespeare (of course!) and announced as their first production *As You Like It*. Ian was eager to play Orlando. He managed to obtain an appointment, went down to be interviewed,
and read for the part.

I awaited his return eagerly, certain that his qualifications of
youth, extraordinary good looks, and an exceptional feeling for
blank verse, would win him his longed-for opportunity. When
he came home he was ominously quiet. He had not gotten the

part. He admitted that he had been very nervous and had read badly.

Neither of us could accept this defeat. Something must be done. I did some quick thinking. Augustus Thomas, the dean of American playwrights, was president of the newly-formed Managers' Association. I had once been directed by him in a short-lived play, and I decided to call him up. I explained that I had recently been married to Ian (our quiet wedding had not been widely publicized) and mentioned our bitter disappointment over the Orlando part. I begged him to let us come to his home and quietly talk it over. He was graciousness itself. We sat in his book-lined study, looking out over a little New York garden blanketed in an early spring snow. It was Sunday morning. New York seemed as quiet as a country village as we sat in the cheery room, with its glowing fire, and talked.

That friendly, civilized interview has always remained in my mind as the one way such matters should be discussed, not the customary brief, uncomfortable session which usually takes place in some managerial sanctum—as coldly impersonal, as rigidly business-like as its occupant is apt to be. How can an actor do himself justice in such an atmosphere? I believe sensitive managers feel just as uncomfortable as do the actors at such times.

Mr. Thomas drew Ian out, talking about the part, making him read bits of it. He then promised to reconsider the matter with his fellow directors. We left, full of hope. A few days later it was announced that Ian Keith had been engaged for Orlando in the impending production of *As You Like It*. We both rejoiced over the reversed decision, but I think he hated the fact that I was partially responsible for the reopened opportunity. This I could understand. We never spoke of it.

He plunged into rehearsals. It is difficult to describe the curious metamorphosis which occurs in a player when he goes into the rehearsal period, into that sphere of the imagination where one's daily self is forgotten, while the ego projects itself into the forming of a purely imaginary creature. I myself have felt it so often, finding it difficult, distasteful even, to revert to the routine of daily living. This explains why some theatre people live a life of isolation, with few outside contacts. I feel sure it was this need of maintaining the reality of the unreal which made Mr.

Belasco live so much of his life within the four walls of his theatre and its studio high above the stage. His continuous success must surely have stemmed from his ability to shut out the world in which we ordinarily live.

Thus I accepted without suspicion or comment the gradual shutting out process which grew, noticeably, as rehearsals progressed, until I no longer felt free to join my husband even at meal times. I heard vague rumors (which I refused to take seriously) of an intimacy developing within the company. The camaraderie of the theatre was, I felt, something which was always being misinterpreted. But one day when I unexpectedly joined him for lunch I felt distinctly uncomfortable.

Then, one afternoon, a very curious incident occurred. The previous spring, during the early stages of my engagement to Ian, I had made the acquaintance of an Englishwoman who had lived much of her life in India where, she claimed, she had developed psychic powers. The previous year she had met Ian and liked him. Since then I had not heard from her. One day I met her taking a walk not far from our apartment. I invited her to join me over a cup of tea. She trudged up the stairs to our apartment, admired it all—listened to my glowing account of my hopes, of our plans. Suddenly, putting her cup down, she looked at me strangely. In answer to my inquiring silence, she began to speak very rapidly— "My dear, I don't quite understand. I am frightened for you. I landed only yesterday; you tell me you are happy—yet all around you I see evil, destructive forces, disaster. What is all this? What is going on?"

I scoffed, a little startled by her obvious sincerity, but she continued: "This play you tell me your husband is in—it will close suddenly, at the very beginning of its run!" She kept looking around, as though seeing things imperceptible to me. "Why should I see this if all is going well with you?" she asked. I felt uncomfortable, to say the least. She left shortly afterward and I never saw her again. In less than a month everything she had predicted had materialized.

It was a month in which I became aware of the inimical attitude being taken toward me by Ian's mother. "I will break up that marriage if it is the last thing I do in this life," she had stated to a friend of hers who warned me of her intention. (I had been a little shocked the previous Christmas by her gift to

Ian of a whole case of whiskey. I was unaware, at the time, of the full significance of that gesture. Later I learned that he had been a rather heavy drinker before we met, but in all the time we were together, during a year and a half of courtship, plus the time of our marriage, his drinking was moderate. It seems almost unbelievable that a mother would go to such lengths to tempt her son back to a weakness that might again make him dependent upon her!)

She consistently refused to have any contact with me. Nevertheless, I frequently urged Ian to dine with her. I knew she must feel lonely deprived of his constant company. Sometimes he did this reluctantly; I can only imagine that there was a good deal of disparaging of me in these meetings. This is pure assumption on my part, made in the light of later developments.

On the advice of a very worldly-wise friend, I determined to give an elegant party on opening night. It might, she said, squelch all the gossip circulating about his attentions to his leading lady. It resulted only in embarrassment for my guests and myself. The two "guests of honor" arrived at the restaurant an hour and a half late, so far from sober that their attempts to dance made them painfully conspicuous. The party broke up, and one of my friends escorted me to our apartment. Ian did not come home.

Alone in the little apartment, I watched day dawn. Utterly spent by the emotional strain of the past weeks I was conscious of a physical pain in the region of my heart, as though a living organ within me had been torn from its moorings. I suddenly recalled the prophetic remarks of my psychic English friend; this must have been the "disaster" she had foreseen as she sat sipping her tea that afternoon. Strange!

Early that morning I left the little apartment to its ghosts of dead hopes and went back to the old brownstone family house down the street. My deepest sensibilities had been mortally wounded. The sudden rejection of the faith and love I had tried to build into the structure of our two lives was a blow to my pride, as well as to my heart. I had known that there would be problems of temperamental adjustment. Superficially, I suppose, I seemed as sophisticated as most people of my generation, but apparently I was not sophisticated enough to take this rejection in my stride. The protectiveness of my family and home life

before my marriage had spared me many an unpleasant experience. Tabloids have made such occurrences commonplace, but
my life hitherto had been singularly free from scandal and
vulgar publicity.

Newspaper headlines began to appear. They were always colored with word-pictures of an older woman luring an unwilling
young man to the altar. Patricia Collinge was furious. It was
from her home that I had gone to church; she and her husband
had been the witnesses. She vowed she would go to the papers
with her version of our wedding. Upon the advice of my attor-
ney, Dudley Field Malone, I refused to give any interviews or to
issue any statements. Nor would he allow Patricia Collinge to do
so. "This case is not going to be tried in the newspapers," he
said.

During this time a woman approached me with proof of her
common-law marriage to Ian in Boston, prior to his coming to
New York. She resented the treatment I was getting, she said,
and wished to make a statement—"telling all"—and proving
that he was far from the unsophisticated lad his mother was
making him appear to be. Again, Mr. Malone imposed silence.
"We are not going to dignify all this muck with any statement,"
was his comment.

A newspaper woman whom I knew slightly had daily stories
in her column about the three of us—Ian, myself and the "other
woman." When I telephoned this columnist and asked her on
what grounds she was basing all these stories, she said, "Mr.
Keith's mother calls me every night after midnight from California and gives me a statement. You have constantly refused to
speak. My paper insists upon material they know will interest
the public, and I have to give it to them. After all, they want to
sell newspapers."

Whenever I am emotionally disturbed, action becomes im-
perative for me. In work I can always find healing, and it was in
work that I sought relief from the unhappiness which clouded
my thoughts. To fulfill a commitment made earlier in the season, I went out to join the Stuart Walker stock company in Indianapolis. In the routine of work my nerves steadied themselves; the daily donning of another identity helped to push into
the background the ugly facts of my real life.

Ian, left free to follow his desires, apparently tired of his new attachment almost as quickly as he had involved himself in it. *As You Like It* had closed unexpectedly soon. Suddenly he turned up in Indianapolis. He demanded to be allowed to fulfill the joint engagement which Mr. Walker had been negotiating with us prior to the New York run of *As You Like It*. Stuart, my friend of long standing, put it to me. I said that I would certainly not wish to keep Ian out of work; it was agreed that he should stay. There were two plays in which we would have to appear together; Maeterlinck's *Monna Vanna,* and Oscar Wilde's *An Ideal Husband*. The irony of the latter title was not lost upon me! I suspect that I even found a certain grim satisfaction in detaching myself completely from the personal relationship while playing opposite him. This detachment is something the layman can scarcely understand, but it can be achieved and helps carry an actor through many an emotional crisis. Both plays were successful; we played them in both Indianapolis and Cincinnati, thus giving us the boon of a two-week's run in each. I remember Mr. Walker's glee when in Cincinnati he could find standing room only in his own theatre. (Greater joy than this hath no manager!) It is a pity that this gifted and sensitive director should have been lost to the legitimate theatre. The Midwest needed the kind of theatre which he provided and which he longed to make permanent. No one person ever did more to develop new talent, nor to offer talents already recognized the chance to expand their range. Although I was far from a beginner by the time I went out to play for him, under the warmth and stimulation of his encouraging direction, I learned a great deal. He worked hard and lovingly, as did all of us when we were with him. We begged him to hold us together and use us to found a permanent repertory company. McKay Morris, George Gaul, Elizabeth Patterson—all of us wanted it.

We had learned, in our previous seasons of working together, how much more fun our profession provides when its members, out of mutual effort, achieve a background of understanding of each other's methods. The pity of our system is that with changing directors and fellow players such effective collaboration is often not possible. Stuart had had some recognition, but the manifold problems of producing on Broadway repelled him. Even in Indianapolis, a year or two later, worn down, he told me of the endless problems which unions had created for managements. He gave up, he told me, when he realized that his stage carpenter was earning more in the season than he, the producer. He relaxed into the cushioned lap of Hollywood which for some time had been inviting him—and the theatre saw him no more.

At the end of that summer stock engagement, Ian and I each went our separate ways. After about a year or two had passed, he attempted to persuade me to take him back and to give him another chance. When I failed to respond he asked Mila to intercede for him. On May 13, 1926, he telegraphed her from Hollywood:

DEAR MILA: GETTING A WONDERFUL START AGAIN. JUST FINISHING BEAUTIFUL PICTURE AND OFFERED ANOTHER ONE HERE ALSO ONE IN NEW YORK. WOULD LOVE TO HAVE BLANCHE HERE AND SEE THIS BEAUTI-FUL COUNTRY IF SHE WILL GIVE ME AN OPPORTUNITY, MEET ME HALF WAY OR IF ONLY CONSENT TO MAKE THE TRIP WILL COME TO NEW YORK FOR HER AND DO THE PICTURE WHILE THERE. WILL BUY HER ROUND TRIP TRANSPORTATION AND PAY EVERY EX-PENSE IF SHE IS NOT HAPPY HERE. TONY KNOWS HOW I HAVE ALWAYS FELT, AND I KNOW IF YOU CAN MAKE BLANCHE SEE THAT I AM HEADED IN THE RIGHT DI-RECTION SHE WILL GIVE ME THIS CHANCE. WIRE AND LET ME KNOW IMMEDIATELY SO I MAY KNOW WHICH ENGAGEMENT TO CLOSE.

I refused to even consider his proposal for a reconciliation and answered in Mila's name:

BLANCHE AWAY. SORRY BUT HAVE NO INFLUENCE IN MATTER CONCERNED. EVERY GOOD WISH. MILA

I could not help being cynically aware of the publicity which this would open up for us both. I had had my fill of that! The cheap and vulgar handling of the whole affair by Ian, and especially by his mother, had destroyed all feeling of affection I had had for him. Yet he persisted.

Our last personal encounter took place in Boston. During the preceding months I had been treated to some minor annoyances

—incidents that suggested that my comings and goings were being spied on. I had reason to suspect that Ian and his mother were responsible for this. As a result, when the front desk clerk called one day and announced that a Mr. Keith wished to see me I decided not to receive Ian in my suite—but went down to meet him in the lobby.

We walked up Huntington Avenue in the cold, bleak Boston air, while I listened to a fairly credible declaration of good intentions, if only I would give him another chance. But my only response was embarrassment, and finally I cut him short by saying, as gently as I could, "I don't want to seem unkind, but you are really wasting your time. I just can't try again. I am no longer in love with you. You and your mother managed that." And I directed our steps back to my hotel. He stayed on for several days longer but it was useless. What I had felt for him as my lover and husband was dead.

Life has a curious way of catching up with one. Several years after that final encounter in Boston, I was rehearsing for a stock star engagement in Cleveland. One of the actors (whose name I don't recall) came over to me as I stood in the wings and said, "Did you hear about the terrible thing that happened to Keith's mother?" "No," I answered, "I haven't even thought about either of them for years." "Well, she was making some synthetic gin in the basement of their house; it exploded and she was burned to death." I could hardly believe my ears. It was too horrible!

Ian married three more times. One of the ladies was Ethel Clayton, the film star; another was a baroness whose name I do not recall, and the last one was an old childhood friend. He returned to the Broadway stage to give two magnificent performances. As Bolingbroke in Maurice Evans' production of *Richard II* he was superb; and again, somewhat later, as Cauchon in Shaw's *Saint Joan,* starring Siobhan McKenna. During the ensuing years he further satisfied his hunger for Shakespeare by playing some of the great roles in college productions, notably at Hofstra College on Long Island, where he was a splendid Macbeth. I believe that had he been seen in these performances, under proper professional conditions, he would have made a profound impression on those who might have used his talents to their mutual advantage, as well as to that of the American Theatre. He was potentially a great actor. I believe that he could have stepped into Barrymore's shoes had he had more self-discipline, a little luck, and sponsors similar to those that John Barrymore had been blessed with.

Ian died in 1960.

CHAPTER 10

THE SQUALL

IF ANYONE HAD the faculty of smelling out a box office "hit," he would probably be regarded as omniscient. There are a few managers whose record would almost prove them to be endowed with this gift. In my early days, David Belasco was one. Yet even the most astute managers sometimes pick a dud or miss a winner. And even a bad play can be a money-maker. The ability to sense the potentials of an unproduced play is rarer than most laymen imagine. I have shown poor judgment more than once.

During the winter of 1925, I met a Spanish lady who wrote under the pseudonym Jean Bart. She confided that she had written a play with a wonderful part for me. Pleasant people whom one meets at luncheons are very apt to have written plays, so I did not take her too seriously, but I did read the script she sent me. I didn't like it much.

Some months later a firm named Jones & Green sent me a play they were planning to produce; it was the same play. It revolved around the household of a Spanish gentleman-farmer who was also something of an artist. A beautiful gypsy girl bursts in on the household seeking shelter from a torrential rainstorm and from her brutal gypsy chief. The mother not only protects her but yields to her plea to be allowed to stay in the house as a servant. They wanted me for the mother. The play was called *The Squall,* the title being symbolic of the sudden storm of dissension wrought by the seductive gypsy in the hitherto happy household. I returned the play with thanks. It did not seem to me to have a chance. The management was persistent. I yielded. There was to be a try-out at Skowhegan, Maine, which had an exceptionally fine resident company. The director was Howard

Lindsay; Dorothy Stickney was the ingenue and Arthur Byron, Walter Connolly, Nedda Harrigan, and Albert Hackett made for a splendid cast. The Skowhegan try-out was voted a success.

Plans for the New York production of *The Squall* went forward. Despite my reservations about the play's Broadway chances, I agreed to do it, as did Dorothy Stickney, Nedda Harrigan, Lee Baker, and one or two others. Nubi, the gypsy, was played by Suzanne Caubet, a dark-eyed French girl who had been the god-child of Sarah Bernhardt. She had an exquisitely seductive figure and gave a good performance. Her father had been a member of Bernhardt's company, and she told us many unhackneyed stories about the Divine Sarah and her shenanigans. Sarah obviously had a rare sense of humor and knew perfectly well what she was about with her strange publicity stunts. Lou Tellegen, the last of her glamorous leading men, told me that he once asked her why she did these "outré" things that attracted so much publicity, and she replied with a grin, "Ca m'amuse."

Almost immediately I began to torment myself with worrying about the play; rehearsal jitters took over. Romney Brent had been engaged for Finito, a zany village boy. He, with tiny, rotund Ida Mulle playing his mother, made an unforgettable picture standing in the arched doorway of the farmhouse in the dripping rain under a huge umbrella, looking like two figures drawn by Goya. Romney's presence in any cast is a source of joy. He bolstered my morale, although he, too, had little faith in the play's chances. "Two weeks after it opens no one will remember that you were in it," he assured me. He was a better actor than prophet. It ran for two years, one on Broadway.

During the pre-opening week in Stamford an interesting bit of directing rescued us from a dangerous moment in the action of the plot. The gypsy girl, having seduced in turn the son and the farm manager, turns her amorous attentions towards the master of the household. Scantily clad, bathed in the glow of the firelight, she throws herself into her master's reluctant arms. The wife, appearing at the top of the curving staircase, sees the scene below and silently withdraws. It was written, of course, to be a poignant and dramatic moment, but the laughter at this point threatened to kill whatever chance the play might have. Lionel Atwill, the director, hit upon a solution. Instead of actually stepping into view of the audience, I moved in only far enough for the candle I carried to throw my shadow on the wall for a moment; from that day on there was not a titter.

For the most part the notices were not good. Some were devastating. Yet Robert Benchley's oft-quoted "Nubi, me good girl, me stay here; me, Benchley, me bad boy, me go home," was turned into surprisingly effective publicity, and quoted widely. The fine Irish hand of Richard Maney, our press agent, exploited it to the full. Money was spent lavishly in emphasizing the sex-angle of the story, and in the middle of the third week business suddenly picked up; we played to excellent houses from that time on, never to what could, by any stretch of the imagination be called Theatre Guild audiences, but to paying customers nevertheless.

Meanwhile fate was preparing a blow from which none of our family ever fully recovered. Absorption in the launching of a new play can blind one momentarily to what is happening outside one's orbit of make-believe. The operation which my sister Mila had undergone at the time of my marriage had only temporarily retarded the wasting disease which should have been dealt with years earlier. Now, I was shocked to realize how rapidly her strength was ebbing.

Both Charlie and Tony had become successful dentists. They had backed a little dress shop for her on Madison Avenue as a small gesture of appreciation of her endless devotion to us all. We had all taken part in getting her started. Enthusiastically we helped her send out announcements, decorate and select her first stock of "ready-to-wear." In the rear she fitted up a sunny work-room in which, with two assistants, she continued to design and make dresses.

I would accompany her on forays into that garment world which lies just west of Seventh Avenue in the upper 30's. It was exciting to see all those lovely clothes and we had many a heated argument over their selection. One day, after we had chosen some twenty dresses and suits in most of which I could visualize myself looking quite ravishing, Mila said, gently but firmly—"Don't you think it might be a good idea to select a few models that you couldn't wear?"

For a few years the shop had been modestly successful and she enjoyed the independence which her work gave her. But now those cheery activities were no longer possible. Soon she had to give up even the few hours' work she had been exacting of herself each day. The workroom continued to be run somehow, for her small staff was devoted to her.

When Charlie told me there was no hope of a cure, the world went black. All our lives we had depended upon her quiet wisdom, her gay courage. Even more than to Maminka, we had turned to Mila for advice. It was as though she were the hub in the wheel of our family life.

She spent her last weeks in my sunny bed-sitting room where we could be with her and surround her with our love. She knew she was dying. I heard her say softly to the doctor, "I'm not afraid to go, doctor. It's just that they all need me so." Even when morphine released any inhibitions she may have had the ramblings of her mind were the expressions of a sweet though feeble gaiety. To the very last she tried to be helpful, striving to sustain our sinking courage.

My evenings at the theatre were filled with dread of what news might greet my return home. Then one midnight, after I had sat at her bedside for an hour or so, as I always did after my performance, I went into the front room for a catnap while Tony took my place by her bed. Presently I felt his arms around me, his face straining to hold back the tears. "She's gone, Sis," he whispered. "She's just gone." I hurried back into the bedroom. She lay peacefully at rest, the suffering body around which I had so often put my arms, still warm. It was hard to believe. I lay wide-eyed on the sofa all through the aching hours until dawn. I saw how empty the world would seem without her; how rich a thing she had made of her simple life. Always she had radiated that loving kindness which two thousand years before was expressed in the command, "Love ye one another." As the morning broke, her sustaining spirit seemed to lift me out of my sorrow, to lead me away from a contemplation of death to one of renewed life.

As the hours passed, I had to let the theatre management have some definite word, as I had no understudy. I knew that Mila, who so loved the theatre, would wish me to carry on, so I sent word that I would play as usual. Closing the play even temporarily would do no one any good, Mila least of all. And she, I knew, would not want me to do it.

I managed the matinee fairly well, resting in my dressing

room between performances. The evening passed smoothly enough too, until the moment at the close of the second act when Dolores throws herself sobbing before the little family shrine, praying for courage and faith. Then the dam broke; the sobs which tore out of me at that moment were very real.

On the day of the funeral friends offered me their care and attention so that I might get through the evening performance. There would be "hot soup, a warm bed and rest" on my return after the chilly drive to the Kensico cemetery. With Lillie Collins and another friend, I started back to town. Soon we realized that we were driving about in circles in a blinding snowstorm. Detour after detour landed us at no familiar road. Of all those who attended the funeral, we had to have a driver who did not know the roads in Westchester. (It seemed that Long Island funerals were his specialty.) It was dreadful—and it was absurd. I began to feel that somehow Mila had taken charge; as though she were saying, "No, dear, you must not go home and lie there brooding for hours. We'll see that it doesn't happen."

The snow fell steadily and was already slush under foot. Finally, at seven-thirty, we reached the environs of 200th Street. The car stalled. The driver announced that something was wrong with the blankety-blank engine. I got out to look for a taxi, but as usual in bad weather there was none to be found. Not waiting to discuss the condition of the car, I dashed through the falling snow to the nearest subway station, caught an express, and half an hour later fought my way through the Broadway crowd to the stage door of the 48th Street Theatre. Jimmy Bell, our stage manager, was peering out into the darkness of the alley apprehensively awaiting me. I ran up the familiar alley, and flung off my wet coat saying, "Please, Jimmy, send out for an egg sandwich on whole wheat and some hot coffee, I'm starving."

The Spanish make-up and black wig went on in record-breaking time. The curtain was not even held. But the final touch of absurdity was provided by the corner drug-store clerk, who forgot to put the egg in the sandwich! I played my performance that night sustained by two pieces of bread, a cup of coffee, and the remnants of a sense of humor.

There was little humor in the task I had to face soon after. As executrix of Mila's estate, I had the responsibility of closing up the dress shop. Inventory had to be taken. I considered disposing of the entire stock to one of those firms which batten on just such situations. I called up one of them. When the gentlemen I sent for arrived, they began lumping the dresses together like so many bunches of carrots, and offered me $1.00 apiece for them. I had seen Mila select them with such careful consideration; I couldn't stand it. Suddenly I knew it must not be done that way. "I've changed my mind," I said to the little men. "Sorry to have wasted your time, but I'm not selling after all." They stared, then withdrew grouchily, doubtless thinking me a bit mad.

Mila, it seemed clear to me, would have wished the dresses to reach the people she had known. I engaged someone to help me, little dreaming what I was undertaking. Before the sale was over my feet were numb from the ankles down; my nerves grew taut, as my temper strained at its leash. Many of Mila's former customers rallied. But as the sale progressed, I learned much about what some women will do to get a bargain! A dress, obviously too small, would be tried on, stretched out of shape, and smeared with lipstick as some customer tugged to get it on. One "stylish stout" after trying on, for over an hour, dresses which had been enormously reduced, finally lumped three of the best together and asked, "What price will you make if I take all three?" I'm afraid I turned fishwife.

Through all these trying weeks the play ran on and on. The theatre became my refuge from the gruelling fatigue, the petty arguments of the long day at the shop. Mere repetition of the performance had brought about a routine smoothness which became my salvation. Again I was able to fall back upon that "adequate minimum performance" which had been dinned into us in the early Belasco days. A curious duality developed in my consciousness, making me feel like a character out of a Pirandello play. Once I entered the familiar stage door and my own face and hair disappeared under the olive grease paint and the smooth black wig of Dolores, she became the real me. My own life during the rest of the day seemed a part which I had been playing; I could shed its exhaustion, its frequent annoyances, because they seemed unreal.

Yet there were pleasant incidents at the shop, too. On a gray, depressing afternoon, a few days before Christmas, a day particularly dreary because the workroom staff had left early to do

Christmas shopping, I sat alone, too tired to go home, wondering what had ever possessed me to take on such a task. The door opened, and in popped a ruddy-cheeked, elderly man with iron-gray hair, looking very prosperous in his fur-collared overcoat.

"Is this the shop where my niece bought some dresses this morning?" he asked. I recalled the similarly ruddy cheeks and Nordic features of a girl who had that morning selected a particularly becoming blue frock. "Yes," I replied. (Oh, Lord, was she going to cancel her order?) "She told me you showed her a number of excellent bargains. It occurred to me that you might help me with some of my last minute Christmas shopping. Now, may we have some dresses in a row? Then perhaps you will be good enough to help me make my selections."

His use of the plural was heartening. I tried not to show my excitement. Gown after gown was brought out as he peered through the show-cases looking for more. When some twenty had been displayed, he said, "Now, let us go through these carefully, and we'll make final selections." Along the line we went, pausing now and then to eliminate one. About two-thirds of the dresses remained, approved. "Those will do beautifully," said Santa Claus, drawing out his checkbook. "After you have verified my check, will you send them out?" And he left. Only about twenty minutes had elapsed since he had appeared. I sat staring at the generous check, for the ones he had chosen had been among the best left in the place. I wondered if I had been dreaming.

Deciding that there must be no anti-climax to that visit, I threw on my things, closed up the shop, and walked home on winged feet, eager to relate my experience to the family. The big brownstone house was dark. A note from Rose was on the table in the dining room where we usually gathered. "Have gone to the country with Charlie," it said. I felt like a deflated balloon. Next morning at ten I hurried to the bank to deposit the check, half expecting to learn the worst. "I suppose—there's some joker in it," I said to the manager. "Will you please call up his bank for me?" He did so. A shade of amusement crossed his face as he was talking. Then, turning to me he said, "I guess it's good, all right." The name, it appeared, was very famous indeed in banking circles.

On the day before Christmas a box of beautiful green and

brown orchids arrived at the shop accompanied by a note saying, "It seems to me that the saleslady, too, should have a bit of Christmas cheer."

As I closed up Mila's shop once and for all I remembered an amusing experience she and I had had some years earlier. It was the period when flat chests and boyish figures were fashionable. My bosom, partly as a result of deep breathing practice, was very high. It bothered me to be out of style—for my evening dresses had to have unfashionably high neck-lines. Then I found a solution—at least for my stage costumes.

From my dentist brother I borrowed some strips of the flesh-colored rubber which dentists then used to protect the tooth on which they were working from saliva. I cut the rubber into strips about twenty inches in length. At each corner I attached a piece of ribbon, using adhesive tape and then sewed the ribbon through the tape, tying all four pieces at the back to flatten myself out. The flesh-colored rubber not only acted as a controlling brassiere, but from a few feet away, and especially across the footlights, they completely masked the split in what my niece called my "boosums."

After I had used the invention for a few months, Mila and I decided that, put together more professionally, this item could be sold in her shop. We had a patent lawyer register it under the name of "The Lovliline." I enjoyed the mirage of a future fortune—for they cost very little to make, only about a quarter, and people gladly bought them for $1.50. One day Mila told me that orders for six to a dozen at a time were coming from the Elsie de Wolfe salon on Fifth Avenue. My curiosity was aroused.

Putting on my most impressive clothes and manner I presented myself at the salon and informed an exquisitely mannered saleslady "I am told that one can buy here a rather special kind of brassiere which Miss de Wolfe. . . ." She interrupted me, "Oh yes, Miss de Wolfe orders them from Paris for a few of her very special clients. It's done, of course, as a favor to them." Very innocently I asked, "Could I see one?" She shook her head regretfully, "I am so sorry," she said, "we have just sold the last one we had to Madame So-and-So. But if you would like to leave an order we could take care of you when we receive our shipment from Paris. It should be here any day."

I thanked her and ordered a dozen. "I'll come for them in

about a week," I said. "By the way, how much are they?" The answer left me gasping—though I managed to control my face muscles fairly well. "Twenty-five dollars apiece." And she bowed me out. I hurried over to Mila's. "Have you heard from the de Wolfe salon?" I asked Mila. "They have just called up to order a dozen for delivery as soon as possible," she told me. We laughed a good deal. The next morning I called to cancel the order. The saleslady did not seem very perturbed. After all, the salon had a large clientele.

Alas, fashions change. The mirage of a fortune melted away. But it had been fun.

With the final turning of the key on the shop, I relaxed into the simple routine of the theatre. There I had a staunch friend in my little Czech theatre maid—one Mizerovska; she was really quite a person. "La Mizerovska," Romney called her, saying that it sounded like the name of a great singer. He adored her, revelling in the freshness of her point of view on matters of the theatre and delighting in her malapropisms. She was the Laurette Taylor of the Czech colony, playing ingenue parts in the same sort of amateur performances which had started me on my career at the Sokolovna. As a matter of fact, *Peg O' My Heart*, she told me, was her greatest triumph. I wish I could have seen her in it; the Irish brogue in Czech must have been something to hear. Tiny, sharp-tongued Mizerovska had the heart of gold one hears of but seldom encounters. The fact that her mother, Dolezalka, had been our family helper for a number of years gave the relationship a warmly personal quality which was a great comfort during the sorrowful events which occurred during Mizerovska's reign. For "reign" it was. She was a born ruler and was very firm with me, despite the fact that she was half my size. In fact, her firmness was directly responsible for my eventual elevation to stardom.

Forty-eighth Street in 1927 was the "street of hits" which 45th Street was to become in later years. Next door to us at the Playhouse, Jane Cowl was starring in Robert Sherwood's first big success, *The Road to Rome*. At the Cort Theatre across the street, Ethel Barrymore was appearing in Maugham's comedy *The Constant Wife*. I really think it was the size of the electric letters in which Jane's name blazed each night that pricked

Mizerovska's pride in her own leading lady; one evening, in a mildly belligerent mood, she came to the point.

"Why is Miss Cowl's name so big on that sign?" she asked. "Because she's a big star. She carries the play." "What does it mean when your name comes after the play's name, like yours?" she asked. "It means that you're a featured player," I answered. "Oh. Then you are not a star?" She looked crushed. "No, in this play, just a featured player." She had her answer ready. "But you carry this play. Everybody says so. Now, Blanchie" (funny how little people always seem to call me Blanchie) "I want you to go right up to the manager's office and make them put your name first." Then she grinned. "Tell 'em I want to work for a star like Miss Cowl's maid does."

I did. It worked. The five-hundredth performance was imminent. The publicity attendant upon such an announcement would be good business, so, as we reached that date, they informed the press that "owing to Miss Yurka's long run in . . . etc.," the management was elevating her to stardom. The workmen climbed up ladders to shift the letters of my name from the bottom to the top of the electric sign, and the Great Progression was achieved. Frankly, I couldn't see any difference in my performance that night. Mizerovska, who had turned the trick, was jubilant; for the rest of the run she was working for a star.

Tragedy seemed to stalk the run of *The Squall;* it even stalked through the aisles of the theatre. One very hot July night, during the last act, I heard a commotion in the audience. Instinctively I carried on, assuming that someone had been momentarily overcome by the heat. Air-conditioned theatres in those days were unheard of.

The moment the final curtain had been lowered I sent Mizerovska out to ask if there was anything we could do. She came back white-faced. "Miss Blanche, the lady's dead; she's lying on the steps in the alley, stone dead." I gasped in horror. Hurriedly getting rid of my make-up and into my street clothes, I sent Mervin Williams, who was playing my son, to find out what had happened. He, too, came back with a startled face. "It's June Mathis, the scenario writer; you know, the one who discovered Valentino. She had a heart attack. They've telephoned the coroner's office; they say she mustn't be moved until they arrive."

Together we went out into the paved alley-way. Miss Mathis' body lay heavy, inert on the stone step. Over it hovered her eighty-two-year-old grandmother who had accompanied her "baby," as she kept calling her, to the theatre. She was unable to realize what had happened. "If you will only let me take baby home," she kept reiterating. "I know I can make her get well. Why don't you let me take baby home?"

The pitiful old voice went on and on while we stood there helpless. The audience, totally unaware of what had occurred, had dispersed; even the morbidly curious had drifted away from the iron gate which barred entrance to the alley-way. Mervin, Mizerovska and I remained. From time to time Mervin would go out to telephone in an effort to reach someone whom the grandmother might know. The coroner's men did not come. Midnight passed. One o'clock! two o'clock! still Mervin and I kept our vigil, the frail little old woman opposing, with iron will, all our efforts to have her taken to her hotel. At last Mervin reported that the coroner was on his way. On the strength of that, grandma let herself be persuaded to return to the hotel where she could get things ready for her "baby." Weary and heartsick, I accompanied her, leaving Mervin in charge of the body.

As we drove uptown, we passed Campbell's Funeral Parlors. I suddenly recalled newspaper accounts of the Valentino funeral there only a year before when crowds of hysterical, milling women had turned the services into a circus. Soon, in these identical rooms, was to lie the woman who had opened for him the golden doors to fame, fortune and adulation such as is enjoyed by few. Life is very strange indeed.

One evening a man whom Mizerovska called "a mad Russian" came by appointment to talk to me about a play. I was fascinated by his incredible vitality and by his thick Russian accent. When I suggested that he leave the play for me to read, he protested. "No, No! I must read it to you!" After my performance that night Gregory Ratoff acted out the whole of *Cafe Tomaso* for me. His performance—replete with movements and gestures —was, I suspect, better than the one the play received later, for it failed. But the exuberant enthusiasm that Ratoff exhibited that night makes his ultimate success as an actor and movie director very easy to understand. He was a very dear person.

Not long after, as I was preparing to leave after a matinee, a woman whom I had known slightly asked to see me. She startled me by announcing that she was about to sue me and the author of *The Squall* for plagiarism.

Sure enough, two years earlier this woman had asked me, through a mutual friend, to read a play she had written and to make any criticisms that might be helpful to her in the form of marginal comments. It is always difficult for me to say no to a beginner. Although the play was excessively long and very amateurishly written I had complied with her request to please our mutual friend. Now this woman announced that *The Squall* was obviously a revamping of her script; didn't she have my handwriting on the margin of her manuscript to prove that it had been in my hands? I and the author of *The Squall* had obviously stolen her story. I was flabbergasted. Fortunately the copyright dates of Jean Bart's play, *The Squall,* settled the question of "plagiarism" in short order. But it was an unpleasant incident and made me reluctant ever after to read un-optioned manuscripts—friends or no friends.

When I told this story to someone recently, I was asked, "But didn't you recognize the similarity between the two plays at the time you read *The Squall?*" My answer must have been quite disillusioning. "No, I didn't notice anything out of the ordinary because there are only about seven plots altogether, and all plays are a rehash of one or another of them."

While walking toward Fifth Avenue one night after the performance, my escort and I were startled to hear the prolonged wailing of many sirens. Quickening our steps we reached the corner of 48th Street and Fifth Avenue just as a long procession of some fifty motorcycle policemen swept down the avenue at full speed.

"Let's follow them!" I cried. Supper forgotten, we leaped into a taxicab and, turning southward, trailed the motorcycles. Block after block sped by until we reached 14th Street. Union Square was black with a milling throng of sorrowful people who were being kept steadily moving by mounted police. Other people kept pouring in from side streets. In and out among the horses the strangely quiet crowd wove its way—a shifting pattern of humanity. Above the muffled sound of moving feet arose a muted, woeful chant:

Sacco-Vanzetti. DEAD!
Sacco-Vanzetti. DEAD!
Sacco-Vanzetti. DEAD!

Nothing else. No other words. No suggestion of rioting. Not even a rough movement. Just a continuous tragic chant, a mournful, hopeless, poignant protest.

Towering skyscrapers surrounding the old square made it seem like the bottom of a well in which human heartache was eddying and lapping against steep, steely walls. It was an awesome sight, and as mere onlookers we felt like intruders.

As we drove toward Second Avenue, cutting across town past the attractive houses on East 19th Street, I could not but marvel again at the close proximity in which luxury and misery find themselves in large cities. In this same street, just off the square we had left, lived two people who represented the old order of the privileged classes with considerable dignity and charm. At the Joe Thomas' house, designed by Albert Sterner, one found what was closer to a formal, elegant salon in the European sense than any other household I have ever visited. The beautifully designed room with its great fireplace and its overhanging balcony made a becoming setting for Clara, the clever diminutive chatelaine, and her tall, good-looking husband.

The drawing room was perfect for music. A splendid concert piano stood in front of a high mullioned window which opened onto a tiny covered patio in the rear. When the windows were open one heard a fountain making its own gentle music. Like some women, this room was at its best after dark when tall candles gleamed against the oak panelling. I saw it once on a Christmas afternoon; in the gray north light it seemed like a theatre set waiting for the footlights and actors to bring it to life. Not a house for children to grow up in. But on a spring evening, when great masses of dogwood filled each dark corner with their graceful branches, that drawing room was really something to see.

It was a salon which gathered many notable people. I remember meeting, one evening, a Frenchman with a keen face, named Paul Reynaud, later to become Premier of France. Painters, writers, musicians, financiers—Clara Thomas drew them all to her with the magnetism of a pretty and intelligent woman who takes the trouble to charm. Molière would have put her into one of his plays.

I recall dropping in one evening after a performance of *The Squall* to find myself in the midst of an international *Who's Who*. Gilbert Miller's look of opulent prosperity seemed to dominate one of the small tables at which supper was being served. Nearby sat Charlie Chaplin. Presently Germaine Taillefere (one of Les Six who did so much to further modern music) played the piano; Ralph Barton, recently become her husband, beamed with pride. Eva Gautier's strangely Javanese appearance added an exotic note to her singing and her exquisite musicianship, while on the balcony Charles Hanson Towne, the well-known wit and columnist regaled me with genial and occasionally astringent comments upon the actors in the pageant below.

When all but a few old friends had left, we gathered around the big fireplace, while Charlie Towne sat at the piano, doing his popular spoofing of Wagnerian music and singers. Someone spoke of lovely Maria Jeritza's new "business" in Tosca—starting the famous aria lying face downward on her stomach—of which much had been made in the papers. I said, "There's only one other way left to do it—standing on one's head. I'll bet it could be done." Charlie bet me it couldn't. Tucking my long skirt tightly between my ankles, I rose slowly to the position of the Yogi head-stand. Throat relaxed, my head resting firmly against my hands, I heard the familiar notes pour into the room. No one was more astonished than I. My delight quickly turned into laughter which ended my singing. Charlie Towne swore it was all done with mirrors.

The parties at the Thomas' house were an oasis of distinction in a society gone wild. What went on in many other circles during those Roaring Twenties was expressive of a brutalized sense of enjoyment in a world eager to forget the war. Speakeasies gave drinking the allure of the illicit. Men, and even women who had never cared for it, drank more and worse alcohol than had probably ever been served to supposedly civilized people. Parties were given at which male dancing partners were at such a premium that "gate crashing" became an accepted practice. The hostess' function was chiefly that of a wholesale liquor dealer operating on a non-profit basis.

But so much has been written about this chapter of American social history that I will refrain from adding my list of 1920's anecdotes. Though I attended my share of parties, I never did acquire a taste for the drunken brawls that so many of these turned out to be. I would return from such gatherings to our house on East 72nd Street with relief, pausing for a minute or two in the familiar hallway to breathe in the aroma of that familiar, decent household.

Of course, there were brave moments too in the 1920's. Who can ever forget the high drama of Charles Lindbergh's lonely flight across the Atlantic, or the outburst of pride and joy which greeted his return? And always, in New York, there was the drama of life in that city: that unforgettable chant of despairing grief for Sacco-Vanzetti in Union Square; the terrible night of the Sherry Netherlands Hotel fire when the high flaming tower beyond the reach of any fireman's hose burned like a torch against the midnight sky.

In January, 1929, I started rather reluctantly on tour with *The Squall.* By now the repetition of those lines was beginning to pall on me. My brother Tony tried to cheer me up. "Go on out, Sis, and make a lot of money!" he said. "Then we can take a real trip somewhere." I can still see him standing beside it in the winter sunshine smiling at me as he turned to go. For some months Tony had been depressed over personal problems, but after Christmas he had seemed to recover his spirits and I left reassured by his buoyant mood.

One evening in Detroit I was feeling particularly elated. Walking back to the hotel with another player and Mizerovska I had been almost foolishly light-hearted. At midnight she came to say her usual goodnight. Her sharp little face was unusually gentle. "Blanchie," she began hesitantly, "they've asked me to tell you—it's awfully hard—there's been a telegram. It's Tony." She couldn't go on, her eyes were brimming with tears. That afternoon Tony had leapt from the window of his fourth floor room. Death had been instantaneous.

There was no hysteria in my deep grief. We had been very close, and I had tried to help him as best I could during those months of depression. When I left New York it was with the happy thought that he had recovered his former spirits and pleasure in life. I was never to know what prompted that tragic act.

I began to long for the end of the tour. Successful as the run of *The Squall* had been, those two years had been marked by so many personal griefs that I knew I needed a long rest. The tour was scheduled to end in Boston in June, 1928. I could hardly wait.

CHAPTER 11

ALHAMBRA BY MOONLIGHT

WHEN THE TOUR with *The Squall* finally ended, I returned to New York faced with the need to make several important decisions. Since our brother Charlie had married and moved to Westchester, only Rose and I now remained at 242 East 72nd Street. The house was really much too large for us, so that when we received a good offer for it we sold it. Reducing the accumulation of many years of family living to what would be suitable for a six-room apartment was a formidable task. Glad as we were to leave behind the sad associations of the past two years, it was a wrench to pull up the roots of so many memories. There was a painful finality in closing up the house in which so much of our adult life had been spent.

During the ensuing holiday I felt as though I were in limbo, waiting for something to show me what turn my life would now take. I had reached a certain milestone; my name was up in lights; I was a "star." I could pause to relax a little. Ironically enough, I had a strong impulse to liquidate my investments, acquire some fool-proof annuities and enter upon a future which might lead me anywhere. I even discussed this with Charlie, who had given up dentistry for the real estate business, but my extreme lassitude made any concrete efforts to organize my life seem beyond me. It was easier to put my savings into Charlie's ventures and let him do the worrying.

I had a little more money than usual: the steady salary provided by *The Squall*, the small royalty on the scenes which I had surreptitiously rewritten, and my share of the money from the sale of the house made me feel more affluent than I had ever been. So I asked Charlie to invest my cash as he thought best, since I had absolutely no sense in such matters. He felt that real estate was the one safe thing. The stock market was going crazy, he said, but people would always want and need land.

We overlooked two essential facts, however; that should deflation come, land values, too, must inevitably shrink and that taxes, like the poor, are always with us. "Fools rush in" was never more true than when we took over some of the wilds of Westchester County.

The combined emotional and physical strain imposed by the two years' run of *The Squall* had left me exhausted. If ever there was a time when a quiet reappraisal of my life's pattern should have been made, it was now. But I have never had sense enough, at such times, to go into seclusion and rest before making decisions. My mental machinery, geared into high, seemed unable to slow down. At this point an acquaintance described a planned tour of Europe which she had decided to join. The prospect of a trip, the details of which one would not have to organize oneself, seemed very appealing both to Rose and myself. Two cheery cousins from Nebraska also seemed interested, so we decided to go as a foursome, feeling that this would protect us from some of the disadvantages of joining an organized tour. Since we had each other, we would not be entirely thrown on the company of our fellow tour members.

Spain was to be our first stop, after which we were to swing northward in a great arc, stopping off at various places before we reached Norway. These two countries especially appealed to my imagination, Spain because of my long stint in *The Squall* and Norway because of my interest in Ibsen.

The sea voyage was dull, but the very monotony soothed my nerves and calmed my spirits. We landed in picturesque Cadiz and then took a train to Seville. My first reaction on that train ride was one of disconcerted disappointment. Could this be the Spain of popular legend? Of the color-drenched Sorolla paintings in the Spanish Museum in New York? Slowly, in brutally increasing heat, we traversed a blazing, arid plain, its monotony scarcely broken by endless rows of cactus. An occasional pyramid of salt only heightened the impression of a sun-baked desert devoid of movement save for the poor donkeys one sees everywhere in southern Spain

In mid-afternoon the breathless heat suddenly broke. A sharp, cool breeze from the mountains swept through the train. We gasped in relief. The mountains were austere and bleak, gaunt peaks which seemed to scorn the softening green of vegetation. At last we reached Seville. Long, cool drinks washed down the dusty memory of salt ditches, and after a brief siesta all four of us sauntered forth into the evening twilight to take a good look at the city. But all memory of Seville fades before the glories of Granada.

Due to the late hour of our arrival there, we could only guess at the unseen beauties of this city. As a matter of fact, that first evening I was obsessed by a desire for just one thing: chocolate ice cream! All through that sweltering afternoon train ride, I had been memorizing the Spanish words for this precious dessert; I grandly ordered it for our whole group—"my treat, girls!" We waited ever so long on our balcony overlooking the sleeping city. When the waiter, whose "Si, Si, Si's" had assured me he had understood, finally appeared he proudly bore on his tray a tall pot of hot chocolate! We nearly died, but we drank it. So much for my command of the Spanish tongue.

We spent the next day at the Alhambra. Its balconies looked out over vistas of mountains. Water from countless fountains trickled through troughs of tiles laid centuries before. We seemed garish intruders in such a place.

To the hotel that evening came a band of gypsies from the nearby caves where they lived. Their leader was a short, stout woman with a strong face which in her youth must have been arresting even though not beautiful. Photographs on sale in the lobby showed her as a wild, primitive young thing. Middle age had buried her in fat, but had not destroyed her magnetism which completely dominated the family group. She sang weird, endless phrases up and down a vast scale, showing amazing breath control, emitting plangent sounds unlike any singing I had ever heard. As she sang, the others chanted an accompaniment. Then they danced in small groups. Occasionally, one of the family would rise from his chair and dance alone; even the old grandmother danced her "pas seul." The climax of the evening was the dancing of a most beautiful girl of about sixteen. I said to Rose: "She might be 'Nubi' herself, right out of *The Squall*."

Just in front of me in the ballroom where the dancers were

performing sat one of the most attractive men I had ever seen—
tall and spare, his clothes beautifully tailored, his fair hair
touched with gray, altogether the grandee. I would have cast
him for what I later learned he was: a Spanish diplomat. As we
left the ballroom, I stepped out onto the high balcony to feast
my eyes on the mysterious beauty of Granada by moonlight. He
followed me. He had overheard me speak to Rose of the youthful dancer's resemblance to Nubi in *The Squall*. With exquisite
courtesy he introduced himself, apologizing for this breach of
convention.

"But I could not resist, Señorita," he said. "In New York I
saw you in this play of which you spoke. Who would have believed that you, so Nordic, could have made yourself seem so
Spanish?" I smiled. "You, too, Señor, are fair, not at all the type
one sees in Spain." His eyes were green. (He explained that the
northern Spaniards are frequently fair; I wondered if they often
were so good-looking and spoke such beautiful English.)

He was to depart early the following day to fill a South American post. Just my luck! I spoke of the wonders of the Alhambra
as we had seen it earlier in the day, beautiful even in the glare of
noon. "How exquisite it must be now," I said, "drenched in
moonlight." "You would go now to see that—if I can manage it
for you?" he asked. I nodded my assent. He disappeared for a
few moments. I said a casual goodnight to the others, then
stepped back to the balcony.

He returned and led me down through the garden to a side
street. In his open car we sped through the warm, lovely night
back to the ruined palace which had housed so many romantic
mysteries. A gate had been left ajar. We wandered through the
fabulous gardens drenched in the magic of silence and moonbeams. To share that unique beauty with someone of rare sensi-
tivity was an unforgettable experience. It seemed as if I had
known him in some other existence—there were no barriers between us. We remained in those enchanted gardens until the
dawn began to glow in the East. By then we were more than
friends, and when he asked me to go to South America with him
it seemed the most natural thing in the world.

"I know this is very sudden," he said, "but why shouldn't it
be? I have so little time to persuade you. We can be married as
soon as we get to my post. Please, Carissima!" The magical gar-

dens glowing now in the light of dawn, the silence and the beauty around us made everything seem quite reasonable. But some streak of Czech sanity fought against my strong desire to say "yes."

If my fourteen months of engagement and marriage could end so disastrously, what could I possibly hope for from this mad, romantic episode, this brief moon-drenched idyl? If I were the heroine in a Shakespeare comedy perhaps we could live happily ever after. But in life things don't happen that way.

Sadly I said goodbye. A few hours later he left for South America, and I never saw him again.

Many years later I learned much about him from the Marquesa Belmonte with whose daughter I collaborated on the adaptation of Martinez Sierra's comedy *Spring in Autumn.* I had been a fool, to say "no." But perhaps not. Somehow I knew that, like Millamant in *The Way of the World,* I was never meant to "dwindle into a wife."

Our cruise proceeded northward. All too briefly we visited Algiers—Naples—Rome—Florence. Berlin, noisy and strident, reminded me of New York. Such fleeting glimpses of cities, of countries, were naturally unsatisfying, yet even these, I felt, were better than having no impression at all.

The shiny brightness of Swiss mountains was a complete change from the grim austerity of the mountains of Spain; different, too, I was to find, from the unspoiled, soft mole-colored freshness of those of Norway, whither our boat was heading. For me there was, of course, a special interest in visiting the homeland of Ibsen, but Norway's charm depended upon no such special attraction. Landing in Oslo, we saw everywhere fresh-faced people unhurried in their enjoyment of clean streets and lovely public gardens.

And what a refreshing change from the monotony of the ship's menu! Delicious lobster, enormous luscious strawberries with thick cream! Music by a fine string quartet. It made us feel that we were in a civilized country, indeed! No theatres were open in midsummer, alas! I did insist that our cruise director make a detour so that we could see the house and room where Ibsen had lived and worked. Everything was just as the great man had left it, hideously Victorian and full of gloom. No wonder his plays were dour. I bethought me of a remark once made by Michael Strange— "If a writer really has anything to say he can say it in any sort of surroundings!"

The cruise brought us all back to Paris where we separated to go our respective ways. Rose and I headed for Prague. It was my first glimpse of Tatinek's homeland. We enjoyed seeing that lovely old city at our leisure, taking pleasure in hearing the language familiar to us since childhood, spoken by passers-by. Tatinek's insistence that we learn something of the language had not been in vain.

The theatres were just reopening after the summer vacations. It is my impression that in European theatres male acting is almost uniformly good. But most of the women I saw left me wondering; they had so little of the personal magnetism which an English-speaking public demands of its favorite actresses. I saw no Cornells, no Jane Cowls, no Lynn Fontannes; in fact no glamorous ladies. Perhaps they were all still away on holidays.

Strolling about the city's coffee houses and streets, chatting with its denizens whenever possible confirmed the impression of my forebears that I had received in childhood. The Czechs are a down-to-earth people genuinely democratic and not overly concerned with "les elegances." There is a paragraph in Franz Werfel's *Verdi* which expresses this beautifully. I feel that only a Czech could have written it, even though it is of an Italian that he happens to be speaking. "The French . . . repelled him. . . . It was the antipathy natural to an earnest, simple nature, distrusting charm and sweetness and luxury—he hated 'grazioso.' "

On the boat coming home Rose and I enjoyed the companionship of Elswyth Beebe. Elswyth Thane she had been when I first met her, and by this name she is known to the reading public as the author of *The Tudor Wench* and *Young Mr. Disraeli*, both of which were made into plays.

Elswyth had married the well-known naturalist, William Beebe. I recall sitting in front of the fire in the Beebe studio on West 67th Street one evening the following winter listening to Will Beebe and Otis Skinner discuss a wide range of subjects. Books, theatre, world affairs were touched upon with what Percy Hammond, the critic, once described as "the high purple of intelligence." In Otis Skinner's personality one felt the aura of fine theatre and gentle living. Mr. and Mrs. Skinner drove me home that night, and Mr. Skinner remarked, "How seldom one is privileged to enjoy such an evening . . . just sitting around a friend's fire and listening to good talk." He continued, "People nowadays all seem to feel that they must be doing something in order to endure the company of their friends. Conversation? Until this evening I had almost thought it a dead art."

On another evening at Beebe's everyone's interest centered on a good-looking white-haired man who was a well-known numerologist. At the sight of the letters which made up my name he looked horrified. "How you ever survived them is a mystery," he said. He begged me to change to another name scientifically contrived by himself. He promised that wonderful things would happen to me if I did. Possibly. But I couldn't take seriously the idea of such a change at my time of life. Will Beebe came to my rescue by suggesting that perhaps it was better to develop the ability to cope with a wrong name than to sail along easily with the right arrangement of letters. At any rate, Blanche Yurka it remains, for this incarnation at least.

CHAPTER **12**

THREE
HIGHSPOTS

W HEN WE RETURNED to New York it was to our new apartment which, like the house we had sold, was on East 72nd Street. It had been exquisitely decorated by Joe Mullen, Romney Brent's friend, assisted by Lewis Martin, an old friend of ours who had gone to endless trouble supervising the remodelling and the installation of the furniture. Not only that, but he had a lovely tea awaiting us. It was the kindest thing he could have done to ease our moving into our new home. Still, pleasant and comfortable as our apartment was, it took us quite a while to get used to having all the rooms on one floor. We were so accustomed to running up and down two or three flights of stairs whenever we wanted anything that for a while I think we actually missed the inconveniences of the old house.

I sometimes think that actresses don't really need homes. Scarcely were we settled in the new apartment when I had an offer to go to Minneapolis to do a stock star engagement for producer Buzz Bainbridge. Knowing his Scandinavian public to be a large one, he suggested that I do an Ibsen season. Naturally I was intrigued.

Starting with *The Wild Duck,* we followed it, in weekly succession, with *Hedda Gabler, Lady From the Sea* and (of all things for me!) *A Doll's House!* I managed the latter by playing it in modified crinolines and heelless slippers. The many diminutives in the dialogue I changed into terms of endearment such as might be used by any husband to any wife; and according to O. E. Rölvaag (the distinguished author of *Giants in the Earth* whom his collaborator on the translation of the book, Lincoln Colcord, had brought to see the play) it was all much as he had seen it played in Norway. There, it seems, even Noras are sometimes tall.

One morning, while I was studying in my room, the telephone rang, and a woman's voice spoke to me: "You don't know me, Miss Yurka, but this is something I felt I had to tell you," she said. "Last evening my husband and I saw you in *A Doll's House*. We have been on the verge of separating for some time, feeling that we were incompatible. After returning home last night we had the first understanding talk we've had in our lives. Seeing that play seemed to open his mind to what was wrong in our relationship. Now we are going to try to go on together. I had to tell you and to thank you." That was all she said. I thanked her and hung up the receiver.

I sat there startled and thoughtful. I had not moved except to lift up the phone. Yet over it there had poured a story of a life which had been altered by the genius of Henrik Ibsen who, so many years before, wrote of Nora and "the doorslam which echoed round the world." I learned once more that great theatre can be a powerful means for encouraging self-awareness and understanding.

I enjoyed the Ibsen engagement for its intrinsic interest, not knowing that it was to prove a preparation for one of my greatest adventures in acting.

How casually an important day may begin! I can still see the morning sun pouring into Shubert Alley, the mid-block thoroughfare between West 44th and 45th streets in New York. Walking through it that morning I ran into Leonard Gallagher, who had been business manager for the Actors' Theatre at one stage of that gallant venture.

"I've been talking to Lee Shubert," he said. "The 49th Street Theatre is empty and he has nothing to put into it. I suggested reviving *The Wild Duck* again. Could you get it ready in two weeks?" I thought swiftly. The Minneapolis Ibsen season was vivid in my mind. What fun it would be to repeat it on Broadway. "If he'll let me do *The Duck* and then a couple more," I said, "I'll guarantee to be ready." "First do *The Duck*, later I'll talk him into doing the others," said wise Mr. Gallagher. We parted, agreeing that he would call me after talking to Mr. Shubert.

Incredible as it now seems, by midnight of that same day I was busy restoring my beloved Ekdal family to life. In retrospect, my temerity makes me shudder. Not only did I have to get together a cast which would inevitably be compared to the original one so brilliantly assembled by Clare Eames and Dudley Digges, a cast whose performance had been rated as "comparable to the best work of the Moscow Art Company," but owing to the very scant budget on which I had agreed to operate, I would have to direct as well as play the part of Gina.

None of the former cast was available. In a way, this was fortunate; I should have been too self-conscious to direct any of my former colleagues. But to stage in two weeks a play with which the cast was unfamiliar was a staggering undertaking.

Dallas Anderson played Hjalmar—a most difficult part to which he brought eager enthusiasm, tirelessly seeking the right inflections, the correct timing, the exact mixture of "ham" and sincerity which that most exacting role demands. It was the first really fine part he had played in many years, though he had once been Maude Adams' leading man. His gratitude was touching and heartened me to devote endless effort in helping him perfect his characterization. We had a believable Hedvig, although no one could quite equal the heartbreaking beauty of Helen Chandler's performance four years earlier.

How we did it I still cannot quite understand, but two weeks after our first rehearsal we rang up the curtain on our opening night as I had promised (November 19, 1928) at the 49th Street Theatre. Always expecting the worst from the critics, I was fully prepared for mayhem. Not quite, perhaps. I knew they couldn't hang me; for anything less than that I should have to be grateful. To my utter astonishment they were kind.

It was delightful to slip into the comfortable honesty of Gina again. There was not the same joy, to be sure, as in the previous playing of it; no Maminka to come home to and say, "Well, Maminka, dear, you gave a good performance tonight"; no dear Mila with whom to share the evenings in the dressing room. Never was the realization of loss so acute as on my return home after that opening night; achievement seemed to have become meaningless.

When the play actually began to do fairly good business (it ran for nine weeks) the idea of following it with *Hedda Gabler* was broached to Mr. Lee Shubert. Again, to my surprise, he consented; a road tour which would enable him to exploit our New York engagement was, it seemed, what had intrigued him in the first place. I have always thought it interesting that Lee Shubert, reputedly so commercial in his attitude toward the theatre, should have been the only New York manager who ever made it possible for me to do three "highbrow" Broadway productions consecutively in one season.

One day—much later—I scribbled this:

> There was a producer I knew
> Whose last name began S-H-U
> Then came B-E-R-T
> And the first name was Lee
> (A name not quite unknown to you).
>
> Actors thought him a hard business man.
> Yet some can vouchsafe, as I can
> He could do the kind thing—
> Things that make welkins ring—
> Like the season when Hank Ibsen ran
> For seven whole months on Broadway.
> Which theatre? Not too far away
> From the Barrymore—Ritz
> (Where Ibsen scarce fits)
> But Lee Shubert allowed me to stay.
>
> Since I feel he was misunderstood
> (For to me he was always so good)
> I want him to see,
> Where e'er he may be,
> How kindly toward him is my mood!

If it had taken courage to try to duplicate the success of the Actors' Theatre *Wild Duck* production, it took even greater temerity to tackle *Hedda Gabler* so soon after Emily Stevens' brilliant performance of two years before. There is a kind of unwritten law in the American theatre that once a player has identified himself with a part no one else should presume to play it. With this I disagree. I think there should be more willingness to challenge comparison in great parts. Surely it must be interesting for a theatregoer to be able to compare different concepts of a great role. We have only to realize that in the Moscow theatres the same play is frequently presented simultaneously by different groups, sometimes on the same night, often with widely contrasting treatment.

I had some ideas about Hedda which were somewhat at variance with the interpretations I had seen. Almost always played as the embodiment of evil from the start, she usually became a ruthless witch, from whom Tesman would, in my opinion, have fled in terror. But I saw her rather differently: as a woman of potentially forceful character who, in another era, given an outlet for her energies, might have been a vital and entertaining member of society; moreover, one whose humor would certainly have been a distinct social asset among the sophisticates of today. But Hedda's restless energies were not viable in the society in which she lived; they festered and eventually destroyed her. She was an example of that evil which is primarily the negation of good, "une vie manquée," as Mme. Lillie expressed it in discussing my concept of the role with me.

In studying the part, I gave considerable thought to Hedda's background. Ibsen has a wonderful way of building up unseen characters in his plays. How clearly one can visualize the two maiden aunts who brought up Hjalmar Ekdal (or Rosmer's dead wife in *Rosmersholm*) from Ibsen's few telling phrases. Yet not once does he mention Hedda's mother; always the reference is to "General Gabler's beautiful daughter." One may infer, therefore, that she was a motherless child, brought up extravagantly by an indulgent father, fêted and spoiled on the assumption that she would, of course, make a good marriage. I can imagine them living up to the hilt of his income, a large one which ceased after his death. Hedda's casual requirement that Tesman provide a villa beyond his normal means, her bored indifference to it on the very first day of her incumbency, indicate a capricious extravagance accustomed to being indulged, with little consideration for ways and means.

Left penniless upon her father's death, we can assume that Hedda had only two alternatives: a dull marriage which at least assured the respectability so essential to her pride; or an affair with Judge Brack whose attentions, we learn, are carefully calculated to stop just short of marriage.

There is more comedy in the play than is generally brought out. The early scenes with the Judge and the photograph album scene with Lovborg; her cross-examining of Thea in Act I and of Tesman on his return from the "orgy" at Brack's—these provide moments of amusing lightness. Every ripple of laughter which Hedda's caustic humor—her *méchanceté*—can be made to evoke, adds immensely to the effect of the tragic scenes which come later. It was the desire to develop these contrasting values which tempted me to do the play. I felt I had succeeded, to some extent, when I read the review by Richard Dana Skinner, the drama critic, who wrote in *The Commonweal:* "We see a Hedda who grows in evil before our eyes."

There was one piece of business in the scene with Lovborg, in Act III, where he tells her he has lost his precious manuscript, which seemed to me to mark the turning point in her character. I staged the situation a little differently from the productions I had seen.

Usually the manuscript is placed on the desk upstage. Ibsen directs it so. But I put it in a large box on the centre table across which we played Lovborg and Hedda's scene. Hedda listens with clinical detachment to his torrent of remorse and despair over his "lost child." Then, smiling indulgently at him as she lifts the lid of the box where she had concealed it, she is about to return his precious manuscript to him and end his agony, when he utters the words: "Thea's pure soul was in that book."

I used to pause for a second, my face stiffening with jealous fury, then, withdrawing my hand, I let the heavy lid fall with a soft, dull thud, a sound which John Anderson said in his review "was like the closing of a coffin lid." It marked the end of Lovborg's hope of regeneration and the end of Hedda's hope of salvation. From that moment her feet are set on the path of destruction. She sends him away with her pistol to kill himself, then burns the manuscript in that marvelous curtain to Act III. Using a fireplace instead of a stove, we got a wonderful effect by my thrusting the edges of the manuscript against an electric hotplate concealed by bits of colored glass which looked like glowing coals. In the slow flames which rose one could almost smell burning flesh as Hedda whispered: "I'm burning your child, Thea! Your child and Lovborg's! Burning your child!"

Usually this scene is regarded as the high peak of the play. Here again I differ. I see this scene rather as the springboard into the mounting tragedy of the last act, where Hedda is driven to her self-inflicted doom. There is even poignancy in her wistful question to Tesman as he sits at the desk, absorbed in reassembling, with Mrs. Elvsted, the notes of Lovborg's book. "Isn't there anything I can do to help, Tesman?" And his preoccupied answer, "No, nothing in this world," shuts off her last chance to escape.

So much for my concept of the part. Its execution was almost wrecked on the opening night by one of those circumstances— usually stemming from some need of economy—which seem to haunt my professional life.

Costumes are my *bête noire*! In ordering the period dresses, with voluminous bustles and draped skirts, I had asked that very soft chiffon velvet be used. My fittings were delayed, as I was not only directing the play during the day, but playing in *The Wild Duck* at night. At last I did manage to tear downtown to Greenwich Village to the Shubert storehouse and costume department. There I found to my horror that the costumes were being made of cheap heavy velveteen. To my shocked protest the fitter replied: "Mr. Shubert says it would be too expensive to do them in the quality velvet you selected; we must use this instead."

I called the office; Mr. Shubert was in Boston. Too angry to use reason, I canceled the fitting, called up the theatre, dismissed rehearsal, and walked for hours through Central Park in the freezing cold, utterly frustrated and ready to give up the whole project.

The next day, somewhat calmer, I went in to see Mr. Shubert. I explained that I could not and would not appear in costumes made of that cheap cumbersome material. "I would look like Barnum's FAT LADY!" I wailed. "But tell me, Miss Yurka, why must you use eighty-nine yards of expensive velvet for three costumes?" I gasped. "Eighty-nine! Who said so?" "Here it is." He handed me a paper. The requisition, which read "eighty-nine yards for each costume" should have read "eight to nine yards!"

Well, that was that! The order went through for chiffon velvet. Unfortunately, precious time had been lost; as the date of the opening drew near the costumes were not ready. "But you'll have them in time," the fitters assured me. On the night of the final dress rehearsal there were still no costumes. Stage hands stood around while I waited; they didn't mind; they were being paid overtime! Finally at 10 P.M., one dress arrived! I rehearsed the entire play in that; the others, they said, would be ready the next day—the day of the opening!

We opened on February 11, 1929. As usual on an opening night, I arrived at the theatre early. Some premonition made me slip on the first-act negligee which was hanging on the wall of my dressing room. It was a fitted full-trained robe of oyster white velvet trimmed with black lace. And it was horrible! Bulky, the lace hastily and badly arranged, it made me look pounds heavier than I'd ever been. Not for this had I been living on raw oysters, black coffee and grapefruit juice for weeks in my effort to turn a healthy Czech-American into a nervous, neurotic-looking Scandinavian!

Frantically my maid and I ripped off the lace; pins were used where there was not time to sew. (How carefully I had to sit down!) In this state of nerves I went out to face one of the toughest audiences I have ever encountered. Never have I felt such frigid unresponsiveness. My first-act laughs didn't come. At the close of the first act curtain I felt I had failed utterly.

Act II began better, and the scene with the photograph album brought heartening ripples of amused response. My nerves steadied themselves. As the play swung into its more dramatic scenes, it gathered momentum, and at the end the applause was fairly good, but my performance, that night, never really recovered from the handicap of that worried first act. The critics were not too unkind.

We played *Hedda* for four weeks. Although thirty-two performances of such a part in a repertory theatre would constitute a success, as a run on Broadway it merely gave us time to prepare the next play.

I was surprised, several years later, in glancing through my scrapbook, to find that several critics received my effort quite kindly. On rereading them, I found them very fair and even constructive, yet at the time they seemed bitterly disappointing. This is one sound reason for firmly refusing to read notices for several days (or weeks, if one has the strength of mind!). Only then one can read them safely; immediately after an opening one's need of reassurance is so pressing that anything except raves seems like condemnation. Instead of being grateful that I had not been called the worst Hedda ever, I was disappointed at the time that my treatment of the part had not registered more effectively and been rated among the best. But this, too, is a fault of our system. One stands or falls on one's opening night performance—one never gets a second hearing, although a performance continues to grow for weeks after the opening.

I have always been amused by one critic's comment on a matter which had nothing to do with me. Ralph Roeder, who had been so good as Gregers Werle in *The Wild Duck,* played Lovborg in *Hedda.* His sensitive face, his Scandinavian coloring, his excellent speech, and above all his fine mentality, made him, in my opinion, an excellent choice for the part of the regenerated writer. One critic grudgingly conceded that although Ralph Roeder played Lovborg well enough, "it would be hard to imagine him the author of an important book." Mr. Roeder, shortly after, made a fool of the critic by creating no small sensation with his first book *Savonarola,* which became, as I recall, a best seller. If only all actors could so gracefully toss a caustic comment back into a critic's lap!

One of the nice things about doing a distinguished play is the kind of people who come backstage. While playing Hedda, I received a note from the actor Roland Young saying that he and Robert Edmond Jones would like to come backstage. Their enthusiasm made me very happy. Bobby Jones urged me to play, one day, Duse's part in D'Annunzio's *La Gioconda.* "You must square those broad shoulders for the mantle of the great ones," he said. I was deeply touched. I knew he was sincere. But I also knew how much of the greatness was Ibsen's. As for D'Annunzio's *Gioconda,* who but Duse could ever play that poignant last scene with the child? A wise actress does not challenge comparison with Duse. Yet, oddly enough, that is exactly what I did in selecting the next play!

With *Hedda* launched, for better or worse, our next effort was to prepare *Lady from the Sea.* Again I had ideas about this play which differed from the only performance I had ever seen, that of Duse who had just done it in Italian at the Metropolitan

Opera House. It was a fantastically large place in which to exploit her talent, especially in this delicate play. I am always surprised that she permitted Morris Gest to push her into doing it.

Duse's *Lady from the Sea* did not seem to me to have any relation to the play as Ibsen wrote it. Exquisite as she was in anything she did, I could not believe in the frail white-haired Italian woman as Ibsen's "strong-swimming, sea-haunted, Scandinavian Ellida," to quote Percy Hammond. Duse was a wraith; it was impossible to visualize her enjoying the surge and tang of Norwegian waters.

The subject matter of the play is far in advance of the period in which it was written. Ibsen seemed to me to have anticipated Freud by many years, for the theme of the play is pure psychoanalysis. It portrays a highly imaginative woman, married to a widower with two daughters. She is deeply frustrated by a suppressed and unfulfilled desire for another man—a man she had scarcely known, with whom she had performed, at dawn beside the sea, a mystical marriage rite before he fled from a crime he had committed. The image of the Stranger, as he is called in the play, haunts her to such a degree that her health and mind are affected. The Stranger comes back after many years to claim her, holding her to the early plighted troth, demanding that she ignore her marriage ties and come away with him. Her struggle against the mesmerism of his insistence reaches a point almost of frenzy. The doctor-husband, having tried all other means to reach an understanding with her, releases her from the necessity of decision by telling her she is free—free from any obligation to him; that she can leave of her "own free will."

Startled, she questioningly echoes the phrase "of my own free will?"—and suddenly the mist in her mind clears. She sees the Stranger as he really is, an ordinary seaman, stripped of the romance and glamour she had conjured up. Of her "own free will" she knows she can stay, happy in the new strength which her husband's generosity has made possible for her.

The play has atmosphere and charm, and the story is a moving one up to the very moment of her decision in the last act. But the final scene I found utterly unplayable because it is impossible to make Ellida's sudden transition believable to the audience. It is this crucial failing which I think accounts for the fact that the play is rarely revived. But I enjoyed bringing it to life again.

A most amusing characterization was given by Florida Friebus as Hilda, the younger of the stepchildren. Her sharp little face framed in black pigtails gave zest to the lusty profanity which Ibsen puts into the mouth of this brat. A young Norwegian professor, introduced to me by Lincoln Colcord, the writer, had helped me to make the translation more fluent. Night after night we three would hurry home from the theatre where I was playing Hedda and sit until dawn trying to recapture the charm and humor which our Norwegian friend assured us characterized the original. Florida's part, it seemed, had especially suffered from Archer's idea of what the well-bred child would say; his translation ignored the fact that this motherless stepchild took perverse pleasure in not being well-bred; she loved curse-words and used them freely. Linda Watkins made an attractive older sister; she presented a charming picture in a costume copied from a book of Norwegian folklore.

As for Ellida, her complexities fascinated me. For me, too, there is a passion for the tang, the movement of the ocean. Having seen and passed through those silent, mirror-like waters of the Norwegian fjords, I could understand Ellida's hunger for the sea.

Of one thing I am convinced: this play, conceived and written so many years before the movies were born, would be much better material for the screen than for the stage. The romantic image of the Stranger, which Ellida's sick imagination has imposed upon the real man as she finally comes to see him, could be conveyed much more effectively by the camera than by any stage actress depending solely on words. Ellida's memory of her child's eyes—"those eyes which used to change as the sea changed"—her obsession that somehow, spiritually, the child was the Stranger's child; the dramatizing of the sea itself as an entity in Ellida's life; all this seems excellent screen material. What Ibsen failed to do in his last act (and in failing left one of his most sensitive heroines to lie all too frequently unheeded on the library shelf) could be magnificently developed by a sensitive movie director, and Ibsen would be "discovered" by a vast new audience. I have always felt that Greta Garbo would be the perfect Ellida. But I understand that she hates the Ibsen plays.

It now became necessary to think about the road tour. My hope of repertory faded quickly. I had had to bring in, even during so brief an experiment as this New York season represented, special people for certain parts. The average American actor is not trained for versatility. Most actors talk fervently of their desire to be allowed to extend their range beyond the confines of type-casting, yet how rarely do they prepare themselves to do this. And not only is this true of American actors. When I approached an excellent English actor, Philip Merivale, to join us for the repertory season to play Hjalmar, Lovborg, and Dr. Wangel, he declined. "I don't care to work that hard," was his explanation. Indeed, the average actor has relatively little incentive to work that hard except for his own satisfaction. For the most part an actor is called upon to repeat the characterization which won him his original success. Still, the dogged determination of an Alfred Lunt, the indefatigable talent of a Noel Coward, the vaulting ambition of an Olivier, seek out opportunities for diverse roles, and such actors are handsomely rewarded. But actors of this quality are rare.

We faced complications. Ralph Roeder, who had played Gregers in *The Wild Duck,* had writing commitments which precluded his leaving town. The new actor whom we had engaged to play the Stranger in *Lady from the Sea* would, of course, have to carry one or two other parts on the tour. But the very first day of rehearsals for *The Wild Duck* he stated, quite bluntly, that he would not rehearse in more than one play! There was no time to break in someone else in all three parts. I had to reassemble the company for *The Wild Duck*—and here I hit another snag. Linda Watkins decided she did not wish to leave New York. We had to find a new Hedvig.

Cecil Clovely, who had helped me stage *Lady from the Sea,* remembered that in a tiny theatre down in Greenwich Village he had seen a youngster with an extraordinary pair of eyes and unmistakable talent. She came up to read for us. My "nose" for undiscovered talent began to itch. She had a strange little face and could look fourteen; that solved half the problem. Her name, she told us, was Bette Davis. Her reading of a scene or two was wonderful. She was engaged. We began to rehearse intensively, as it seemed wise to break her in before leaving the home-theatre, so to speak. I did not know until I read her autobiography recently that she had gotten up out of a sick-bed for that "audition."

I had decided not to rehearse her fully in the big emotional scene, where Hedvig weeps hysterically over her father's leaving her. I have a theory that if a part is fully embodied up to such a point in a play, the climax can safely be left to the inspiration of the moment, for a first performance at any rate. I realized, of course, that it was a risky thing to do with such an inexperienced youngster, but I followed my hunch and merely told her to let herself go when she came to that spot. But on the opening night, even I was not prepared for the torrent of emotional intensity which racked that frail body as she lay face downward on the sofa, crying her heart out; some of it was sheer first night nerves; but out of that dynamic little girl grew the Bette Davis we have come to know on the screen—the spark was clearly visible from the start.

We toured only *The Wild Duck* for the remainder of the season. It was a season in which I had used my talents and energies to their fullest capacity—a wonderful season never to be duplicated or forgotten by me.

Looking through old reviews I found a notice on that Ibsen season that appeared in the May issue of *Theatre Magazine*. It made me wonder all the more at my disappointment at our reception. For surely we were well received.

In the midst of a season that has been pronounced by practised producers one of the worst in theatrical history, Blanche Yurka has completed, practically single-handed, an entire Ibsen season on Broadway. She has proved, by the success of her venture, that the great Norwegian is no longer just a "highbrow" in the public mind, but is one of the most popular playwrights of the day. Miss Yurka, under the sponsorship of the Actors' Theatre, has successfully directed and starred in *The Wild Duck, Hedda Gabler* and that poetic psychological drama, *The Lady from the Sea,* last seen in New York as a part of Eleanora Duse's repertoire, in Italian.

The success of Miss Yurka's Ibsen season makes Bernard Shaw's dream of a real Ibsen Theatre come true at last. Also it prompts this foresighted actress to make plans for another Ibsen season, in which she will produce *Rosmersholm, A Doll's House* and *Lady Ingar of Ostraat,* which has never been done in this country, though it is the Norwegian dramatist's one perfervid hair-raising melodrama.

The following January, 1930, I played another guest engagement for Stuart Walker, this time in Cincinnati. We did Stuart's long-dreamed-of production of Daudet's *L'Arlesienne*, the climax, Stuart said, of his whole career. A powerful play, its effect is greatly enhanced by the music which Bizet wrote for it—music well-known to radio and concert audiences as "The L'Arlesienne Suite." Relatively few people realize that this suite was originally written as incidental music for this classic of the French theatre.

L'Arlesienne is a folk-play depicting French peasant life in the area called "the Midi"—a region described in Alphonse Daudet's short stories about the natives of Arles. Stuart had always wanted to produce it, but the expense of the orchestra, singers, and dancers necessary for the betrothal scene had made its production by a stock company seem impossible.

Now at last he decided to risk it. He used the excellent translation made by Charles Livingood, a Cincinnati business man who had spent much time in Arles and was familiar with the life that Daudet depicted. Interestingly enough, the character who gives the play its title never appears. She is the maleficent creature who drives the son of Rose Mamai (the part I played) to suicide because he cannot endure life without her. Harry Ellerbe as the son was a poignant figure; Russell Hicks as the wise old shepherd made an unforgettable picture in his long white beard which gave him the look of a French Walt Whitman. Leon Ames played a brief but powerful scene. On the opening night we had thirty-two curtain calls. We played to packed houses for two weeks. Stuart was radiant, and the whole experience was gratifying to every one.

One night while still in Cincinnati, I was startled from my sleep by a long distance telephone call. It was from a young man named Francis Carpenter. He had played a bit in the original production of *The Wild Duck* and as far back as that we had discussed the amusing possibilities of an ancient Greek comedy called *Lysistrata*. Now, five years later, it seemed that there was a chance of our doing it—he was negotiating with some people he knew in Philadelphia about a possible six-week Theatre Festival there. If it proved successful, the whole project might develop into a permanent theatre. Would I please contact him immediately on my return?

I did so. Knowing the young man to be prone to extravagant attacks of imagination, the whole plan seemed to me a bit over-ambitious, to put it mildly. But all theatre financing is inexplicable to me anyway. I went along with him to the extent of making a few trips to Philadelphia; one of them took me to the peaceful book-lined study of Dr. Howard Horace Furness. I found him not only a charming gentleman of the old school, but an enthusiastic supporter of our Festival idea. So, when a few weeks later, the young entrepreneur told me that the whole matter was settled, with Dr. Furness as chief sponsor, I was delighted, and, I might add, a bit surprised. I had never been able to raise money for anything.

We had all agreed that our Festival season should consist of a program of comedies. "Laughter Through the Ages" was to be our slogan; for once, an art venture would shun the Tragic Muse. Dr. Furness was evidently more in love with the general idea of the Festival than familiar with the specific plays we had selected for our season. We planned to start with the Aristophanes' farce, *Lysistrata*. One day, while en route to New York for a conference, he perused the translation in a college text book. He was startled, I was told, at the "stag" humor of some of the lines and situations. However, we all knew that an adaptation would have to be made (since in its original form the play would have run only about forty minutes), and we hoped the adapter could modify, somewhat, the bawdier aspects of ancient Athenian humor.

May I say, in passing, that plays in those ancient days were produced primarily for male audiences, no "ladies" in our sense of the word, supposedly, being present. The hetaerae, the ladies of easy virtue—who according to report were ladies of exceptional education as well as beauty—attended the plays openly. But respectable women were presumably absent, occupied with their household duties, so that their sensibilities did not need to be considered. Whether they sometimes sneaked in, one can only surmise.

It was agreed I should direct the play, as well as play the title part. I sounded out a few players to find out who was available. With our limited funds it would be necessary to plan simple but, we hoped, beautiful productions for the three plays we were planning to do. I recalled an austere setting in which an illusion of great space had been achieved by Norman Bel Geddes for the Players' Club production of *Julius Caesar*. Something of that sort would be perfect for the "hill of the Acropolis" on which all the action of *Lysistrata* takes place.

Childishly unaware that economy was no part of Bel Geddes' great gifts, we went down to his studio to lay our plans before him. His imagination seized upon the *Lysistrata*—I question whether he ever gave a thought to the others. Conference followed upon conference. I was usually present since I was to direct the first play and was therefore startled, one evening, to learn over the telephone, that Mr. Bel Geddes had signed contracts with Dr. Furness not only to design the setting but to direct as well.

I must point out, lest I appear woefully inept in my appraisal of his directorial talents at this time, that Bel Geddes' previous undertakings in the producing field had been dire failures. Everyone knew that on one occasion several years before, Otto Kahn, the banker, blessed with a boundless enthusiasm for the theatre, had backed him in another project to do three plays. The entire backing, I was told, was used up on the first production, a picturesque but slight comedy, the values of which were swamped under the magnificence of an over-sumptuous setting. Bel Geddes the director had been defeated by Bel Geddes the designer. He needed epic plays on which to expend his imagination, and for him *Lysistrata* was ideal material. Our plans for simple settings evolved into a gigantic production which not only employed his dynamic energies to the utmost, but used up all our backing as well.

Further complications developed. The cast which I had originally planned to engage (and in some instances had even approached) was rejected by Bel Geddes. As the days went by, my efforts to learn what was happening were met with evasions. I began to feel myself an intruder in the whole setup, and presently, in the interest of harmony, I asked Dr. Furness to release me from our verbal agreement. Fay Bainter was engaged in my place. She, along with Ernest Truex, Sydney Greenstreet and Miriam Hopkins, proceeded to bring the fabulous old comedy to life. It opened in Philadelphia before a distinguished and not-a-little-startled audience. The names of many staid old families were on the list of sponsors who had simply lent their support to a Theatre Festival launched by Howard Horace Furness.

But, alas, he was not there to enjoy the vindication of his faith in the classic theatre. Even prior to his affiliation with the venture his heart had caused his physician concern. One night he passed quietly away in his sleep. His death was naturally a great shock. Commitments had gone so far, however, that his heirs decided to carry through the contracts for which the estate was now responsible.

After a successful run of several weeks in Philadelphia, *Lysistrata* opened in New York. Fay Bainter, having previous commitments, was replaced by Violet Kemble Cooper.

Sitting out front on the opening night, I grew very humble. For seven years I had peddled the idea of bringing this wonderful old farce back into the land of living, lusty laughter. That night I knew I could never have done it so magnificently. The beautiful swaddling clothes provided by the gifted father who had adopted it could have been designed by no one else.

With this production, Bel Geddes proved himself a superb director. The taste he showed in his selection of the cast—his effective handling of large groups of older men and women—his choice of beautiful girls for the younger ones, all contributed to an evening never to be forgotten. Steps of varying heights rose from below stage-level in the orchestra pit to a platform two-thirds the height of the stage. Up there were the doors to the Temple, behind which the women of Greece had barricaded themselves. The lighting, as it gradually developed from the darkness before dawn to full daylight, gave an impression of immense space against the sky-blue cyclorama.

Stuart Walker used to say that he judged an actress by the way she walked up and down stairs. Indeed, it is no slight accomplishment to descend a flight of steps without looking down when there is no railing to hold on to. The uneven distance between steps in *Lysistrata* made it necessary to develop a kind of sixth sense; in order to move freely up and down one had to keep the torso uplifted so that as little weight as possible rested on the feet.

With the success which Bel Geddes brought to what I had thought to be my *Lysistrata,* my resentment faded, and when I was called upon to take over the title role in September, I was glad to do so. It was really thrilling to realize that modern audiences on the island of Manhattan were laughing at the same humor which had "mowed 'em down" in Athens over two thousand years before.

One evening on coming to the theatre, I was amused to see on

the marquee the electric sign reading: "2444th Year." I heard a
passer-by mutter, "Some run!" I played *Lysistrata* for five
months. With an orchestra, dancers, and an expensive cast, the
operating costs were very high, so that when business dropped
off for several consecutive weeks the lusty old play closed. It had
made money for everyone concerned, bearing out one of my pet
theories that given as fine a cast and production as is assumed
necessary for the success of a modern play, a classic can show box
office results. To achieve this, however, all the elements of showmanship are needed, and these rarely are available to a "library"
play. When, as in the case of *Lysistrata* and *The Wild Duck,* a
really fine cast is assembled and the producer uses the best resources of the present-day theatre, the result is apt to make theatre history.

As so often happens to me, my joy in the success of the play
was tragically marred by death. My brother Charlie like so
many others, was a victim of the 1929 crash. He saw every bit
of his life's savings melt away, leaving his family of five penniless. His suicide left us with endless problems, heartbreaking
property losses which grew into a nightmare; it was difficult not
to become obsessed by them.

One source of warm comfort to me was the growing friendship and devotion of producer Arthur Beckhard and his wife,
the singer Esther Dale. These two sturdy, courageous human
beings pulled me through many a trying time in the ensuing
years. They had the gift of laughter and an abundance of patience and understanding. After the closing of *Lysistrata,* Arthur knew how important it was for me to be kept busy. He put
me under contract and began searching for a suitable play.

Arthur Beckhard was the only manager I have ever worked
for who undertook to plan the management of my career with
any continuity. He was very loyal to those in whom he believed;
I was fortunate enough to be one of them. His faith in my ability was heartwarming, his analysis of my shortcomings keen and
helpful.

Had the success of his first managerial venture, *Another Language,* been followed consistently by others, many actors would
have enjoyed the sort of benevolent leadership which all of us so
sorely need. He produced one other success, *Goodbye Again,*

and then a number of failures. His most important contribution was to bring to New York the interesting and talented young people who had founded The University Players in Falmouth, Massachusetts.

Charles Leatherbee was the original organizer of the group which included Joshua Logan, Bretaigne Windust, Henry Fonda, Margaret Sullavan and Jimmy Stewart, not to mention Myron McCormack, Kent Smith, Mildred Natwick and several others. All of them eventually made an impact on Broadway, a brilliant group of people whose respective talents won them notable recognition.

My own appearance under Arthur Beckhard's management profited no one as much as myself. I learned a great deal. Arthur's insistence on naturalness led me to strive for this quality in my own speech. With his help I worked on this problem. I had never really concerned myself with how a character sounded —only with how she thought and felt in a given situation. But Arthur made it clear to me that in my case this was not enough; that I must face the fact that the modern ear is not accustomed to as wide a range of voice as I habitually use even in my private life. My effort must be to condense that range and seek for readings so simple that for the ear of the average listener they would have the undisputable ring of truth. In fact, I was faced, for the first time in my life, with the paradox that in order to sound spontaneous I must become completely studied in my acting.

Early in the spring of 1932, I received yet another important phone call. Again, an enthusiastic young man's voice asked for an appointment. Robert Henderson came to see me. He was making arrangements for his annual dramatic festival at Ann Arbor, Michigan, and invited me to come out for two weeks as one of his guest stars. Mr. Beckhard, to whom I was under contract, agreed to let me go as the New York season was drawing to its close. Henderson and I talked over possible plays, as well as a few impossible ones. By what process of elimination we finally decided upon Sophocles' *Electra* I no longer recall. I think it was his idea.

The translation we decided to use was by John Tresidder Sheppard of Cambridge University. It had an astringent fluency which made it seem more colloquial to the modern ear than any of the others we read. I shut myself up with it and plunged into the woes of the house of Atreus. What good performances I give (or seem to myself to give) at this stage of preparation! Tears stream down "the visage wan"—the part and I have a wonderful rapport. Seldom does one fully recapture that first fine frenzy of creative imagination, but it is wonderful while it lasts.

Before opening the Ann Arbor season, Mr. Henderson decided to tour for a week of one night stands. *Electra* was to be the opening bill at Ann Arbor. Mr. Henderson solved the difficult problem of the Greek chorus by a compromise, giving most of the lines to individuals, only occasionally making use of choric speech. Such orchestration of the spoken word is infinitely difficult, and the labor of training a chorus in the brief rehearsal period permitted us by our labor union was one of our great problems. (When Rondiris, the great Greek director, brought his production of *Electra* to New York, he told me that the chorus had been in training for three years!)

I did not see our set until the dress rehearsal in New York. When I saw the shabby canvas doors of the palace of Agamemnon, my heart sank with the velocity of a disconnected elevator. How could one possibly make the play live against such an implausible background? The set was simply awful! But there was nothing to be done. We were advertised to open in two days at Jordan Hall in Boston under the auspices of the Harvard Drama Association. Obviously, this setting was the best Mr. Henderson's budget permitted. I swallowed hard and said nothing. What could one do?

Arriving in Boston, we learned that the performance was sold out. Three hundred people had been turned away. The following evening, before the performance, we were told that some three hundred more persons had been turned away. Despite the hopelessly inadequate scenery, the marvelous old masterpiece held its audience in tense silence, and the lovely intangible feeling of success was in the air.

In the Boston of those days one could always look forward with interest, even if not unmixed with apprehension, to the keen, erudite reviews of H. T. Parker of the Boston *Transcript*. He spoke his mind as follows:

Her words come bitter off her tongue . . . [her] gestures are restrained frenzy. . . . Suddenly . . . the cleared mind . . . the purified imagination . . . the beauty that is called classic. . . . In Miss Yurka's cry—her speech, her actions . . . the Sophoclean exaltation —the deep measured classic beauty. To classic beauty Miss Yurka is adding classic splendor.

During the following week's tour the daughter of Agamemnon trailed her dusty robes through some strange places. There was one lonesome matinee in Kalamazoo, I remember, where we played to thirty people. But for the most part we had good houses. By the end of the engagement the percentage on the gross which my contract called for came to over a thousand dollars—a brave sum for so highbrow a venture. It was the first time I had ever earned that for a week's work.

The week in Ann Arbor was delightful. The Lydia Mendelssohn Theatre is one of the most attractive and well equipped in America. There was a little walled garden in which one could study, and even occasionally rehearse—a far cry from the customary summer stock surroundings.

Electra opened the Ann Arbor season with distinction; we were warmly received. Playing this exacting role daily was exhausting, but fortunately there was no time to be "tired but great" after the opening night. Rehearsals for Sil-Vara's *Caprice,* the second bill in Mr. Henderson's schedule, began at 10 A.M. the next day. (I had seen Lynn Fontanne's delightful performance!) The play's sophisticated gaiety and cynical fun was a refreshing change from *Electra*'s grim rages. The audiences' enjoyment at such a play is infectious. And I adore playing comedy!

Because of some delay in his bookings, Mr. Henderson asked me to stay on another week to play Congreve's enchanting Millamant in *The Way of the World.* Ernest Cossart was coming out to play Sir Wilfrid Willful. I was delighted to accept; rarely does one have a chance to appear in an Eighteenth Century comedy!

Speaking Congreve's delicately humorous phrases was like playing Mozart on a spinet. Ernest Cossart was deliciously droll. I loved the exercising of an entirely different set of mental as well as physical muscles. Millamant provided me with a fascinating experiment in a new and delicate style. The voice took on subtle inflections; gestures and movements had to be attuned to these and to the charming dresses of the period. The enchanting scene in which the hero and heroine discuss what each will require of marriage should she yield to his wooing and consent to "dwindle into a wife" is as amusing today as it must have been to the audiences of two centuries ago. What a pity that a program of distinguished plays such as these cannot be offered to the American public except in sporadic spurts. It is in engagements like these that I have found most of the enjoyment I have had in my work.

The following autumn, Mr. Henderson, stimulated by the success we had had with the *Electra* on tour, determined to risk putting it on for a series of matinees in New York. But this time, he promised, there was to be no shabbiness. It was to be a first-rate production. James Reynolds had just returned from Greece with a series of drawings of characters from *The Iliad* as he imagined them to have looked; the ancient Greek heroes seemed to him people he had known; he agreed to design our setting and costumes. I was thrilled.

I persuaded Katharine Cornell to lend us Joyce Carey, Charles Waldron and John Buckmaster from her *Barretts of Wimpole Street* cast. Mr. Buckmaster's magnificent physique was perfect for Orestes, "that golden youth whom great Mycenae yet shall see." All three were enthusiastic.

Casting Clytemnestra was a problem. Aline MacMahon agreed to play it, then was called to Hollywood. Mr. Henderson even had the temerity to approach Margaret Anglin, who would, of course, have been superb. She declined, which was understandable in view of her own personal triumph as Electra several years before. But Robert's temerity reached a new high when in his desperation he finally decided to approach Mrs. Patrick Campbell, then appearing in a play which was about to close. By this time I was so involved in the effort to train the chorus into some sort of effectiveness, so frantic over the growing prospect of our never finding a Clytemnestra at all, that he might have engaged an orangutan for all I cared. As the rehearsals developed there were moments when I almost wished he had!

Rehearsing with "Mrs. Pat" was an experience, to put it mildly. Her personal idiosyncrasies are, of course, well known. Even at that age—she was in her seventies—she was a fascinating and provocative creature. Traces of her beauty were still perceptible, though she was a far cry from that willowy vision with the great dark eyes framed by clouds of dusky hair that I had first seen the day of the Modjeska benefit in my opera school days. She could be ever so charming when she chose to be, and for the first few days she actually was. But, as she admitted, she hated to rehearse so that she would arrive late, work for a little while, then interrupt anyone's scene to suggest that we "break for the day." "You all look so tired," she would say. We humored her considerably, for we knew we had to cope not only with a woman of advanced years, but one who was almost as famous for being difficult as for her artistry. Although, for that matter, her age was something one seldom thought about except to resent the demon, fat, which so obscured the beauty still evident in her glorious eyes and her interesting face. Because of these latter assets, it did not seem incongruous for her to be playing the vivid and impassioned Queen.

The first day she insisted upon my having tea with her after rehearsal. "You look so tired, my dear," she said solicitously. I was, so we dismissed rehearsal and bundled ourselves into a taxi. She directed the driver to take us to "that great railway-place where they serve you such marvelous oysters."

My first "tea" with "Mrs. Pat" proved to be an oyster stew at Grand Central Station! Sipping the rich hot cream she exerted herself to be amusing, and I succumbed readily to her humor and her charm. Blithely I hoped we should continue to get along. She came to rehearsal only when it suited her and completely repudiated the strong, utterly unromantic treatment of the play which we were trying to achieve. She announced her intention to play Clytemnestra "for sympathy," and used her remarkable voice with an exaggerated lyricism completely out of consonance with the stark realistic key in which we had planned the performance (and in which I was playing), insisting that poor Clytemnestra had been very badly treated by her violently antagonistic daughter. Had not Agamemnon's sacrifice of Iphigenia more than justified his wife's becoming a partner with Aegisthus to his murder? Electra, in her opinion, had shown lamentably bad manners in declining to accept the Queen's revenge gracefully.

"But," I tried to point out, "Sophocles didn't write it that way. Unless there is bitter antagonism between Electra and her guilty mother we have no play!" I found myself, in our big scene, hurling invective against a remote, soft-voiced woman seemingly made of cotton wool. In desperation, I sent an S.O.S. to my friend Howard Lindsay, who had once staged the play for Miss Anglin, asking him to take over the direction from Mr. Henderson's somewhat hesitant hands. We hoped Howard's authority might have some effect. He came for a few days, then whispered to me: "It's no use, baby, you're sunk! Just give her her head; she'll take it anyway," and disappeared, leaving us to our problems.

In agreeing to do the stage designs, Jimmy Reynolds had stipulated that there were to be absolutely no changes made in the costumes; they were archaically correct, based on research he had done in Greece. But he reckoned without Mrs. Pat. She remodeled her costumes ruthlessly, discarded the tall Cretan headdress he had had made, and substituted one of her own design. To his furious protests, she replied, "My dear young man, you really can't expect me to wear that chest of drawers on my head!"

Blithely she went on altering the costume to suit her own ideas. As a final touch, she wore gold evening slippers with high French heels; they clumped noisily as she moved up and down the palace steps supported by two handmaidens. Outraged, Mr. Reynolds insisted that his name be stricken from the program and refused to come near the production again.

Our funds were getting low; we had had no full dress rehearsal. Dress rehearsals cost money. In my despair I remembered a woman who was a patron of the sort of thing we were trying to do. Although I knew her only slightly, I called on her. I explained the danger of our attempting to open without a dress and light rehearsal. She said, "But of course, my dear, you must have a dress rehearsal. How much would it cost?" A few minutes later I found myself in the street with a generous check in my hand. In four figures! I was breathless with surprise and joy. I had never done such a thing before, nor have I since. It seemed a sign that all might yet go well.

At the final run-through, Mrs. Pat decided to change all her positions. Wearily, I assented, merely begging her to tell me where I might reasonably expect to find her in our scenes. At this she swept out of rehearsal in majestic fury, her little dog under her arm, and we did not speak again during the entire run.

But how could I have dreamed of the major catastrophe lying in wait for me? Brooks Brothers had made the costumes. For the long scarf with which Electra covered her drab robe, I wanted a dark cloth stained with many colors, colors which might once have been beautiful but had grown faded and blurred. It was suggested by Brooks Brothers that the colors be sprayed on; would I, for the dress rehearsal, use a substitute so that they might have an extra day in which to set the dye? I agreed.

Our matinee series started in a downpour of rain, but word of a sold-out house comforted us. On entering my dressing room, I saw the beautifully dingy colors of Electra's shawl; it looked like a faded peacock's tail; the dyers seemed to have done a splendid job. With several last moment matters awaiting my decision I did not bother to try it on. At curtain time, using almost no make-up, my hair disheveled, I wrapped myself in its folds, leaving only Electra's white face showing, and went on stage. We began the play. Crouching in the shadow of the palace steps, I spoke Electra's first lines:

> Oh holy light of Heaven, and air,
>   earth's equal partner,
> How many dirges of my singing have
>   ye heard!
> How often have ye seen me—beating my
>   breast until the blood flowed. . . .

The house was hushed in attentive silence. The long mounting speech carried me along. With my first gesture, my arms emerged from the shawl. To my bewilderment I saw that they were gray-black, as though covered with soot! What could it mean? Had the paint of the set against which I had been leaning not been dry? Frantically covering my arms, I surreptitiously tried to rub off the grime with my shawl; the next gesture showed my arms blacker than ever. My horror mounted. Slowly I realized that the colors which had been sprayed on the shawl were coming off all over me. This, in a play in which Electra never leaves the stage! As I continued to pour out the lengthy speeches, my thoughts raced ahead to the final scene in which Electra has to fling herself into the arms of her long lost brother Orestes who, alack and alas! would be clad in the most beautiful costume imaginable made of pure white felt. In my mind's eye I could visualize the black smudges which my arms would leave as I clung to him. I quailed. Still, the endless full-page speeches had to be uttered; how I remembered them I shall never know. But on flowed the story of hate and vengeance. Finally with Clytemnestra and Aegisthus safely murdered the curtain closed; the ghastly ordeal was over.

The ovation at the end of the performance proved that a great play can hold an audience even against such unpredictable odds. People came back in droves; their congratulations seemed warm and encouraging. A few expressed bewilderment about my make-up.

Speaking to her friends through the open door of the adjacent dressing room (I had given her the courtesy of the "star" dressing room) we heard Mrs. Pat's purring voice: "You really *liked* it, darlings? Fancy! How could you possibly?" I was past minding and went home spent but grateful that the seeming disaster had apparently not been fatal to our project. But the next morning's reviews proved me wrong.

Here was meat for wise-cracking reviewers. The "Anthracitic" Electra was dwelt upon; variations on this theme were made amusing, to everyone, I presume, except its victim. The packed, attentive house, the ovation we had received at the end, were not even mentioned. By the time I had read the major reviews I felt utterly crushed. My disappointment turned to rage. How could I have anticipated such a catastrophe? The Furies themselves were against me! Why go on trying when such unforeseeable circumstances could defeat one's best efforts? I wanted to give up acting for good. Once more I sat up in bed, my face streaming with tears at the didos of unkind fate. But this time the tears were not for Electra, they were for Yurka. Fortunately, we had announced only three matinees a week. By the next scheduled performance I had myself in hand.

Investigation proved that Brooks Brothers had failed to "set" the dyes; through someone's negligence, the order to do so had never been carried out. I substituted a plain black cloth for the offending garment which was consigned to limbo. I wished I could send Brooks Brothers there too.

Burns Mantle praised the play, noting that "There are few flaws in the revival. The cast is as near perfect as need be." Attendance was good and we added extra matinees to our announced schedule.

Once the shock of my mishap wore off, the warmth of our audiences' response rewarded us for our efforts. Even Mrs. Pat became gracious again and tried to "make up" to me. But I had had enough. We never became "friends" again.

CHAPTER 13

YOGA PAYS OFF

ROBERT HENDERSON'S SUCCESSFUL Ann Arbor
Festival had led to his appointment as director of the Detroit
Civic Theatre. This was the successor to Jessie Bonstelle's Detroit Stock Company which had once had a girl named Katharine Cornell as one of its cast. When Robert invited me to
play Portia in *The Merchant of Venice* during his 1932–33 season, I was delighted because I had evolved some quite different
concepts of how to play two of her scenes. Mr. Henderson liked
experimentation, so he gave me a free hand. We had an excellent Shylock in Francis Thompson.

As I saw it, the first Portia-Nerissa scene should take place in
Portia's bedroom. At the rise of the curtain Nerissa comes in
quickly and draws back the draperies to let in the morning light.
She sets a cup of chocolate on a table beside the bed, at which
moment Portia stirs, sits up, and stretching her arms says, "By
my troth, Nerissa, my little body is aweary of this great world!"
Presently Portia rises, slips into a robe, crosses to the dressing
table and runs a brush through her golden locks (Portia must be
a blonde), and the dialogue continues to its delightfully sophisticated end.

This treatment makes possible several charming, natural bits
of business—far more believable and interesting than the customary staging of the scene (at least as I have always seen it)
where the two women usually sit opposite each other in two period chairs and make set speeches.

My delight was augmented by the little seven-year-old daughter of the wardrobe mistress who asked to see the play again because "I want to see Miss Yurka's golden hairs."

Russell McLauglin's review made me want to dance:

. . . the big event of the evening . . . is Miss Yurka's Portia. The celestial phenomenon called a blue moon affords few theatrical experiences like it . . . to sit under a scholarly woman whose talents embrace humor, romance, dignity, and poetry; whose reading of the most casual line, since it is a great voice declaring great literature, sends tingles down the spine; whose domination of the famous Trial is such that it must needs thrill and excite spectators who can recite the scene from start to finish. Miss Yurka is the stateliest, soundest, and most Shakespearian Portia who has trod Detroit stages these many years.

I mentioned that I had several ideas about the parts. The second was a new treatment of the courtroom scene. I have never been able to believe that Portia could walk in—undisguised—and not be instantly recognized by her husband. To my way of thinking she must look totally different. So I planned to wear a dark wig, glasses and a small but not unbecoming dark moustache. Thus she might "get away with it."

Mr. Henderson agreed that it might be fun to do it that way. So all was arranged. I really did look different. But the dress rehearsal revealed the sad fact that there was not enough time between the scenes to make the make-up change, so I had to abandon my glorious idea! Perhaps one day they'll make the play as a movie when they can take all the time in the world.

During the depression, the Works Project Administration reached out to include actors in its scheme of providing a sustenance wage in return for public services. Under the aegis of the WPA various theatre groups were formed, some of which launched admirable productions. Among these was Orson Welles' production of *Macbeth* with an all-Negro cast; Elmer Rice also participated as one of the directors. WPA made possible experimentation in new forms which might require weeks of training—far more than was ordinarily possible because of financial limitations.

One day a friend brought Eva Sikelianos to see me. I recalled that some years earlier I had read an article in the *National Geographic* describing the fabulous production of *Prometheus Bound* which she and her husband, the poet Sikelianos, had put on at Delphi, in Greece, in 1927. This quixotic adventure had been made possible by the generous squandering of practically the whole fortune which she, as Eva Palmer of Chicago, had inherited.

The preparations, she told me, had taken two years of dedicated work, involving most of the inhabitants of Delphi. Materials for costumes were woven by hand, in beautiful primitive colors. A young Greek, George Bourlos, was selected to play Prometheus, although he had had no theatre experience but was blessed with a beautiful resonant voice. She trained him and apparently achieved remarkable results.

Years later when she came to see me, during the depression, she was desperate. She was now a widow. All her resources had been drained by the Delphi Festival, and she needed to work. I had what I thought was a bright idea. "Your work requires time. Actors at long last are getting enough from the government to live on. You will need many weeks in which to train them, and this is a priceless opportunity to combine all these factors and produce something new and beautiful." She brightened up. "But I know no one. I wouldn't have any idea how to go about it," she said. "I'll find out and arrange for you to meet the right person," I answered. I did and left to go on tour, hoping to see exciting results on my return.

I had no word from her, and when I returned and made inquiries, I learned that her group had disbanded at her request. When I finally got in touch with her, she said that she found the actors assigned to her impossible to work with; they had no interest in the kind of training she proposed to give them; they failed to turn up at rehearsals, or arrived late; she finally gave up. Too bad, I thought. A fine project grounded needlessly.

She died in Athens in 1952. A great dreamer and a great lady!

Early in July of 1933 I went to Falmouth, Massachusetts, with the Beckhards to do summer stock with the now famous University Players. A number of new plays were to be tried out, among them one called *Carry Nation* by Frank McGrath. It was a chronicle play about that hatchet-throwing enemy of the Demon Drink, an oddly assembled pen portrait of "the Kansas Cyclone." Esther Dale Beckhard had decided to abandon her singing career for acting, and her husband offered her the opportunity to do so in this play.

The try-out in Falmouth was an incredible undertaking for a summer stock company, involving as it did sixteen scene changes and a cast of fifty-two players. The ordinary run of stock productions are usually tried plays that have been rendered fool-proof by the time they reach the Samuel French catalog. This one called for an extraordinary coordination of effort. The supporting cast included an unknown actor, Leslie Adams, who made a genuine hit as David Nation. Broadway's recognition of his talents a few months later lifted him from a lifetime of obscure trouping into the sunshine of success. Unfortunately his triumph was short-lived, cut off soon after by his untimely death.

Carry Nation was well received by the Falmouth audiences, and Arthur Beckhard decided to bring it to Broadway. Although he had established his reputation as director of *Another Language* and *Goodbye Again,* he asked me to continue to direct *Carry Nation* for the Broadway run. The idea appealed to me. But though I had already had my trial by fire in directing the revivals of *The Wild Duck* and *Hedda Gabler* at the 49th Street Theatre, tackling a brand new play, and one as complicated as this one, was something else. I knew it was asking for trouble. Still, Arthur was persuasive, "Esther will be more comfortable working with you than with me," he insisted, "I'm too close to her and I make her self-conscious."

So I let myself be persuaded. Esther and I were warm friends. I had studied singing with her and knew that she was an intelligent and tireless artist, and that we understood one another. We plunged into work. Our common knowledge of musical terms proved helpful, as Arthur had surmised it might. Whenever it seemed difficult for her to fix a piece of business or to hold to the reading of a scene, I would say, "Look, Esther, it starts at middle C, goes up to F, then drops back about an octave. Try to hold it like that." Or, "Try doing the whole scene 'sotto voce.' It's in a minor key. That's its value as a contrast to the bravura of the following scene." I was speaking her professional language, and she was wonderfully receptive.

But we were not without problems. After our out-of-town try-out, we had a very trying session with the author. It was his first play and Arthur and Josh Logan (who was playing a small part and helping vastly with the direction of several scenes) felt, as I did, that numerous changes were needed. Since the Broadway production was scheduled to open shortly, there was some urgency in getting together with the author and having him make the revisions before we started our rehearsals.

On a Saturday night we drove down from Falmouth, arriving in New York about 3 A.M. Then we settled down with the author explaining and arguing—very courteously, I might add—why these changes were necessary. We worked on until noon on Sunday, by which time the author reluctantly agreed to make some changes. When he left he was clutching two sheets on which we had typed our suggestions. He was to get the new version to us as soon as it was done; in the meantime we would hold off on our rehearsals.

On Wednesday, three days after our meeting, the author reported that he was ready. Eagerly we waited to see what he had done. He handed us the two sheets we had given him and an additional one he had prepared. There were a few minuscule changes of dialogue—nothing more. Josh and Arthur exchanged looks of despair. Like so many first-time authors this writer seemed unable to change any of his lines—nor would he let anyone else touch them. There was little to be done.

On opening night I watched Esther from my place behind the orchestra rail. Within minutes it was clear that she had the part well in hand. Her previous experience with concert audiences kept her nerves steady, and she held with authority to the pattern which we had worked out. As her first scene progressed, I heaved a huge sigh of relief and remembered what Mrs. Fiske had once described herself as feeling during the first half hour of a performance by Réjane, in Paris—"I could have left the theatre then," she said, "secure in the knowledge that her part would be perfectly played for the rest of the evening."

The play received mixed reviews. One critic made much of the fact that the director was a woman. "It is particularly appropriate that Miss Yurka has directed this play because . . . it is a play about a woman and the entire action is centered around the leading character of Carry Nation." He did add: "Though Miss Yurka would be the first to deny . . . any particular kinship with or special understanding of the mentality that characterized Carry Nation, it still seems reasonable that a play about a woman ought to be directed by a woman." Actually he did go beyond this bit of nonsense to say something about the presentation of the play:

Miss Yurka has striven in "Carry Nation" to find an appropriate
middle ground in her method so that the play would not seem to be
either a quaint and ridiculous old tintype . . . or . . . a piece of
stark realism. Mostly her efforts have been to make Carry Nation a
human understandable figure, not just someone out of the American
history books.

Although the play ran for only six weeks it succeeded in launching Esther as a dramatic actress. She was to play many roles on
the screen for the rest of her life.

As his next venture, Arthur decided to produce Susan Glaspell's play *Comic Artist* which he had bought for me. While this
was being discussed, I received a call from Guthrie McClintic.
Katharine Cornell was planning her first step toward the classics; she announced Andre Obey's *Rape of Lucrece,* which had
been produced in Paris with great success by a group called, I
believe, Les Quinze. It was a new treatment of Shakespeare's
poem. Eventually Mr. McClintic decided to call the play simply
Lucrece. I thought this a mistake; it seemed to me to be side-
stepping the main subject which was, after all, a rape. He invited me to play one of the two narrators. Mr. Beckhard graciously agreed to postpone the production of *Comic Artist.*

Miss Cornell, as always, assembled a distinguished cast. It included Brian Aherne and Robert Loraine. The latter, having
seen the Paris production, became a human reference library for
us. Robert Edmond Jones designed the settings and costumes.
There are few things more stimulating than working with such
first-rate talents.

The European success of Obey's play had been due in large
part to the simple earthiness of both the lines and the settings.
Although Thornton Wilder's translation retained this naturalness of expression (also characteristic of his own play *Our
Town*), Robert Edmond Jones' designs departed lavishly from
the almost monastic austerity of the original sets. He designed
sumptuous costumes and used Roman columns to create a styl-
ized interior within which the actors moved through imaginary
doors, using imaginary props. But this was not done consistently. Later in the play, Joyce Carey carried on a real water ewer
instead of an imaginary one. Several people took exception to
this. Nevertheless, the artistic concept of a magnificent Renais-

sance tapestry brought to life resulted in stage pictures of extraordinary beauty.

There were those who felt that this richness of decor swamped the play which the French producer had treated more like a primitive painting. We had only crude flashlight pictures of the original production, which made it difficult to judge. Les Quinze had had little money to spend on their production; McClintic had plenty for his.

Rehearsals were a joy, as they usually are for me; it is the creative period. Guthrie McClintic's sensitive direction was always especially helpful to women. Much of his work with "Kit" (as almost everyone called her) naturally took place in private. One sensed his molding of her performance as it developed in detail at rehearsal.

Obey's theme was the immolation of a noble Roman woman as seen through the eyes of two abstract figures, the Narrators, who framed the human story with their cosmic commentary. The two Narrators wore half-masks. Presumably unseen by the other characters, they moved about through the action of the play, commenting upon the protagonists—their behavior, their simplest household activities, as well as their larger significance. Robert Loraine, as one of the Narrators, expressed the masculine viewpoint. I, as the other Narrator, voiced the more sympathetic, compassionate, eternally feminine view. Our half-masks of dull gold and our simple bronze-green draperies gave us both a sculptured appearance.

My own acting assignment was full of pitfalls. Arthur Beckhard had warned me to guard every inflection lest my voice become "beautiful" in the wrong place, letting the reader become aware of sound rather than sense. I wanted to avoid, above all else, any elocution, any pyrotechnics or "artiness" in voice or posture. The danger of these was inherent in the part. I tried to hold my voice on the simplest "level of every day's most quiet need." The gold masks made facial expression impossible, and one had to rely entirely upon the voice. And on the body! I began to diet strenuously, and during rehearsals dropped ten pounds—via the buttermilk route—so that I could wear the clinging bronze jersey robe "sans everything" underneath—and succeeded in looking really sculpturesque! I had my reward when Maurice Goldberg, the famous photographer, came backstage to say, "It's the first time I have ever known of an actress who could make her thighs speak."

We did a preliminary tour of *Lucrece* in Detroit, Buffalo and Cleveland. One of the Cleveland reviewers wrote:

Blanche Yurka has a voice that ripples on like globules of silver, or —say—moonlight on water. She interrupts—explains—comments, philosophizes, and while sitting there, a lonely figure, she is worth dozens of revolving stages, and scores of scenes. Last night she read poetical lines as they sounded when that greatest of our contemporaries the late Eleanora Duse, recited long speeches by D'Annunzio. Here was the supreme histrionic achievement of the performance.

After three weeks out of town, we came into the Belasco Theatre. It was like a home-coming for me. As I walked onto the stage and looked out into the dim auditorium, I remembered the first time I had stood on that stage. I seemed to see, reflected in the glass-partitioning at the back of the lobby, the frightened youngster doing the scenes from *Magda* for the gentle voiced David Belasco. So many years ago, on that same stage, he had nodded encouragingly and said, "The voice is of good timbre; now to learn to act." And in this play the voice was too good and had to be restrained.

Our opening night was, of course, brilliant as are all of Kit's first night audiences. All through the four-week run exceptionally interesting people came backstage. We all loved the play. I believe it is one of Miss Cornell's favorites.

The critics, alas, found the play dull and said so, not once, but repeatedly, making it difficult to live down the first bad notices. Katharine's part was relatively short, too short for her public which wished to see more of her for its money. There was also the possibility that those who came looking for the sensationalism suggested by the original title of the story felt cheated by the classic austerity of its treatment. Sitting close to the footlights I used to study certain faces in the audiences as they drifted through various degrees of bewilderment. Occasionally a gentleman seated in the very first row, full of cocktails and too heavy a dinner, would start nodding into his shirtfront. The impulse to lean toward him from my place on the forestage and poke him awake with my toe was almost irresistible.

Personally, I felt that three things militated against the production's success. The first was Obey's failure to establish the relationship of the two Narrators—wandering presumably unseen through the settings—to the play until the second scene. It seemed to me that the lines of the opening scene in which a group of soldiers compare the relative virtue of the various generals' wives should have been assigned to the Narrators. Then their commentary at the opening of the play would have balanced their touching speeches at the end. Instead, the dialogue of the soldiers started the story in a kind of "Road to Rome" atmosphere of realism into which two strange masked figures suddenly intruded to wander through the action for no prior well-established reason. Had the soldiers' lines been spoken by the Narrators, and had the audience known at the beginning what these two figures represented, the device would, I believe, have been accepted and enjoyed—or at any rate understood.

My second hunch is that Tarquin should have been a figure of horror—physically as well as dramatically, so that his very glance at Lucrece would have seemed a desecration. Beautifully played as Tarquin was by one of the handsomest of leading men, the audience, I think, had a lurking suspicion that Lucrece didn't quite know when she was well off. Brian Aherne made a magnificent picture in his sumptuous costume—and the audience simply couldn't feel as sorry for her as she did for herself. Even a modern playgoer, however, might have cringed at the sight of a slimy, bloated lecher trailing his vileness across the stainless classic purity of Kit's Lucrece.

Finally, I have the temerity to think that had the rape scene been played in a dim light, with the turmoil of the actual struggle taking place behind drawn curtains, the hideousness of the attack would have created horror in the mind of the onlooker. Instead, the lighting, beautiful though it was, made it perfectly possible to see what was *not* going on, thereby defeating the intention of the scene. It was, after all, a play about an ugly deed of violence, and the audience should have been given the breathless moment around which the play was built. This moment would have heightened the effect of Kit's exquisite readings in the first and last acts. Her voice in that last act was of an unearthly beauty. Her white face, framed in its black cowl, must have made Phidias yearn to reassemble his ashes that he might immortalize that tragic mask. With so many elements of beauty captured in the play we all hated to see it shelved. But after four weeks we had to close.

If only our theatre system did not make it so expensive to experiment that practically no top-drawer producer is free to do it! Post-mortems are futile, of course, but it is interesting to wonder how the changes I have suggested might have affected the fate of this play.

After we closed in *Lucrece,* Mr. Beckhard proceeded with his postponed production of Susan Glaspell's *Comic Artist.* It is the sort of play which should be done in repertory—one of those delicate and sensitive studies of contrasting characters which is not likely to fill a theatre eight times a week, but which might easily fill it two or three times.

Both Arthur and I loved the play and its Cape Cod atmosphere. It is about a portrait painter, Steve Rolf, and his wife, Eleanor, who have left behind the confusion of city life and found contentment and a peaceful life on Cape Cod. Their marriage is threatened by the arrival of Steve's younger brother, Karl, a cartoonist, and his beautiful wife, Nina, whom Steve had once loved. Eventually Steve has to choose between Eleanor, who is middle-aged and motherly, and Nina, who is young and passionate. I played the role of Eleanor. Susan Glaspell had written the play several years earlier, in collaboration with her husband, Norman Matson. There was a delicate scene in Act II between the younger brother and Eleanor. Mr. Beckhard had staged it behind a gauze curtain to enhance the effect of a breathless summer night, lit only by an old Cape Cod lantern set beside the steps on which sat Eleanor sorting out beach plums as she talked to her young brother-in-law. He was the title character. In a return to Belasco realism, Arthur had gathered a family of moths which fluttered about the light of the lantern and finally flew distractingly against the gauze which hung between us and the audience. One witty critic, who had found the play dull, insisted that the moths had come out of the manuscript.

We opened at the Morosco Theatre but moved to the Empire a week later. As I stood on that wonderful old stage I thought of the colorful figures who had peopled it in the years since I first sat in that top gallery on Saturday afternoons to see Ethel Barrymore. Looking into the miror in that famous star's dressing room I saw, not my face, but those of many others; Ethel, Katharine Cornell, Doris Keane, Maude Adams, even the Divine Sarah. My pleasure was short-lived. We stayed there only a week. Nevertheless, I was pleased with Robert Garland's comment in his *World-Telegram* review:

Not since her memorable performance in *The Wild Duck* has Miss Yurka been more impressive. . . . Her Eleanor Rolf is as right as her Gina Ekdal was. Three dimensional, motivated from within, you grow to know Eleanor as well as Miss Yurka does. Consequently she is as real as real. When the play is going on her problems are your problems.

Comic Artist was a play I liked immeasurably. In the weeks I had studied and played Eleanor I learned to appreciate her beautiful sanity, her decency and her understanding; when we closed it was like losing a dear friend. What an escapist one must be, to be able to live so fully within a creation of someone else's imagination!

Again, the next summer, we all went to Falmouth, finding rest, despite the work schedule, in the balminess of the Cape Cod air, the swimming at Silver Beach, and the camaraderie of that group of gifted young people.

Arthur decided to try out the play which Nena Belmonte and I had translated from the Spanish of Martinez Sierra. Called *Spring in Autumn (Primavera in Autoño)*, it is a simple story characterized by that naturalness which is the special charm of Martinez Sierra's writing.

The heroine was refreshingly earthy despite her prima donna pretentiousness. The play ambled along slowly as Sierra's plays are prone to do. During the Boston try-out after Cape Cod, Arthur decided that it was necessary to create, somehow, a more strenuous conflict. There was much doctoring of the plot with the result, I think, that we lost the original charm of the play, replacing it with fustian. It was hard for me to realize this when immersed in playing, since one's whole endeavor as an actress is to believe what one is trying to make an audience believe. To combine this with the critical detachment necessary for play-doctoring is not easy.

The heroine, a prima donna, had left her husband and baby girl years before to make a career as a singer. The husband had brought up the child in a peaceful home atmosphere and had just about persuaded himself that their serene life was the better for the mother's absence. However, the daughter, having fallen in love with a neighboring lad, insists upon at least a seeming reconciliation with her mother for the sake of appearances. The mother consents. She arrives, upsetting their peaceful lives with her entourage, her irregular routines and her distinguished visitors from Madrid. Eventually the husband and the singer are reunited, although I, for one, never believed it could last.

We had trouble in casting the part of the young Spanish diplomat who is in love with the mother and daughter successively and who finally woos and wins the latter away from her yokel sweetheart. Our problem was temporarily solved when Kent Smith played it. He was charming, but before long he had to leave for another play; Cesar Romero succeeded him and was in turn followed by Charles Leatherbee. Mildred Natwick played one of those long-suffering secretary-attendants to a prima donna with delightful acidity, and Esther Dale was the husband's housekeeper who ruled him ruthlessly. Those two gave a rich, mellow flavor to the modest little play.

The most talked of episode in the play was the moment in which I stood on my head, singing the first notes of "Vissi d'arte, vissi d'amore." The situation in the play called for an exhibition of extravagant behavior which would shock the rather conventional husband, yet command a certain amused respect on the part of everyone else, including the audience. The head stand which I had learned from my Yoga teacher years before and had brought to a point where I could do it with complete security seemed just what was needed. At least Arthur thought so. (I had told him of my stunt of singing while upside-down at Clara Thomas' years before.) I am sure audiences counted on my skirts falling, but knowing they couldn't, I had no qualms. The laughter and applause which greeted this piece of "business" each night testified to the audience's enjoyment of the stunt. Robert Benchley, the critic, said in his review, "If that won't bring you into a theatre, I don't know what will." But it didn't. We ran only six weeks. The temperamental prima donna theme was definitely outmoded. And when I saw a performance of the play later in summer stock (minus the head stand) I was amazed to realize how thin the play really was. But at the time we played it, I loved it and wept copious tears when I had to pack up my make-up and leave Elena and her tantrums behind me for good.

CHAPTER **14**

A DIP IN THE ISIS

AS THE NEW YEAR—1934—approached my prospects were dreary. Broke, discouraged, exhausted by the endless financial worries imposed by my brother Charlie's death, I grew to dread the sight of my mail, to shudder at the ring of the telephone. The world seemed peopled with the ghosts of fruitless hopes and the faces of the dear ones who had gone. Worst of all, there was no play for me on Mr. Beckhard's list and so no income.

Yet before the year was done I was to enjoy a kaleidoscope of luxurious privileges, varied landscapes, and acquaintance with people and places I had never dreamed I would encounter. Sunlit Bermuda at Easter time; London in all its gray fascination; Malvern, Oxford, Stratford; Paris, Warsaw, and—towering above all else in the impression it made on me—Russia!

Early in January a young man from Yale University asked for an appointment to talk about a play. Halstead Welles, who was one of the stage directors for the Yale Dramatic Association (he later directed the first American production of *Murder in the Cathedral*) had spent considerable time in Russia. There he had seen the Moscow Art Theatre production of Michael Bulgakov's play *Last Days of the Turbins,* a daringly sympathetic study of a White Russian military family engulfed by the onrush of the Bolshevist Revolution. He told me that on the opening night in Moscow the play's nostalgic charm was so potent that many a good *tovarish* was reduced to tears. When this kind of response continued, orders came from "higher-ups" that the play be

withdrawn—this at the height of (and because of) its success.
But a little later, some potent influence was brought to bear and
the ban lifted, whereupon the performance of this work became
a highlight of the Moscow Art Theatre repertory.

At Yale, too, Halstead Welles had to have a ban of sorts lifted
when he decided to sponsor the American premiere. He wanted
me to play the only woman's part, the lone sister in a family of
military brothers of varying ages. But a long-standing regulation
at Yale forbade the employment of professional actors or actresses on the Harkness Theatre stage. How Hal managed it I
don't know, but finally, one blustering snowy night I walked
into a dimly lighted rehearsal room for our first reading of the
New Haven production of *Last Days of the Turbins*.

Never had I seen so many men in one room! There were big
men and little men; some were obviously football heroes, others
obviously not. How could I have guessed that somewhere in
their midst was a tall husky blond lad named Sonny Tufts who
would later go to Hollywood and become one of the movie
stars? Or a man named Stewart Alsop, who is one of our finest
columnists? Surrounded by all that impressive masculinity I
suddenly felt very shy. To cover it I said, "Are any of you as
scared as I am?" Then I took refuge in a corner with Hal and the
friendly young men who were to play my brothers, and the rehearsal began.

I thought the script charming. The characters of the brothers
and the officer friends were beautifully drawn; the little country
cousin humorous and lovable. The lone woman in their midst,
the sister, was sympathetic and gently authoritative. Around
these principals swirled some two hundred lesser parts: cadets,
revolutionaries, insurgents and rabble. The stage settings were
an outstanding achievement; the department of stage design
ranks very high at Yale.

This New Haven premiere attracted a surprising amount of
attention in New York. Distinguished Yale alumni came traipsing up, among them the impeccable Lucius Beebe, (if one could
conceive of the magnificent Mr. Beebe ever "traipsing!") and
several New York managers. I was again impressed by the fact
that when New York theatre people really want to see something in the theatre, nothing can stop them. The weather had
been awful; blizzards blew the snow into high banks so that the

train service was unreliable. But through the snow they came to see the play, interested in its possible value for New York.

Despite the limited acting experience of my colleagues, I enjoyed rehearsals. The character parts were especially well played. Again I wondered whether there is anything to this acting business after all, since occasionally amateurs do it so well.

Except for the love scenes! The sister I was playing not only had a husband whom she didn't much like, but a suitor whom she obviously did. My leading-man-lover was very tall, very good looking and very, very stiff. The love scene called for a long and passionate embrace; two to be exact. My "suitor" did the business in gingerly fashion. It was a vital scene; played self-consciously it would get a laugh, and a laugh at that time would be ruinous to the performance. Seriously worried, I asked Mr. Welles one day to let us rehearse that scene by ourselves. When the others had all been dismissed, I went into action.

Years ago I had heard a great director say that playing comedy was a matter of arithmetic; I set out to see if playing a love scene could be similarly handled. "Look, Fritz," I said, "the first time you kiss me, bring your face close, place your lips on mine, and count three before you take them away. Then, for the next kiss, count eight. Let's do it quite mechanically, several times in succession." I managed to keep my face straight. He grew less and less self-conscious, and when we finally played the scene in performance, bathed in firelight, Fritz turned on his arithmetic sex appeal and held the audience quite beautifully. It was not, perhaps, quite flattering to me to have to achieve my effect thus, but when playing with an inexperienced colleague, I thought it safer to rely on mechanics rather than on romantic impulse. Toward the end of the run, Fritz explained, after an especially realistic performance—"Sorry, I forgot to count!"

During the two weeks we played *The Turbins*, I examined many of the Russian magazines with which Hal Welles' study was littered. All in Russian, of course. The more I heard of his impending holiday in Moscow, the more keenly interested I became. But how to manage such an expensive jaunt? The financial strain under which I had been struggling put such a trip outside the realm of possibility, yet I felt that I must get away for a while or my soul would wither.

Then I remembered that a year or two before, the New York

Drama League had asked me to become the nominal head of a group of its members, organized to make a two-months' visit to England. A course of study in London with the distinguished teacher, Dame Elsie Fogarty, which all members would attend, would be one of their privileges. Later there would be visits to Malvern and Stratford for the Theatre Festivals held there each year. When the offer had first been made, two years previously, I had declined—a little haughtily, I'm afraid. Now my thoughts came back to it.

Immediately on my return from the *Turbin* engagement in New Haven, I called up the pleasant young woman who had first broached the subject to me two years earlier. Would she like me to consider doing it this year? "You are sent from Heaven," she cried. "Dean—who was to head the group—has just had to cancel. We have been frantic! Please come down to the office at once!"

Her enthusiasm was infectious. I explained, over the luncheon table, certain of my limitations: that theatrical "trouping" under the aegis of a company manager spoils most actresses in regard to such details as tickets and luggage; someone, I warned her, would have to herd me as well as the others onto the right boats and trains. She seemed not to mind anything:

"We'll send along Jay Gould who has made the trip before," she said.

"And Russia?" I queried hopefully.

"Well, even that might be arranged."

It was settled that we would sail for England late in June; though there would be no salary all my traveling expenses would be provided. It was manna from heaven.

Then more manna from heaven. It started one rainy day in February when, much against my will, I dragged myself down to a midtown hotel to be a guest at one of those publicity luncheons always being given in New York for one purpose or another. (Because I am facile at "thinking on my feet," I am frequently called upon to speak. Rose called it being "fed by public subscription.") When my turn came I spoke of the new charm pervading the social picture since women of mature years had been taught to safeguard their natural beauty through intelligent care. "There is a kind of beauty at every age," I pontificated!

A dainty little woman sitting next to me (whose name had escaped me) glowed with enthusiasm and approval as I sat down. And well she might, for she told me, presently, that she was Elizabeth Arden. We chatted in a friendly fashion. The luncheon over, we drifted into the hotel lobby. It was pouring cats and dogs outside. While I stood waiting for a taxi, Miss Arden's car rolled up; she offered to give me a lift. As we drove eastward through the gray, teeming Forties, she told me that my speech had expressed what had been her life-work. But she was disturbed, she said, that I, myself, looked a little tired and worried. Would I not, to please her, be her guest at her salon, where they would "quickly erase that tired look?" I knew it would take considerably more than a facial treatment to obliterate the lines left by my worry over our Westchester County real estate problems, but she was so sweet about it that I consented.

I presented myself at the salon, and after my treatment I walked over to thank the salon manager. "Oh, but your treatments have only started," she said. "Miss Arden has given strict instructions that you are to continue with us until she is satisfied with the results." She continued, "You are also, Miss Arden says, to have the exercises, the body massages; so please make plans to take them three times a week, until further notice." I gasped.

Elizabeth Arden, I've learned since, did nothing by halves. For three months I luxuriated in the sybaritic comfort of that charming salon, where clever, knowing fingers practice their magic in the scientific cultivation of potential beauty. Under the manipulations of experts my figure grew slim as a birch tree, my face become daily more firm and fresh. I began to feel myself (at long last!) becoming glamorous. Elizabeth Arden's pioneering in the field of Beauty Culture has had far-reaching results; her generous kindness to me taught me to appreciate the humanity of one of the most remarkable business women of our time.

Still another windfall came my way. Elswyth Beebe called me to say that she and a wealthy friend of Will's had planned to join him in Bermuda for Easter. For business reasons the friend's plans had had to be abandoned, but as Elswyth's health had been bothering her, Will felt that someone should accompany her. Would I take the friend's ticket? Being free to go, who wouldn't? I accepted with alacrity. Bermuda in the spring! Paradise *with* plumbing!

It was a delightfully informal visit. In the Beebe house opposite Nonesuch Island we read favorite stories aloud to each other, we sunbathed and, for exercise, we painted all the house shutters and screens bright green. Under Dr. Beebe's supervision, I had the thrilling experience of walking into the sunlit silence of the ocean floor twenty feet below the surface clad only in a bathing suit with one of Will's undersea helmets resting on my shoulders. As my footsteps led me deeper and deeper into these quiet undulating blue-green depths, fish of various sizes peered at the clumsy intruder and moved about me in graceful curves. I realized that, for the moment, I was in a world entirely without angles, a noiseless world into which the wavering sunlight filtered softly, while all around me reigned a silence like no silence I had ever known.

In my delight at my surroundings I lost my sense of direction. Which way did I go to return? I stood still and heard my voice in the helmet saying audibly, "Sister, this is no time to lose your head!" Slowly, I moved about until I became aware that the water was growing more shallow. At last I emerged, to find Dr. Beebe and Tee Van, his assistant, waiting to help me out. "Well, were you scared?" asked Will. "Oh, no," I said blithely. "Just for a minute I didn't know in which direction to go—to return." "You poor fish," said my distinguished host, "you had only to look upward and follow the oxygen tube." That had never occurred to me.

Will himself had begun to dive several years earlier. Elswyth recently wrote me some of the details of these early dives.

. . . the first short dive in the bathysphere was made on June 6th, 1930—this was the one where the bathysphere leaked, but Will decided not to n-o-t-i-c-e and reached 800 feet, before coming up, to find he was sitting in a pool of greasy water! The second dive 4 days later went to 1426 feet. In 1932 they began the dives on August 31st. That was the year the door blew off in the implosion, when it had been sent down empty—fortunately. On September 22, 1932, which happened to be our wedding anniversary, they did the dive for the NBC radio men, which was broadcast over combined networks. The third year of dives was 1934, when they went to the record depth of *3028 feet,* which used so much cable that half the drum on the deck of the tug was left bare, and John drew the line and said Would they please come up. They did.

Since then, of course both Barton and Piccard have I believe been deeper, but no man was equipped as Will was to record and render into exciting prose what they saw.

Will described these experiences in his book *Half A Mile Down*.

Returning from Bermuda, I plunged with renewed energy into preparations for the European tour. But I had moments of trepidation. Much as I wanted to make the trip, it meant accommodating myself to about twenty-seven people of all ages and varying degrees of temperament. Fortunately, I like people, and since enthusiasm for the theatre had attracted them to the tour in the first place, we had that interest in common. Finally, to my great joy, I was told that the Russian trip was possible!

The boat trip was calm and uneventful. Jay Gould, a young teacher from Troy, was our official cicerone. He handled small crises with a calm sanity which endeared him to me for life. His attentions were spread about the group with infinite tact, which I tried to emulate. On shipboard he and I rotated from one table to another so that no one might feel slighted.

We reached London somewhat later than we had expected. Getting the members of the group installed in their various hotels took most of the morning, so that neither the group nor I reported to Albert Hall, where classes were to be held, until afternoon. Dame Elsie Fogarty was highly offended, especially by my failure to report in, even then. (I expect she had concocted some especially caustic strictures for a "leader" who led so badly.) She asked Jay Gould for an explanation of my absence. "I don't think she plans to attend the classes," Mr. Gould explained. (It had never occurred to me to do so!) "Well, really!" was her indignant reply. And she was justified. We *should* all have been present at the opening class that morning even if we had had to cover the last hundred miles at sea by walking over the waters. At the very least, Jay Gould should have telephoned her from Southampton and notified her of the delay in our arrival. She was a very great teacher. And contact with greatness is not to be missed.

Nevertheless, I foolishly continued to absent myself from the sessions, having other diversions which attracted me more. I had several charming and "important" friends in London whom I wanted to see as much as possible. I lunched frequently at The Ivy, where the great and would-be great of the London theatre foregathered daily. There was a certain cachet in being seen there, I learned.

Finally, Mr. Gould felt it incumbent upon himself to explain to Dame Elsie that I was a "stellar player" of some recognized achievement on Broadway, known especially, he said, for my voice and style in classical plays. Dame Elsie was evidently impressed and somewhat mollified and promptly invited Jay and myself to dine with her—in style, I must say! I found her a most agreeable and interesting hostess. Much of her work, incidentally, was with doctors in hospitals doing therapeutic work. Throughout the remainder of our tour of study with her (which took us to Oxford and Malvern) my relations with her were friendly, but slightly chilly! I attended no classes.

The two weeks in London passed swiftly, and then we moved on to Stratford-on-Avon. Stratford's historic charm has been marred by its having become such a tourist's mecca. The performances at the handsome but overly modern playhouse were smooth, though not brilliant. But I loved my small hotel adjacent to the churchyard where Shakespeare was buried at that time. The Avon flowed gently through the grounds, whispering to Sweet Will of peace and immortality.

Malvern was much gayer. The plays on the Festival list were of varied character and interest. But it was people who made up the excitement of those weeks—Bernard Shaw striding through the streets of the town or up the slag-covered hills; Sir Barry Jackson as the cordial host at a huge garden party to which all and sundry were invited—the festival tourists wearing nametags for identification. Among the attractive young actors in the company who were cordially interested in the young girls in "our gang" was a good looking young man named Errol Flynn. I don't remember anything about his acting.

Actually, the program offered was not more impressive in material or players than some of those done by Robert Henderson at his Ann Arbor Festivals, or Stuart Walker in Indianapolis. But the combination of Shaw and Sir Barry Jackson, plus well-organized international (and far-reaching) publicity, brought people to the Malvern Festival from all parts of the world.

After two weeks there we moved on to Oxford primarily for the verse-speaking contest. Here was a program which held my enchanted attention, perhaps because I had struggled so hard with the choruses in *Electra,* spending days trying to achieve color and clarity in the combined voices. And I had seen Lee Simonson trying to cope with a similar problem in *Man and the Masses* and being only moderately successful. But these non-professional English folk, who had been preparing for the contest all through the year, trying to capture the inner as well as the obvious beauties of great poetry, were really dedicated to a noble and worthwhile effort. Groups numbering from four to twenty-four came from all parts of England to compete for honors. Points were given for interpretation, for memory, for enunciation and several other qualities. The judges were a group of famous poets and several actors of distinction.

The competitive sessions began at ten in the morning; there were also afternoon sessions. The poetry ranged from the ancient to the most modern, and the treatment was left entirely to the taste and imagination of the groups themselves. It was most interesting to hear the identical poem done in half a dozen different ways and by differing numbers of people. And to perceive the many aspects of technique which were analyzed by the judges: tempo, unity of style, mastery of the poet's concept and chosen form, vocal coloring—of all these one became increasingly aware as the contests continued.

Between sessions we browsed among the beautiful buildings of Oxford or wandered through the university gardens. Everywhere one saw the rich heritage of centuries, beautifully preserved. My diary speaks of frequent bicycle trips along the towpath which ran beside the Isis. One of these jaunts had an ignominious climax for me.

Early one evening Jay Gould and I started out on our bicycles single file on the towpath. He led, I followed, feeling fresh (and looking charming, I thought) in a white linen suit and gloves, my white bag in the basket on the handle bars. The shallow river was crowded with punts of students enjoying the soft English twilight. As I reached a narrow bridge I saw a woman and two children walking toward me. Right or left? Quick! Which side did one take in England? My moment's hesitation was shared by the bicycle; there was a wrong turn of the wheel and into the water I went, basket and all—down, down into the muddy ooze! The immaculate white purse floated away, my blonde bangs hung, dripping mud over my nose. I stood up in the shallow water, a sorry sight. One wag among the students asked solicitously, "Can you swim?" I answered, furiously but grandly, "Need one, in this mud bath?" and swished my way to the embankment where I and my bike were hauled onto dry land.

An abject creature, I stood there trying to make up my mind to mount and follow after Jay. Suddenly he appeared. Glancing back he had missed my spotless whiteness gleaming in the twilight. As he retraced his way to look for me he saw a small crowd gathered around a woefully mud-streaked figure. To his eternal credit he refrained from even a ghost of a smile. "What on earth? . . ." "Don't worry, Jay," I hastened to reassure him, "I couldn't drown, it's too shallow. And they call this a river! They should see the Hudson or the Mississsippi!" Then I added, bitterly: "But it's the ignominy of it! I feel such a damn fool."

He took his clean handkerchief and wiped the mud from my dripping fringe of hair. Then he looked at my hands. "Do one thing for me, please take off those gloves." I removed their sorry elegance. "I'm getting on, again, at once," I said. "I've got to prove to myself that I can ride." Jay was quietly adamant. I walked my bike to the hotel, first swearing him to secrecy. Slipping around to the side entrance I encountered one of the girls in my group. "Want the bike, Fran?" I said. "I'm going in."

Bicycles were scarce, and we shared them whenever we could so she saw nothing surprising in my offer nor, in the dark, could she see my bedraggled condition. She accepted with alacrity. But as she hopped on the leather cushion she remarked, "Funny— this seat feels damp." "Oh, just the night air," I casually threw over my shoulder. "You know what English night air is like." I went upstairs and took a long, hot bath. Next day at tea time she spoke of it again. Jay kept heroic silence until I told the story with gusto. Jay's version always ended with, "Oh, the ignominy of it!"

Back in London the group disbanded. I installed myself at Brown's Hotel, in Dover Street, recommended to me by an American friend as being the habitat of "nice Americans and minor royalty." I never did meet any of the latter, but I fell in love with an apple-cheeked little page boy—the "buttons" of the place—who always greeted me cheerily as I walked into the rather old-fashioned lobby. At tea time, especially, when small tables were set out before the two glowing fireplaces, there was a cozy, friendly atmosphere which I loved. Cappy Weller, one of the tour members, and her grandmother were stopping there too.

CHAPTER 15

A RUSSIAN
DIARY

FOUR OF THE youngsters had decided to let me take them on to Moscow for the September Theatre Festival. I was delighted. There was much discussion and a last minute delay in the decision of one of the girls, which resulted in our losing the reservations we might have secured earlier. But finally, at noon on August 25, 1934, we sailed down the Thames on *Sovtorgflot Sibia*. My diary of the trip has its melancholy overtones:

Friday, August 24th:

Night before sailing. Read the Carveth Wells book on Russia, Kapoot. *He paints frightening picture. At 3 a.m. got jittery, went to Cappy's room, awakened her wanting to consider calling the whole trip off. She assured me I was "nuts" and sent me back to sleep.*

Saturday, August 25th:

In cold daylight prospects seem somewhat less grim. Reinforced my morale with an Arden treatment and got down to dock at noon. (Contrast between sybaritic Arden salon and the Sovtorgflot Sibia *almost more than I can bear.) Dear Mrs. Close came to boat with huge basket of canned food, lest we starve in Russia. God, that boat! Looked as though it might fall to pieces. Cappy's grandmother, down to see her off, pointed out a large hole in one side of the ship. (I think she blamed me personally for it.) Again whole trip went* Kapoot *then and there. A battered little tub it seemed after our trans-Atlantic liner. I*

had visions of myself on the floor of the slate gray Baltic Sea
without a Beebe helmet! Not a soul of the crew spoke English.
(Very wise of them, if you ask me!) Girls' relatives stared at me
so piteously, I began to feel that I had built the so-and-so ship.
Girls themselves good sports. After weeping relatives said what
they believed to be farewell forever, we sailed.

Owing to our little Debbie's indecision about whether she
would go to Russia, no space was left for us but Tourist-Third
cabin. Steep steps like a ladder led down to our quarters in the
bowels of the ship. One old lady promptly fell down and almost
broke her neck. Down in our stateroom things looked even
grimmer. Six in a cabin (an English girl added to our five); we
are separated only by a wafer-thin door from crew's dining
saloon, where we too ate. Each time we emerge we are practically
belched into the teeth of the diners. No running water in the
cabin. A chance to try out proletarianism with a vengeance.

With the help of a blessed bilingual professor from Chicago,
named Harper, I argued indignantly with officials over being
put in such quarters, only to be informed that this was the only
cabin available when we applied, boat having been booked solid
for four weeks. Decided that if my mother could cross the Atlantic in a forty-eight day sailboat, we could certainly brave the
Baltic on a five-day steamer. All the bolstering of other people's
morale left mine limp; I retired into our sardine box sans supper at 6 p.m.

Sunday, August 26th:

Woke up to find sun shining. Thank God! Breakfast raw
salmon and so-so coffee. Girls behaved like angels. Cappy
Weller positively radiant with sense of adventure. Fran Rein-
hart sane and cheery. My two debutantes wistful and silent.
Further arguments with ship's powers. Results: only single remaining seat at First Class table (class distinctions on a Soviet
boat? Oh, yes!) being conceded to me, I offered it to the members of my group. Cappy and Fran haughtily declined it. By this
time they had grown fond of some of our proletarian tovarishi.
They would have none of class privilege. I decide this trip provides an ideal chance for me to fast, so we let the two debutantes
take turns at First Class meals. Peace reigns. Retired to sunny
corner to read Great Offensive and ponder over importance of
being adaptable in this changing world.

Monday, August 27th:

Awakened early. Stifling air in cabin suggests Black Hole of Calcutta. Made hasty exit and found public washroom accommodations even more malodorous, so I returned to the cabin where I persuaded everyone to renounce face-washing "for the duration." Contributed large bottle of Elizabeth Arden skin tonic, to be used communistically (and economically) instead of water; other necessary concessions to nature to be performed in stolen trips to First Class lavatories. Evolved a personal plan of going to bed at nine, thus getting three hours sleep before my tovarishi turn in; then rising at five, thus escaping several hours of nauseating air in crowded little cabin. By now girls have found soul-mates: Cappy's an attractive Russo-American engineer who played Brahms and Cesar Franck on a gramophone for us. Fran's expansive joie de vivre encompassed two English boys—intelligent and nice. One of the debbies fascinated the Chicago bilingualist. He proves most interesting on the subject of the Soviets, having been over during the Revolution and sixteen times since. I move in majestic aloofness amongst them all, wishing to God the damn trip was over, although I am beginning to like the down-to-earthness of most of my fellow passengers. Feel that ideas, not stencilled formulas of thought, are circulating among them. Funny to think that probably just the opposite is true. Amazing, too, how one gradually adjusts to a different standard of living. Temporarily, anyhow.

Tuesday, August 28th:

Everybody growing friendly. Two charming people (Mr. and Mrs. Charles Ferguson, of New York) brought a ray of sunshine into my gloom. They had seen me in The Wild Duck *and in* Lysistrata—*which bolstered my morale. (What hams we actors are!) Hubert Griffith, London newspaper man, made a short speech to assembled passengers on Russia. He referred to St. Petersburg. From the back of the room a heavily accented voice corrected him. "There is no such city any more. You are referring to Leningrad."*

Studying Russian. Awfully difficult language, even though somewhat like Czech. Believe if I could hear it spoken constantly I should learn it by ear. Rich and beautiful in sound.

Wednesday, August 29th:

High, rolling sea and gloomy, gray day. Bea frankly very sea sick. Even I a bit squeamish. We all went up on deck. Mr. Griffith administered straight vodka; instantly all felt better. English boys, Russian engineer, Frank and Cappy brought up basket of supplies so kindly donated by Mrs. Close in London. Picnic lunch on deck and more vodka. Has it all over "Mother Sill's." All grew very gay in spite of wind and high seas. Girls and English boys huddled together in protected corner, so we christened them "Animal heat units number one, two, three and four" in true regimented fashion. We sang and did some exercises. Even Bea recovered her spirits. As though in response to our gaiety, the sun came out.

Thursday, August 30th:

Boat twelve hours late, owing to head winds. What a business packing bags in that crowded stateroom! Entered Kiel Canal at 4 a.m. Sky like a Turner painting. All very pretty. Breakfasted on cheese and red caviar. Actually tasted good. Fraternizing with Russian fellow-passengers at dawn broke down last inhibitions. Sat up on front deck in sunshine chatting with all sorts of people. Struggling to cope with extra letters in Russian alphabet, I said to Cappy's engineer, "Now that the 'powers that be' in Russia are out to modernize things, I wonder they do not adopt the alphabet used by the rest of the world." He smiled as he replied, "The number of outsiders who will try to learn Russian is hardly sufficient to justify asking one hundred and eighty million people to change their spelling, is it?" I felt properly squelched. One forgets the numeric size of those incredible Russians.

Friday, August 31st:

After standing in line to get back money and passports (the joy of seeing those again!) got my first view of Russia. Kronstadt (scene of famous mutiny) bleak in sunlight. Leningrad very unimpressive from the water. Piles of lumber all over lading piers. Had forgotten that Peter the Great built the city on piles set into swamps. On the pier a native band greeted us, which was cheering.

Saturday, September 1st:

On landing, a nice girl guide took charge of us immediately. Customs people very friendly. On tables set up in the station wonderful values in furs, jewelry, petit-point squares and dolls (of which I bought several) and all sorts of objets d'art. I made up my mind not to load up on souvenirs but regret, now, not having bought a brooch containing handsome star sapphire for about sixty dollars! I assumed it was "phony," not knowing that sapphires cannot be imitated. After customs business was attended to, Lyda, our guide, put us into handsome Lincoln car and away we went to Hotel Europa. Terrific thrill at realizing where we are. Shock of seeing streets full of people with feet tied up in sacks, and in rag-bag clothes, but with such nice faces! Buildings very shabby, plaster falling off them, windows either empty or hung with bits of worn lace curtains which are even more pathetic looking.

At hotel huge, comfortable room with alcove bed and bath, furniture all very massive. Bathroom obviously not in frequent use, rust stains in tub, towels cut down from what were formerly linen sheets. After a marvelous supper, which it took us two and a half hours to get, several of us, including Professor Harper (the bilingual Chicagoan) walked through the crowded streets. We saw no one who could be called even moderately well dressed, but their faces were cheerful, healthy looking and purposeful. We walked as far as the famous Alexandrainsky Theatre. Very handsome. In the midst of its park, is a huge monument showing Catherine of Russia on top, supported by her seven lovers below. (I said that I thought the positions should be reversed.) I was told it was the only imperial statue allowed to remain standing because the people are fond of the old girl.

We approached the theatre. I begged Professor Harper to use his Russian to get us permission at least to see the lobbies. He did so with such effect that the manager ushered us into the auditorium and found us seats in what looked like a packed house. It was one of the biggest thrills I had in Russia—seeing that first proletarian audience. Working people in shirts and sweaters, apple-cheeked old Babushki with kerchiefs tied under their chins, earnest, short-haired girls in sweater-coats, all watching the performance with such rapt attention that the tovarish next to me did not even know I was holding his cap on my lap until the end of the performance when he reached for it and found—me! In a five-galleried salle, obviously designed as a background for military uniforms, laces and jewels, one saw a house packed to the top with men and women in workers' uniforms. A very thrilling sight. I recalled a steel-engraving I had seen of the pre-Revolutionary days when officers in full-dress regalia always had to remain standing until the Czar arrived and ladies wore, I was told, the largest jewels that could be imported.

The play, insofar as I could judge, was not very good, and in the acting I detected a slight odor of ham, but the audience was most attentive.

Walking home after midnight we stopped in at a grocery store, still open and still crowded with milling shoppers. We noticed a can of apricots priced at the equivalent of eight dollars. In reply to my questioning as to who could afford to buy an eight-dollar can of apricots, Professor Harper replied that a Russian family probably saves all month and then has one as a spree. I give up. Bewildering to try to understand how these people can afford anything. The double ruble standard makes it, of course, very confusing. Valuta rubles are worth about eighty cents apiece, and are the only things foreigners are supposed to, or indeed allowed to use. If one can get hold of boot-leg rubles and is able to spend them, one gets marvelous values. The shops will accept only "valuta" from a foreigner. Ruble business all very complicated, but Professor Harper tells me that this is one of the few countries that has beaten the foreign exchange game.

We continued to stroll through the streets until the wee small hours; the crowds seemed undiminished. When do Russians do their sleeping?

Sunday, September 2nd:

Took sight-seeing tour with Lyda, our guide. Leningrad's former elegance sadly depleted. Broad avenues and former palaces in pathetic state of disrepair. Mohammedan Mosque with blue mosaic dome and doors very picturesque. Guides always point out with pride new workmen's dwellings. They look like our flats at home, the sort of housing the average worker in America takes for granted. I said something to this effect to our guide. She said coldly, "Of course, Madame, I know that is not true." I told her I only lied about important *things.*

Back at hotel at 3 p.m. for dinner. Service is slow and one wastes endless hours at table. Food good and portions very generous . . . too generous. I hate to think of the hunger which must result somewhere in order to produce such an effect for the tourists. Cigarettes and wine are absurdly cheap. Wine for eight at dinner today was forty-five cents.

After mid-day dinner went to anti-religious museum. Met Professor Harper who explained many things to us. All agreed that propaganda effect was childishly inadequate. Posters, pictures and exhibits intending to show how Church had exploited workers were stuck about everywhere with singularly unimpressive effect. Mosaic portraits of saints and holy family; the dome entirely covered with gold leaf. Guide told us this church cost millions. Walked home, pestered by beggar boys in rags, but must admit that at a word of reproof from a Russian passerby they scampered. The state presumably wishes to give impression that they have no beggars. Yet one read in our papers at home of gangs of homeless boys. Leaving Leningrad, we barely made the train for Moscow. Recall Chekov's play Three Sisters *and their longing for a trip to Moscow. Slept well. Breakfast—tea in train compartment—with nice English girl who described her work at Oxford Theatre as most unsatisfying; student body not interested in "good" Theatre, she said, so theatre had to cater to local yokels. Reminded me of playing at Poli's in New Haven; there, too, the students practically ignored us.*

Monday, September 3rd:

Arrived in Moscow at 10 a.m. Rooms at the National Hotel were huge, clean and fairly comfortable. After breakfast we all felt better. Hotel personnel friendly and to me, very sympathetic types—the Slav in me, I expect. Delightful surprise to be greeted in the lobby by Hal Welles, Dick Hawkins, and T. Edward Hambleton, who had been so good as the country cousin in the play In the Days of the Turbins *when I appeared with the boys at Yale. They had been on the lookout for me. Hal is occupying the apartment of Ralph Barnes, the New York correspondent. The boys took me for my first walk across Red Square to see Lenin's tomb. Long queue waiting to go in. His body is magnificently preserved. Afternoon a whirlwind of sight-seeing with a rather trying girl guide who was obviously reeling off a "line" which she had learned by rote, naturally. View of the Kremlin from the opposite side of the river was something! Golden oriental towers shining in the sun. Streets all torn up with subway construction; everywhere building going* on like mad. *Stock in shops pitifully meager and shoddy. Only Torgsin stores (which cater only to visitors) carry "luxury" goods and their prices are astronomical. You can feel the Oriental origins of this city very strongly, also the tremendous determination of these people. Those in Moscow somewhat better dressed than in Leningrad. Yet, one morning as a friend and I stood outside the hotel waiting for a conveyance, a sweet-faced woman looked at us—turned to look again, and smiled. She came back a step and said, in excellent French, "I am not staring in rudeness. It is such a pleasure to see ladies in such pretty dresses." I blushed. (Those old clothes which I had purposely brought so as not to embarrass anyone!)*

Most exciting feature of afternoon was Youth's Day celebration; bands of youngsters from six to twenty marching like Sokols, singing as they marched. All walked beautifully, purposefully. Was torn between desire to see youths parade before Stalin and seeing the performance of Prince Igor *at the Bolshoi Opera House.* Igor *won! Production sumptuous and ballet, of course, superb. Thrilling effect as supers leap across stage carrying huge banners. Norris Houghton was there and joined us. Took all four boys back to hotel for supper. Meal schedule incredibly flexible: Breakfast from nine to three, lunch from three to ten, dinner (or supper) ten p.m. to three a.m.! No one ever seems to go to bed. Food well prepared and lots of it. But the thought of those eight-dollar cans of apricots once a month haunts me.*

Sent off letter given me by Robert Milton to Stanislavski, but he has just recovered from serious illness, so there's little hope of my seeing him.

Tuesday, September 4th:

Saw exhibit of stage models at Museum of Theater Arts—very rewarding. Extraordinary range of style in designs. One of the real thrills of the visit was seeing a performance of the original production of Last Days of the Turbins *at the Moscow Art Theatre, and seeing it, moreover, with my own New Haven Turbin family flanking me on either side! To actually sit before that simple gray curtain with its famous sea-gull decor, to be able to follow every word of the dialogue, to even indulge ourselves in a wisp of pride over what Hal had done in staging one particular scene! Well—we beamed at and nudged each other to our hearts' content. The actress playing my part was handicapped by a shiny chromium tooth which gleamed like a spotlight everytime she opened her mouth. I felt sorry for her.*

After the performance we were guests of the author at a supper which, I'm afraid, cost him many a meal afterwards. He lived in two small rooms—Hal told me on the way back to the hotel, that the fact that Michael Bulgakov had two rooms showed the respect in which the government held the author. It was, Hal said, a rare privilege.

Next day, Museum of Revolution: learned a lot about Marxism from the guide. She quoted Lenin: "Early revolutions failed because unorganized. . . . A successful revolution is an art, not an emotional orgy. It must be studiously planned and executed with coordination and precision. Violence against individuals alone (such as various assassinations of earlier days) accomplishes little; it is the capitalist system that is the cause of social and economic inequalities." And lots more of the same sort of talk. Back to hotel worn out with accumulated impressions.

In the evening my will came into mule-headed conflict with the Soviet Intourist dictatorship. It happened thus: On the day of my arrival in Moscow after studying the schedule of performances, I had explained to the Booking Bureau that, since my interest was in acting rather than in the dance, I should prefer to see a play instead of a ballet. They agree to arrange it. (My group had been scheduled for Swan Lake at the Bolshoi Ballet.) Going down at seven to pick up my ticket for whatever play they had arranged for me (performances begin at 7:30 p.m. in Moscow) I was astonished to see that it was for the ballet!

"But we discussed this matter days ago," I said. "Only this afternoon I was assured the change had been made." Alas, they said, no tickets for the theatre had been available. They were sure I would enjoy the ballet. I assured them I had enjoyed it very much, more than once, in New York; on this occasion, however, I wished, as I had explained ten days before, to see a play. They tried to dissuade me. I was firm. Endless telephoning ensued. They pleaded with me to go to the ballet, assured me I would not enjoy any play quite as much but I insisted I must be the judge of that. The other guests all left for their various theatres. Finally I announced I was going upstairs to write a report to my Drama League "sponsors" for the trip.

Whether the mention of "sponsors" had an effect I do not know, but no sooner had I reached my room than word came to me that "Comrade Tairov, of the Kamerny Theatre, had graciously agreed to put an extra chair in his private box."

Of the line of cars that had been waiting to take people to their various theatres not one remained. Would I, they said, kindly be seated for half an hour until one returned? I kindly would not, I said, miss the whole first act, because of their oversight. "What about that empty limousine parked in front of the hotel?" "That is Ambassador Bullitt's car, madam. He is at the Bolshoi Opera House just around the corner." Suddenly I felt a proprietary interest in that car. I had met Mr. Bullitt the night before. Feeling sure, too, that my Westchester taxes must have contributed considerably to the upkeep of that limousine, I scurried out and accosted the chauffeur: "I'm an American; I know Mr. Bullitt. Because there's no way to get to the Kamerny Theatre I'm missing the first half of the play. Could you possibly run me up there?" A nice American voice behind a wide grin said, "Sure, I've nothing to do until the opera is over." He helped me into the car and we swept away leaving the hotel people gaping. If the ambassador ever found out, I hope he didn't mind; I feel we made a distinct gesture of democratic cooperation for the enlightenment of at least a few citizens of the Soviet Union.

The play at the Kamerny was O'Neill's Desire Under the Elms. *The performance was interesting, though scarcely suggesting New England. It did not blot out of my memory the performance I had seen in New York of Walter Huston and Mary Morris. The theatre itself is lovely, simple gray walls, soft indirect lighting, undecorated proscenium, perfect sight lines from every seat, fine depth to the stage. How I'd love to work in such a theatre! Alexander Tairov charming—a man of wide range of culture and warm enthusiasms. Between acts had tea in his study with several other visitors, all very friendly. We talked in French. How I blessed Mlle. Sesso for my grilling in French verbs!*

Wednesday, September 5th:

Went with Mrs. Ferguson to twelve o'clock matinee at the Children's Festival Theatre, directed by a young woman named Natalie Satz. Biggest thrill of whole festival. Small theatre, gayly decorated; on curtain a garland of romping children. Walls of auditorium similarly decorated. Play: The Negro Boy and the Monkey, *an imaginative tale of a little boy living in the jungle who saves a monkey and adopts him as a pet. In the course of showing the vicissitudes of these two, as well as some of their happy experiences, one realized that the author was teaching racial tolerance, kindness to animals, etc., as well as providing an engrossing story and much amusement for her audience of children. Their enjoyment was infectious.*

Prior to the beginning of the performance youngsters had been assembled in the theatre lobby. There two young Communists, a boy and a girl of about eighteen, taught the children games which involved movements similar to those I was to see presently used by the actors they would be watching. This concentration on the interests and development of children is something which impresses one very strongly here. The government realizes, of course, that these children are the citizens of the future. What impressed me most was the fact that in organizing this theatre for children the state used only their finest professional actors, playwrights and musicians. There are no child performers and no make-shift productions. They feel that the taste of the child is established during those early years and that nothing but the best, given to them in terms of gaiety and beauty, is good enough in this formative period. It was a joy to see the children explode with laughter over some of the adventures of the amazing little dancer who played the part of the monkey. Mrs. Ferguson and I were deeply moved by what we saw. Natalie Satz, the director, says there are plans to send similar units all over the Soviet Republics. The children seemed to adore her.

Had tea at Hal's flat where the other guest was an aristocratic Russian woman, whose family, Hal tells me, looked down on the Romanoffs as upstarts. Afterwards went to Jewish State Theatre which is considered very remarkable by Muscovites. Did not enjoy its noisy eccentricity. So left the Jewish Theatre after first act and went up to Kamerny again, to see Tairov's production of Sophie Treadwell's Machinal. *Being familiar with the play makes it easier to analyze the method of production. The impact of this one was terrific. Have not been so moved since my two-hour hysteria in Bayreuth after Gulbranson's Brunhilde. Superb imagination shown in Tairov's production. Be-*

hind small interior sets, similar to those Simonson used in Goat
Song for the Theatre Guild, were great towering skyscrapers,
painted on the backdrop. From time to time they would light
up, then fade out. This gave the impression of the ebb and flow
of activity taking place in a great city. The din of machinery
was used as a kind of orchestral accompaniment to the action of
the play from time to time. At certain crises in the story, great
headlines, projected in shifting cinema pictures, gave one the
sense of newspaper commentary on the tragic story. All these
elements combined to stress the individual inadequacy of "cette
pauvre petite" as Madam Koonen, who played the heroine, described her; a creature hemmed in by the barrenness of her
under-privileged existence, her limited opportunities for happiness; crushed and eventually destroyed by the machinery of the
law and of modern living conditions. The final scene was quite
different from Arthur Hopkins' treatment in New York, where,
after the death-dealing electric switch has presumably done its
work, the stage was suffused with a glowing light into which
the heroine walked.

In Tairov's treatment, as the girl is led away to her execution
chamber, her cries of protest are drowned out by the din of
clattering typewriters, clicking telegraph keys; and all over the
backdrop newspaper headlines flash in a crazy pattern of movement. The tabloids have the last word. The impersonal cruelty
of it flooded my soul with such an overwhelming sense of pity
that sobs rose in my throat. I felt I was going to disgrace myself.
I bolted and hid behind a door leading backstage. Rubenstein,
Tairov's manager, came upon me there, crying my heart out,
and took me upstairs to Tairov's study.

My response to the play seemed to touch them both. Vodka
was administered and after I had recovered a little from my
attack of Weltschmerz, we sat and talked for a long time about
art and humanity. Alice Koonen, Tairov's wife and leading lady,
joined us after the performance. All drank Russian tea and
talked about theatre, religion, and life as only Slavs can talk.
Madame Koonen is a sweet woman with a sensitive face. Offstage
looks very tired (as well she might be, playing the repertory she
does at the theatre), but on stage she creates an extraordinary
illusion of beauty. She seemed to me the one glamorous actress
I saw in Moscow. Curious how little of that quality one sees in

the plays considering how much of it is to be seen in the ballet productions . . . except that the national concept of beauty has perforce been altered in the stressing of utilitarian as well as proletarian policies. After all, to maintain glamour costs money.

Cappy, one of the girls, who had stage ambitions, asked me to find out whether she could stay on and study in one of the acting studios. I inquired of Tairov what it would involve. His reply was illuminating: first, she would have to speak flawless Russian; "we are very particular about speech in our studios." Then, if she were accepted as a student, she would undergo a rigorous four years' training: body work and dancing, voice work, theatre techniques, history of the theatre. Of course, during those four years she could be dropped at any time if her work or her talent did not satisfy her teachers. But assuming that she did graduate she would be sent out to act in a provincial company, probably as part of the unit with which she had been studying, before she would be acceptable to any of the major theatres in Moscow or Leningrad. Cappy gave up the idea.

Find myself returning to the Kamerny because it represents for me a happy compromise between the realism of the Moscow Art tradition and the grotesque experimenting of some of the newer theatres. There is a spacious nobility in Tairov's handling of classic themes, yet the modern note pervades all of his productions. He, a man of charm and virility, of rich culture and fresh ideas. Our chats took place on the top floor of his theatre in the comfortable green room. In the center stood a round table with plates of cakes and sandwiches and a steaming samovar. There we'd sit and talk till dawn.

I learned in Russia something of the privileges to be enjoyed by artists of my profession. Today I was asked to come in to the office of the hotel manager. Someone, it seemed, had told him I was an "artist of the classic theatre" in my own country. With charming courtesy he conveyed to me the pleasure it would give the management to extend to me, as a courtesy, all first-class privileges—the use of Lincoln limousines instead of buses for transportation, and white tickets instead of red ones (or perhaps it was the other way around) in the dining room. I did appreciate the kindness he offered and thanked him. But because these privileges could not be extended to the rest of my party, which was understandable, I declined. Nevertheless I was

*touched by the graciousness of their gesture towards me as an
artist. They recognized the achievements of their own players
of rank by conferring titles such as Honored Artist of the Republic, and other variations on that theme. It is good to have
some form of recognition; acting takes on a much-needed dignity thereby. But it gave me a tiny moment of amusement, in
my regretful refusal, to be able to take, two blocks from the
Kremlin, a stand against the enjoyment of special privileges.*
Thursday, September 6th:
   *Yesterday saw a propaganda film showing reclaiming of
swamp lands for agricultural purposes. In the lobby Mrs. Ferguson presented Ernst Toller to me. When he learned I was an
American actress he said, "Do you know the Theatre Guild?"
"Oh, yes, very well. I've even played for them." "So? Did you
perhaps see my play* Masse: Mensche?" *"Oh, yes, I saw it . . . I
appeared in it. I played the Woman." We staged a small jubilee
right there in the lobby!*
   Sniffled through Twelfth Night. *Comedy scenes brilliantly
played. All romantic scenes made deliberately ridiculous by
casting Olivia as a slightly faded lady, seeking the favor of a
Viola dressed to look like a plump soubrette out of a Christmas
pantomime. This treatment probably expresses the Soviet anti-
romantic viewpoint. I disliked it until I suddenly realized how
phony the whole Viola story has always seemed to me anyway.
It is one of my less than favorite Shakespeare plays.*

   The diary goes on and on. So I clamp it shut and go on to my
most thrilling experience in Russia. I touched greatness!
   The matinee of *Marriage of Figaro* began at noon. This production fulfilled one's dream of perfect theatre. Such charm—
tempo—color! It was the original Beaumarchais play (without
music). The audience consisted mostly of workers enjoying their
weekly day of rest. They rocked with laughter and responded to
every nuance of the sophisticated comedy. The handsomest costume I have ever seen on any stage was that of the Duke Alma-
viva, in French blue, and brown leather, studded with silver. His
makeup and voice were distinguished to the nth degree. One
can sense this even when not understanding the language. During the first intermission, a nice-looking elderly woman came
down the aisle to ask if I were Madame Yurka. She spoke in

French. "If convenient for you, Monsieur Stanislavski would be honored to see you after the matinee." I assured the gentle-voiced envoy (obviously the pearl of secretaries) that the honor would be mine, and spent the remainder of the afternoon trying to control my excitement. My companions were even more excited than I. My almost forgotten letter of introduction to him was to bear fruit after all!

I assumed I was to see him for a few minutes in his office at the theatre. Instead, I was ushered out to his car and driven to his villa in the suburbs. It was the only house I had been in in Moscow which seemed to be in a state of good repair. The same conspicuous tidiness was evident within, and an air of comfortable spaciousness as well. One or two elderly Russian servants passed through the foyer as I waited to be announced. They might have stepped out of a Chekhov play. A quiet dignity pervaded the atmosphere. I felt as though I were in the home of an important state official. As a matter of fact I was! In Russia the theatre does serve the State.

The soft voiced secretary led me into the loftiest, most spacious study I've ever been in. The first impression was of thousands of books. Books everywhere. Tall books, small books, manuscripts, magazines, but nowhere a sense of disorder. The silence, the peace, created a mood of lovely detachment from an outside world in the throes of change. Presently, emerging from this background, beautifully in scale with his lofty surroundings, stepped the tallest, most exquisitely gracious and distinguished human being I had ever met. Stanislavski came forward to meet me. What a man! Such clear eyes, such gentle distinction, such "depth and breadth and height."

Salvini, grandson of the famous actor, and Stanislavski's lady-secretary were the only other persons there. Presently, Stanislavski mentioned having seen me play the Queen in *Hamlet*. "She looked very beautiful," he said to Salvini. "Younger than her son." This, with a mischievous gleam in his eye. I blushed as I had that matinee day when he first said it to me. "I must explain," I said. "You see, I was always being cast, in those days, in parts much older than I was. I resented it. Besides, I had just married a man younger than myself. I wanted to look as attractive as possible." Both men smiled. I suspect that, as directors, they had both had similar experiences with the female ego. I was touched that he remembered me at all.

We discussed (in French) the world theatre from many angles. Stanislavski explained that the Revolution had changed the character of his audiences. As he talked it became obvious that he was meeting this social challenge with a mental flexibility which showed no evidence of his 70-odd years. He spoke interestedly, sympathetically of the new public to which they were now playing. His remarks conjured up an extraordinary contrast. I had been subconsciously aware of it at the matinee. I realized that I was seeing a play originally designed for the amusement of aristocratic, highly sophisticated audiences, and now was being presented to an audience largely composed of workers, most of whom had never been within the sacred precincts of that playhouse prior to the Revolution. Yet they apparently were not missing a single point of the humor of Beaumarchais.

I quote from an account which Stanislavski, himself, once gave of the problem which this new public presented:

Faced by an altogether new audience which we did not know how to approach. . . . We were forced to begin at the very beginning, to teach this new spectator to come into the theatre at the proper time, to sit quietly, not to talk, not to smoke, not to eat.

From his tone, I gathered that Stanislavski found fresh stimulus in reaching out to these unjaded minds and hearts, and I could well understand this, however much he might miss—as I did, in imagination—the aesthetic and pictorial aspects of that former public. An artist's joy in his work is in direct proportion to the eagerness of his public to receive that work. Enthusiasm clad in sweaters is quite as heart-warming as that stirring under a necklace of diamonds or an officer's uniform; it is conceivable that it might be even more gratifying.

We touched on the effect his various books had had on the acting profession all over the world. And especially in the United States. "But most people, directors as well as actors," he said, "do not realize that in those books I have not been dictating to them a method which they must use in order to act as we do. Your whole theatre practice is conducted differently; you are not allowed the time to work as we do. You must evolve a method of your own." And I remembered what he had said to someone (to whom, I no longer remember). "It is not surprising that you have relatively few great performers; the miracle is that you have any."

He went on: "My books are written to record the manner in which we have worked—to explain as nearly as possible why we worked that way, and with what results." I explained that I had always suspected this to be the case; that I had frequently commented to myself when studying his books: "Why, that's just what I do! No book ever told me to think it through that way!"

He smiled again. "I have tried to explain this to the young people who come here, now and then, to study with me. They are eager and intelligent, but not always wise in their application of my principles." All this was said in the gentlest possible manner. "And what do you do," I asked, "when a student proves to have no talent? After all, there must be some who are mistaken in their ambitions." "Oh, we weed them out very soon," he said. "I do not believe in anyone nursing false ambitions."

And I remembered Tairov's remarks on Cappy's ambitions to become a student: "At the end of a few months we appraise the potential." My mind swiftly recalled Dr. Damrosch's blunt advice to me. This attitude is fundamentally the kindest.

Among other things, he mentioned that he had changed his method of direction and his approach to a play in the last year or two. Then he went on to explain why. Formerly, he said, the company had spent many weeks reading the play, analyzing the motivations of the characters, their hidden life, so to speak, experimenting with various ideas of interpretation—above all, talking, talking, talking about it all. "All this," he said, "tended to create a kind of mental constipation. I now feel it is better to get on our feet and begin to do the play itself much earlier." I was tempted to say, "Much as we do at home," but I suppressed the impulse.

What seemed remarkable to me was the mental resilience which enabled a man in his seventies to say, "From now on I must do it another way." But thoughts of age evidently had no place in Stanislavski's thinking. In discussing one of the great Salvini's guest engagements at the Bolshoi Theatre (an enormous opera house) years before, when Salvini was playing a repertory of *Hamlet, Richard III,* etc., Stanislavski said, "He was not very old at that time; he was, I think, only 73." This attitude about maturity in art seems characteristic of their thinking over there, in spite of the fact that it is a country dedicated to youth.

There is a refreshing difference from our standards of interest. The assumption in the Russian theatre is that youth and youthful achievement are interesting only as a beginning; a promise; not as a substitute for accomplishment. It is presumed that an important talent will reach its fulfillment only with maturity, and that only a matured and proven talent justifies recognition and acclaim. *Ars longa—vita brevis* (Art is long—life is short) is an indisputable statement. In Russia promise is greeted enthusiastically, but only as promise. It must be carried through to its fruition before the laurel wreaths are handed out. And never, I am told, do the actors cease that searching, that experimenting, that disciplining of voice and body essential to continuous growth. There would seem to be no place in their mental picture of a living artist who uses his laurels as a pillow on which to rest permanently. Stanislavski, himself, when in his seventies, announced to his dressing room companions, "Now, at last, I can control my voice!" Complete theatre units worked together for four years in all departments of production, so that when they were graduated they represented an already coordinated ensemble. Then, in some outlying theatre, each could work intelligently along lines developed during its period of preparation.

One felt the surge of vitality in all these projects; one glimpsed a theatre world in which ambition could find an outlet in hard, continuous work. Vastly better, I thought, than putting one's energies into trying to be patient, courageous, philosophical through dreary periods between jobs. These are the bane of the average American actor's life.

The corners of the high, book-lined room became shadowy as twilight crept in. We had consumed vast quantities of tea; two hours had slipped by imperceptibly. I hated to leave. It seemed that I would be relinquishing something which contained the reality of all my dreams of ideal theatre; a place in which to recreate "The reality of imperishable and exalting things" under the guidance of an artist of incomparable rectitude.

Next day I went back to Tairov's Kamerny Theatre with several other visitors, including a Czech group from Prague, to hear Tairov discuss his coming production of *Egyptian Nights*. They showed us interesting Masonic designs and explained their use of them. We went backstage on a tour of investigation.

As we walked across the cellar under the stage, one of the

Czech visitors, Dr. Mojzis, director of the National Theatre in Prague, suddenly turned to me and asked whether I would be interested in playing in Prague. For years I had dreamed of just such an opportunity—how proud Tatinek would have been! I was sorely tempted. But the part Mojzis wanted me to do was Nazimova's role in O'Neill's *Mourning Becomes Electra,* and the difficulty of memorizing that endless dialogue in Czech seemed too overwhelming. Regretfully I turned it down.

My visit to Russia had a rather amusing and very pleasant aftermath. In 1935, shortly after my return from Europe, I received a telephone call, asking if I would honor Ambassador and Mme. Troyanovsky by attending a reception they would be giving in Washington on March 28. If I would care to recite one or two poems after dinner, he would be most appreciative. Would I, the voice said, allow the speaker to call on me and extend the Ambassador's invitation personally? I said I would be charmed and we set a time.

A few hours later my visitors were announced and into my apartment came two of the tallest, handsomest Russians I had ever seen. They introduced themselves as Embassy attachés and conveyed, in excellent but accented English, the Ambassador's appreciation and pleasure at my acceptance of the invitation. They handed me an envelope containing tickets for a drawing room on the best train running to Washington on the day of the reception. Then they bowed themselves out, after assuring me that they would meet me on my arrival in Washington.

They did, looking taller and handsomer than ever. They ushered me out of the station to a waiting chauffeured Rolls Royce limousine which drove me to my suite at the Clarendon Hotel (where I had never felt I could afford to stay when playing engagements in Washington). At the hotel I found beautiful flowers in my reception room and roses beside the bed in the adjacent room. I felt quite important.

After a short nap and dressing slowly, I opened the door to a bell-boy who presented me with a box containing an orchid corsage. (It looked very pretty on my simple black evening gown.) My limousine was waiting, he said. I descended (no attachés this time!) and was driven the two blocks to the Russian Embassy.

I found it surging with beautifully dressed people. The Ambassador and Madame Troyanovsky greeted me graciously and presently I was escorted to a large, handsome dining salon, where a long table seating about eighty people was spread with sumptuous food. My table partner was a rather talkative gentleman who spent the time, for the most part, in extolling the values of his Russian Motherland and who assured me it would be wise to invest some money over there. I told him that being an *American* artist, I didn't have any to invest.

As we left the dining room, Madame Troyanovsky suggested that I might like to be alone for the half hour or less it would take to assemble and seat the guests in the ballroom where the artists (a violinist, a pianist and myself) were to perform. I retired to a little room nearby and contemplated my navel for a while as I rehearsed mentally the little group of poems I was to recite; two love poems of Elizabeth Barrett Browning and Poe's "Annabel Lee," which I had heard Mrs. Patrick Campbell recite so beautifully at the benefit performance at the Metropolitan when I was a student at the Opera House.

Soon I was notified that everyone was seated; I sat through the violinist's performance, then arose and "did my act." It was graciously received, and a large armful of American Beauty roses was brought to me as I bowed.

About two hundred people had been invited to the reception after the program. We all re-entered the dining room where the long table was again groaning with marvelous zakuski, fruits, and salads galore.

Later, as one of the attachés deposited me at my hotel entrance, he said: "Madame Yurka, the Ambassador thought you might care to stay on for a day or two of sight-seeing. Please feel free to do so as his guest. The car, of course, is at your disposal for as long as you care to stay."

I managed not to faint and carried my armful of American Beauties upstairs and deposited them in a tubful of cold water to keep them fresh until morning. I returned home at noon the next day. "Enough is enough," I thought. "Let's not be greedy."

Touched and delighted as I was by the attention showered on me because of the Russian respect for artists, I was nevertheless haunted by the contrast between my experiences in Moscow and Washington. In order to entertain Hal Welles and me after we had seen the Moscow production of *The Turbins,* the cast had

had to pool their ration cards to provide us with a simple supper. In Washington, the tables had groaned under the weight of the feasts offered to the Embassy guests. Somehow it didn't seem right.

CHAPTER **16**

LONDON
INTERLUDE

WHEN MY LITTLE group disbanded in Paris, I decided to go on to London for a couple of months. Cappy came with me to rejoin her grandmother there. On the last afternoon before leaving Paris, I found, at a sale, a lovely Camille Roger hat and a smart broadtail shoulder cape. They almost cleaned out my money reserves. To avoid paying duty, I wore them both on the channel steamer which we had learned was the cheapest way to cross to London. I looked very chic in my Paris purchases. As we were to land in England at four in the morning, Cappy and I sat up all night. Two sinister-looking Portuguese were the only other passengers. In the dim gray dawn, we stood in line at the Custom Officer's desk. I must have seemed oddly resplendent in my new Paris finery.

"How much money are you bringing into England?" asked the Customs man. "Two pounds," I answered. He looked up, startled. "Two pounds? Isn't that very little, Miss?" I knew Romney Brent was in London and would be good for a loan until money could reach me from America so I blithely replied, "Perhaps, but I know where I can get plenty more in London." His eyes took in the chic new hat, the charming broadtail capelet. "Well, Miss," he said finally, "I expect you know your business." His tone left no doubt as to what he thought my business was.

Brown's Hotel in Dover Street was still asleep when we arrived. I deposited my bags. Since the dining room was closed we went out in search of coffee. It was a clear, sunny morning and the solid prosperity of those London streets and buildings gave one a comfortable sense of security. Later, as Bond Street filled with a stream of well-dressed, marvelously fit-looking Englishmen, I decided that Englishmen, at their best, are really something quite special to look at.

I put through several telephone calls and found all my friends in London vastly interested to hear about my visit to Moscow. One or two of them urged me to stay on and see what might turn up for me in the acting field. So, with my Drama League return-ticket tucked away in the hotel safe, I settled down at Brown's for my own personal siege of the London Theatre. Two of my friends, Mary Ellis and Romney Brent, had made warm berths for their talents in the hearts of Londoners. Perhaps I could do the same. The slower tempo at which people lived fitted my temperament better than the hectic pace of New York. I felt I should like to become a part of it all. Mary introduced me to her agent. With such sponsorship there was reason to be hopeful.

During my earlier stay in London I had seen as many plays as possible, and on my return from Russia I resumed my theatre-going. I saw Gielgud's glorious *Hamlet* performance—saw it again and again and understood why he was so popular. He was more princely than John Barrymore, although he lacked Jack's impish humor and fabulous good looks. Gielgud's reading of the line "Rest, rest, perturbed spirit" was unbelievably touching.

On the whole, though, the English theatre in the early summer of 1934 seemed to me somewhat less vigorous than what I had left behind at home. Rather silly little plays of a type which we had long since outgrown seemed to be enjoying considerable success. This impression was heightened on my return from Russia. The rugged vitality which characterized the Moscow stage made the British theatre fare seem pretty anaemic.

Like so many visitors, I fell in love with English country life. I spent long weekends at the home of Lady Betty Hawkins, the American-born widow of Anthony Hope. His *Prisoner of Zenda* and *The Dolly Dialogues* had years before made him a popular author. The brick and timber manor house with beautifully cared-for gardens stretched alongside the heath. During the day the sun poured through casement windows into the chintz-hung drawing room. In the evening the candlelight, the soft-spoken servants, my gay red-haired hostess and her tall witty son, David, were like something from one of the novels written by the late master of the manor, whose *Dolly Dialogues* still made good reading for us during those leisurely evenings in front of the fireplace.

Barry Jones, an actor who had frequently played with Jane Cowl and had later toured in America and Canada in several of Shaw's plays, arranged an interview for me with G.B.S. I was very excited that morning, dressed carefully, topping my costume with the wide Camille Roger hat. It blew off completely in the blustering wind which swept up the river and I arrived, blown and quite unkempt at Shaw's sunny Chelsea study, at 10 Adelphi Terrace, overlooking the Thames.

He sat before his immaculately tidy desk looking pink and white and clean as a freshly-bathed baby, and asked questions about Russia in a most beautifully modulated voice. My association with the plays of Ibsen interested him, but he too, like Romney, advised against making my London debut in an Ibsen play. His attitude surprised me a little as he had been a vociferous defender of Ibsen in his early days as a dramatic reviewer. Perhaps time had taught him the futility of tilting at windmills. Needless to say, I did not argue with him. The interview was pleasant enough, though scarcely to be compared with the stimulating one I had had with Constantin Stanislavski. I think Shaw found me quite uninteresting.

But I feel that Shaw was much more high-minded than he permitted himself to sound. One senses this in those early acerbic reviews he wrote as a drama critic. He was constantly demanding higher quality of players and playwrights, coining the phrase "Sardoodlum" which he contemptuously applied to the plays Sardou regularly turned out for Sarah Bernhardt. And there is a fine concept of responsibility for his great gifts in the following few lines, released by him on his eighty-eighth birthday:

I want to be thoroughly used up when I die, for the harder I work the more I live. I rejoice in life for its own sake. It is a sort of splendid torch, which I have got hold of, for the moment, and I want to make it burn as brightly as possible before handing it on to future generations.

Despite my various contacts, nothing developed professionally in London except a chance to do a bad play at the Gate Theatre, a tiny box of a theatre located under the Charing Cross Station. Had the play been a good one I should have leapt at the offer, but Romney persuaded me that it would be a mistake to make such a start. And the stage was so small that I should have filled it quite too completely just by myself.

One day Mr. Carol Sax, whom I had known in New York, called on me. He said a few ladies of pacifistic leanings, among them Sylvia Pankhurst, were interested in the idea of doing *Lysistrata* in London. If I'd like to do it, they would find backing. I met Miss Pankhurst and we agreed on terms. But first, a new version had to be made, since the one used in New York had been vetoed by the Lord Chamberlain, the censor of the London Theatre. So, with much effort, and invaluable critical help from Mr. Sax, I set to work making an adaptation which might, with luck, get by the Lord Chamberlain without losing too many of the sure-fire laughs with which five months' playing had made me familiar.

I sat up in my tiny room under the eaves at Brown's Hotel combing through the various "pony" translations which Mr. Sax had collected for me. There were five. I restored some of the fine anti-war speeches which had been deleted in the New York version in the interests of bawdy humor. In the original, Aristophanes did more than ridicule war; he lashed out at it in speeches which have a strangely modern ring. At one point Lysistrata cries out:

We know nothing of war? We—whose wombs bear the burdens of giving you sons? We, who face death gladly each time we bring forth life—only to have you again dedicate it to death?

Aristophanes did more than laugh at war some two thousand years ago.

The script finished, Mr. Sax actually succeeded in getting the Lord Chamberlain to pass it. Lewis Allen, Gilbert Miller's capable stage director, knew of a beautiful, scarcely-used setting for a play called *Acropolis* by Robert Sherwood which had opened and closed so quickly that no one had had time to see it. He thought it could be had cheaply and could be safely used again. We interviewed several actors and actresses. But, suddenly, one day word came that the ladies were growing worried over the

Blanche Yurka in The Lawmakers, *a society melodrama by Jules Goodman*

Ian Keith

Blanche Yurka at the time of her marriage to Ian Keith

For my mother with much love
from her mildly incestuous son —
John Barrymore —

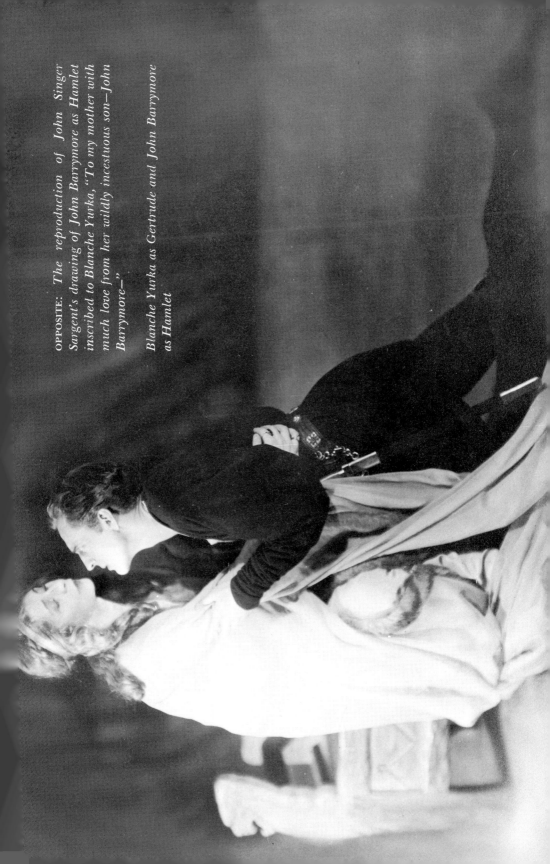

OPPOSITE: *The reproduction of John Singer Sargent's drawing of John Barrymore as Hamlet inscribed to Blanche Yurka, "To my mother with much love from her wildly incestuous son—John Barrymore—"*

Blanche Yurka as Gertrude and John Barrymore as Hamlet

Alfred Lunt

Lynn Fontanne

Blanche Yurka in the Theatre Guild's production of Franz Werfel's
Goat Song

*Blanche Yurka as
Dolores Mendez in*
The Squall

*Blanche Yurka in her
Paris dress: "The prettiest
dress I've ever owned."*

Robert Loraine and Blanche Yurka as the narrators in Lucrece

Blanche Yurka as the Nurse in Romeo *and* Juliet *in which
Katharine Cornell played the role of Juliet*

OPPOSITE: *Blanche Yurka at Elizabeth Arden's Salon*

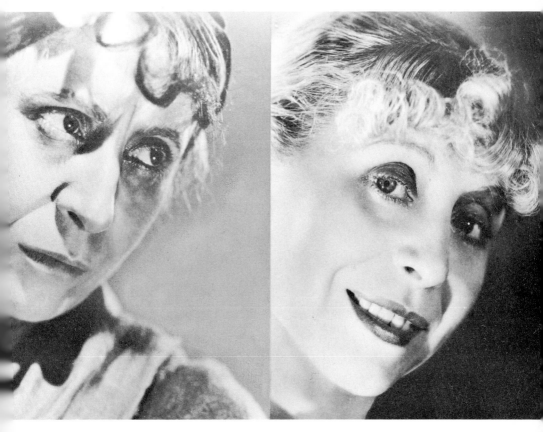

Mme Defarge/ Blanche Yurka—"A Tale of Two Faces"

OPPOSITE: *Blanche Yurka as Mme Defarge in the Tribunal scene from* A Tale of Two Cities

ABOVE: *Blanche Yurka with Frank Lloyd Wright at the dedication of the Hartford Theatre*

Edith Hamilton

*Blanche Yurka
as Mrs. Wendel in the
New York revival of
Dinner at Eight*

Blanche Yurka

impending Christmas holiday slump, at which time, they told us, nothing did business but Christmas pantomimes. Would I mind postponing the whole project until the early spring?

I did mind. Acting on a sudden impulse I tossed my Lysistrata script into my trunk, booked passage on the *Berengaria* and on December 4, sailed for home. There were few passengers on that December crossing—about eighty in all. This had the advantage of making the trip more restful. I enjoyed long walks around the deck with a very distinguished fellow-passenger, Senator Robert F. Wagner. We had met casually during a radio broadcast a year or two before. He told me that he had booked a round-trip passage on the *Berengaria* in order to escape interruptions while he drafted what has since made history as the famous Wagner Labor Act. During our promenades around the almost empty decks I learned something of the careful study and thoughtful consideration such a man gives to the political problems with which he is faced. I found myself wishing I knew more about such matters. And I found him charming.

He questioned me about my Russian trip and I dwelt at length on the Government-supported theatres. We, too, I urged, could have them in America, if such encouragement could be made available to our theatre workers as seemed to be extended to the "honored artists of the Republic." The seed planted in these talks bore fruit the following summer.

Frequently I had shared with two friends of mine, Mary Stewart French and Amory Hutchinson, both of whom had long been active in cultural affairs in Philadelphia, my vision of an American theatre which could stand proudly among the theatres of the civilized world.

After my return I expressed my enthusiasm for this idea even more vigorously. The moment was ripe to ignite their enthusiasm into action. They decided that something must be done and proceeded to rally round themselves a distinguished group of supporters from all of the arts and letters. Beginning in Philadelphia these two women carried their campaign to Washington, armed with a letter from me to Senator Wagner, begging him to assist them in any way he could. He responded nobly, enlisting the interest of his congressional colleagues—opening doors which needed to be breached, including those of the White House. Undeterred by a hot summer and countless discouragements, they finally reached their goal. In July of 1935, Franklin D. Roosevelt signed the first charter ever granted to a theatre organization in America. The American National Theatre and Academy became an established fact. It had as its dedicated objective: "To extend the living theatre beyond its present limitations by bringing the best in the theatre to every state in the Union."

There was only one difficulty. The Charter did not carry any financial subsidy with it. In its early years ANTA was served entirely by unpaid enthusiasts who gave of their life's blood and strength—and their ability to live on next to nothing—in order to make its purposes a reality. Robert Breen, Robert Porterfield and many others, worked night and day to further the growth of this organization. In the course of its expansion, many important people became interested in ANTA. In its more recent development it has evolved money-raising techniques which have paid, however modestly, the salaries of the dedicated people who work for it. Its story has been told in an interesting brochure entitled *The ANTA Story* which is obtainable at ANTA headquarters. In 1968 ANTA's perpetual money problems were finally solved when the National Committee for the Arts assumed the burden of ANTA's financial responsibilities.

CHAPTER 17

MME. DEFARGE ARRIVES IN HOLLYWOOD

During the winter season of 1934 I attended a very exciting first night, with Elizabeth Arden as my guest. Katharine Cornell's appearance as Juliet in her first attempt at Shakespeare (I imagine that her role in *Lucrece* had been a preliminary exercise for this) was in itself a major theatrical event. As usual she surrounded herself with a most distinguished cast. It included two of her former leading men: Basil Rathbone as Romeo and Brian Aherne as Mercutio. A very vigorous young man named Orson Welles played the truculent Tybalt splendidly.

On opening night the characterization which, after Kit's Juliet, was on everyone's lips was that of Edith Evans as the Nurse. She brought a rich fruity quality to the role. At her stipulation the part was uncut. Even the "keening" scene was retained—the scene in which the Nurse discovers Juliet lying on her bed, seemingly dead. This gave the part an importance and emotional values never revealed in any performance of the play I had ever seen.

Shortly after the opening a sudden death in her family made it necessary for Miss Evans to return to England. Mr. McClintic invited me to replace her. I was both flattered and frightened. Miss Evans' performance had been acclaimed; following her would be a tough assignment and an interesting challenge.

Never having played anything remotely like the fat, bawdy
old Nurse, I had to re-adjust my thinking. I buried the slimness,
so laboriously achieved at the Arden Salon the previous season,
under the required thirty pounds of padding. I even wore it
while rehearsing in order to acquire the waddling walk and la-
bored movements of the character.

Mr. McClintic and Katharine were infinitely patient with my
fluctuations between hope and doubt as to the wisdom of what I
was undertaking. Could I justify my temerity in following so
brilliant a performance? And if I did succeed, was it wise to play
such a "character" part? Would I ever again be allowed to play
anything else? But despite all this vacillating I agreed to be
ready in ten days' time.

On the day I was to enter the cast an early run through the
lines with the stage manager went smoothly. At 3 P.M. I went up
to the studio of Madame Daykarkhanova, a Russian actress who
knows everything there is to know about makeup. I had not the
slightest notion of how my aquiline features and rather deep-
set eyes could be turned into an apple-cheeked old face which
would seem to belong to the fat, rolling body beneath it. I
watched her fingers work a miracle. It took two hours, but, by
clever high-lighting and shadowing she painted out my face and
in its place created little pig eyes, double chins and full brick-
red cheeks. But on my return to the theatre for a final line rehearsal with Jimmy Vincent, the stage manager, I suddenly
found that I could not remember a single consecutive speech.
Terror gripped me. I tried again. It was no use. Jimmy looked
helpless and counseled that I go up to the dressing room "to rest"
until the performance. "You knew it perfectly this morning.
Please don't worry," he said. I stretched a blanket on the floor
and as I lay there, trying to muster courage to ask for a second
postponement (knowing full well I wouldn't do that) Maminka's remark came back to me: "You're nervous when you don't
work; you're nervous when you do. What do you get out of it?"
Rose came in to join me. I couldn't speak to her.

Half hour was called, fifteen minutes. Horrible premonitions
swept over me: I would "dry up" and one couldn't fake Shakespeare. I would ruin Kit's beautiful performance as well as my
own future. Why had I ever imagined I could do such a part?
My woolen robes were less heavy than my heart as I went down

to sit on the darkened stage to await my cue. It came. I began to speak. I heard a cracked old voice (my own, incredibly changed) calling:

"What, lamb! what, ladybird!—God forbid!—Where's this girl? What, Juliet!" And before I knew it I was launched on the long garrulous nurse's speech. In a moment or two I heard that loveliest of sounds, laughter! My heart lifted. Again that ripple out front; a few lines later still again. It was the sweetest of music to my ears. Terror evaporated like mist before the sun. The scene went beautifully; the lines rolled out as though I had been speaking them for weeks. The mental mechanism, released from stage-fright by that first ripple of laughter, functioned without a halt. As I came offstage, Jimmy Vincent hugged me and Kit squeezed my hand; the swift change of scenes allowed time for nothing more.

The lovely play went on to its more lyric beauties; again, in the garden scene, heart-warming laughter. The rope-ladder scene, with its keening and tears, held no terrors for me; Guthrie's moist eyes at rehearsal had reassured me about that.

At last the performance was over. Back in my dressing room where only a few hours ago I had lain on the floor stricken with foreboding, I doffed the huge skirts and the heavy padding. A few swift smears of cold cream and I saw my own face emerge, greasy but happy. There's no sense to it all, such depths of fear, such heights of relief, but I've never been able to keep a sensible middle path between the two; those who can are lucky! I pinned three corsages of gardenias down the front of my coat, and Rose and my loyal friend Lillian Okun and I went joyously out to celebrate in a hamburger joint on Eighth Avenue. I had had nothing to eat all day and I was starving.

After my fears and apprehensions it was very warming to see Burns Mantle's review of my performance:

I was much pleased with the performance of Blanche Yurka, who has succeeded to the role of the Nurse. It might be expected that the First Tragedienne would bring intelligence and authority to the reading of any role, but that she should also touch it with a proper comedy sense and fall so gracefully into the perfect timing that characterizes this whole Cornell production is quite within the best, or Edith Evans tradition.

When the great ones agree to toy with minor roles it frequently happens that they either overplay to attest their greatness or patronize the part to prove their superiority. Only those of a true quality are equal to the test. Blanche Yurka belongs.

John Mason Brown, who admitted that he had had his doubts as to how I would fill Dame Edith Evans' shoes, concluded his Two on the Aisle column, entitled, "Blanche Yurka's Excellent Performance of the Nurse in Miss Cornell's 'Romeo and Juliet'" by writing:

Capable as Miss Yurka is throughout, she rises to true magnificence in the scene in which she discovers Juliet under the influence of the Friar's drug and thinks her dead. Her cries . . . are sobs that stab the heart. They are final proofs of the shading and variety which lend such vocal color and interest to Miss Yurka's characterization as a whole. And they find her at this moment outdistancing her predecessor and endowing the scene with a poignancy that even Miss Evans failed to bring to it.

Romeo and Juliet continued its New York run for nine more weeks. Katharine's triumph was complete and her warm joy in it was infectious. I, for one, had been charmed and moved by Basil Rathbone's Romeo. Some of the critics had been of a different opinion, but watching it repeatedly from the wings, my first impression was, if anything, intensified. In certain scenes I thought him the best of the six Romeo's I had seen. Especially in the bedroom scene his tender, muted reading was so convincing, so touching, that I never grew tired of listening to it. Some Romeos, in this scene, use sufficient voice to rouse the Capulet household a dozen times. As for the balcony scene, it is usually done in a key which would ensure the "death, if any of my kinsmen find thee here" of which Juliet was apprehensive. Not so with Basil Rathbone. He played the whole scene in a muted voice which nevertheless carried perfectly. He was very moving, too, in the scene in Mantua, when word is brought to him of Juliet's death.

The whole performance was one which could be watched night after night with pleasure. Brian Aherne's Mercutio was brilliant both in voice and appearance. Only Katharine's desire to play a series of other parts that season prompted her to terminate the run while business was still good. I said goodbye to her and "honey nurse" with a heavy heart.

What a surprise my next assignment was to be! In the official listing of my career I see a brief line: "In 1935 appeared in a film, *A Tale of Two Cities*. But in that year's diary:

A new world has opened up; a sun-drenched, dazzling white world which may mean escape from the treadmill of financial worries of these past five years. This is the turning of road. Faith! If only one held closer to it.

It all happened unexpectedly, with no preliminaries. Romney Brent had been playing the Spring Festival in Ann Arbor with Nazimova. She told him that she had received an offer from Hollywood to play Mme. Defarge in a screen production of Dickens' *A Tale of Two Cities*.

"But I am not right for it," she said. "I am not big and strong enough. It should be someone like Blanche Yurka. You know her, don't you? Tell her to put her agent on it at once. I understand everyone in Hollywood has been tested for it. It is a fine part and she'd be perfect."

I was excited and grateful to her for the suggestion. My agent was notified and arrangements were made for a test in New York at a small studio in West 54th Street, which was used for East Coast tests. Two scenes were required. One: the wineshop scene with Barsad; the other, the denunciation of Darnay before the Tribunal.

One afternoon while on my way to consult the makeup man I heard the now familiar lines spoken by a very familiar and famous voice. I peeked through the curtains of the Test-studio and caught a glimpse of another actress being tested in the Tribunal scene. She was wearing the tidy dress and smooth hair of the wineshop keeper's wife of the previous scene. But I had the firm conviction that by the time Madame Defarge had been carried along by the tide of revolt and bloodshed to the Tribunal scene she would look very different from her usual tidy self. Sleepless nights, battles in the street, the violent overthrow of all order and decency, might well have turned her into a disheveled fury, ruthlessly seeking and finding revenge after eighteen years of implacable waiting and endless knitting.

So, in preparing myself for that second scene, I loosened the smooth black wig, made it dank with oil, ran my hand across the floor and smeared my face with dirt; then I ripped the cotton neckerchief with my fingers until it hung in ribbons. The test director looked startled when I appeared. "Good God! Isn't that going too far?" he asked. We argued. I explained why I felt that she'd look like that. He continued to protest, but at last, grudgingly, he yielded. "Well, honey," he said, "it's your funeral."

We worked over the scene for several hours. He grew more and more interested and, at the end of the test, he was calling me "Blanchie"—always a good sign. Jack Conway, who directed the picture, told me, later, that it was the startling effect of that virago suddenly sweeping onto the screen which "sold" me to him and to Mr. Selznick, the producer, who clapped him on the back, exclaiming, "That's it! That's what we've been looking for!"

The part had been regarded in Hollywood as the plum of the season, and all my friends considered me lucky, indeed, to be chosen and to make my debut on the screen in such an important role. I felt I had been richly rewarded for insisting upon following my hunch about the harridan makeup! Later I was told that sixty-seven actresses had been tested for the role.

Mr. Selznick insisted that I fly out to Hollywood at once. It was my first long airplane flight. No later one could ever match it. As the great wings lifted me slowly and powerfully up into the sunset, the world grew more and more like a map. Tiny houses, gardens, rivers; streets filled with automobiles which looked like crawling ants. Then clouds and moonlight. I was too excited to sleep. Presently, the dawn rose over the painted desert to complete the picture of a world seen by me for the first time.

Flyers should be poets. Here was the instrument through which Man's eternal quest for new worlds had found glorious fulfillment. The stop in Albuquerque filled my lungs with air like no other air I had ever breathed. Airborne again, we approached high, snow-clad mountains. Finally, through a milky ceiling, we eased down into the Glendale California Airport as gently as a homing pigeon.

Rooms had been reserved for me at an hotel surrounded by gardens. After a few hours rest I went out to the Metro-Goldwyn-Mayer Studio for my first interview. Everywhere I encountered eager friendliness. I was given a sight-seeing tour over the lot and shown charming bungalows which housed sumptuous dressing rooms. To anyone accustomed to the rudely functional aspect of most *theatre* dressing rooms, these were fantastically elegant; it was hard to imagine anyone *working* in them. Only one room was utterly simple and unpretentious. "Whose room is that?" I asked. They told me that a Miss Helen Hayes had used that one; she didn't want them to redecorate; said she didn't care where she dressed. Her attitude seemed to puzzle my guide. I found it refreshing.

Only established stars rated the magnificent suites which had been shown me. My own was smaller but attractive enough in its green chintz, with a white leather sofa. Madame Defarge's coarse peasant costumes seemed shockingly out of place, so I always spread a sheet over the couch before lying down to rest. After all, white must be kept white.

On my arrival I was sent to the Costume Department. They had made me simple dresses of a peasant type, but of new material. This struck me as false. I went to Mr. Selznick's office and said, in effect: "This woman would not have had a new dress in ten years. It is necessary that the dresses she wears show this. I don't think it can be done by applying aging treatment to this new material." I suggested that the Dress Department find some old, used dresses, rip them apart and use the material for my costumes. He agreed. It was done. The dresses were perfect.

Once I had been outfitted and my makeup problems settled, I was free to have a good time, as my scenes had not yet been reached on the shooting schedule. I lunched almost daily at the Vendome, then the most popular restaurant in Hollywood. Everywhere I saw faces one had seen only on the screen. I was as excited as any "fan." There were old friends there, too, Stuart Walker "regulars": Beulah Bondi, Elizabeth Patterson, Spring Byington. "S.W." himself was a director at Paramount.

Shortly after my arrival the Basil Rathbones gave me an exciting party. Mrs. Rathbone's parties had become legendary. On this occasion I really did feel myself in the midst of *Who's Who* in Movieland. Through the lovely rooms drifted theatre-people with whom I had played: Freddie March, now far removed from the Fred Bickel whose part in *The Lawbreaker* I had salvaged for him; Bette Davis, my dynamic little Hedvig in *The Wild Duck,* now rapidly growing into a movie star of first rank; and

Basil himself, who had become the most effective of all the screen villains; Cesar Romero, who had been my Spanish lover in *Spring in Autumn* was now the Latin heart-throb of countless celluloid heroines. It was all very exciting. I am sure two-thirds of the guests did not know nor care for whom the party was being given; Ouida Rathbone was giving a Party and that was enough!

But these social diversions were only the icing on the cake. My real interest was in the studio in Culver City. I was delighted when the call came to get to work. Our director was Jack Conway, a gaunt Irishman with a long, wistful face. He made things easier for me by saying modestly that his chief hope was to keep my whole performance as good as my test had been. This, I knew, was to reassure me; I was well aware that it would have to be much better. But he couldn't have been kinder. He freed me from camera-consciousness by telling me to forget about the camera and play as I would in a theatre which had only one row of seats. He'd watch out for the rest.

Despite my confidence in Mr. Conway, the first day before the camera was an agonizing experience. We started with a scene which occurred in the middle of the picture. Frantically nervous, I simply could not remember the few lines I had to speak; the camera seemed a juggernaut which would roll forward and crush me if I failed to please it. This silly fright wore off before long. My chief problem was to remember that round eye of the camera. Mitch Lewis, who played my husband, used to whisper, "Don't act for me back here; that little machine in front of you is all that matters."

Then there was the knitting. Never having held a knitting needle, I had to learn how. MGM sent a woman to teach me. Early and late I practiced, carrying my knitting bag everywhere and concentrating in silent frenzy on achieving speed and smoothness. I had many free days between studio calls due to the fact that there were actually two stories: the English one, centering around Sidney Carton, and the French one which focussed on the characters involved in the Revolution. It seems incredible that in my first ten weeks in Hollywood I actually worked only seven days. On off-days, like a busman on a holiday, I would haunt the studio watching the work of Ronald Colman, Edna May Oliver, Basil Rathbone and other interesting players in that truly remarkable cast. There was so much for me to learn by studying their economy of method. Holding the eyes steadily open was one thing I noted while watching Mr. Colman: I had not realized how often one blinks until I saw my own rushes at the showing of the first day's work in a small viewing room. I learned to keep my eyes steadily open.

It was helpful to be facing my first camera ordeal behind a character makeup. (It made me less self-conscious.) Vocally I kept remembering one word: simplify. As the shooting progressed there were out-of-door scenes in the streets of Paris, through which two thousand extras poured. On those days some twenty cameras rolled simultaneously. Visitors filled a small wooden platform; I met stars, newspaper people, distinguished foreigners; other stars working on the lot would slip over to see the excitement.

My sister, Rose, had come out to join me for the fun. I had found a treasure of treasures in a combination secretary-girl-Friday and stand-in, the youthful, capable mother of a lovely girl whose name has since become very familiar: Jinks Falken-burg. Micky herself was an ex-champion in amateur tennis. Jinks, as well as her two younger brothers, had practically been born with tennis racquets in their hands, and they seldom put them down. All three children did an occasional day's work in pictures; Jinks had appeared in a few small parts. She had the beauty of a young Diana, bypassing the gawkiness of the mid-teens through the coordination which stemmed from her athletic prowess. An excellent swimmer as well as tennis player, she actually was the ideal "all-round American girl" which she grew to symbolize for her fans.

In mid-June, in the midst of a busy afternoon's shooting, I suddenly remembered that it was my birthday. Deputizing to Micky the assembling of "the makings" I invited all and sundry to repair to my dressing room at the end of the day to help me celebrate my first birthday in movieland. Cameramen, hair-dressers, actors and assistant directors, all sat on the floor as well as on the few available chairs. The ace cameraman, Ollie Marsh, who seldom spoke a word, yielding to the potency of Micky's milk (?) punch (made in the water cooler) broke his usual taciturnity for the first time in our acquaintance. Brian Aherne, picked up en route to the dressing room, sang us an

Irish song. Everyone was very gay. It was ten o'clock before we finally left the lot. I did not know until later that entertaining on the "lot" was "verboten." I guess allowances were made for a greenhorn.

On my arrival home the clerk said, "Miss Yurka, there's the biggest box of flowers I've ever seen on your sofa." And it was. Six-foot stems on magnificent American beauties and a card saying: "What a hell of a way to spend your sixtieth birthday!" signed: Jack Conway. I thought it was a lovely way!

The fight scene between Edna May Oliver and myself took two days to shoot—and after it was over Miss Oliver and I were definitely spent. Fights between women on the screen have been done often since then and with increasing ferocity, but ours was the first and caused a mild stir. Getting an effect of violence without the actual use of it is a tricky business but even so it was a very strenuous physical involvement. When it was all over both Miss Oliver and I took to our beds for several days to recuperate and she swore she would never do another such scene. I was rather proud of myself because after I was "killed" I remem· bered to keep my eyes wide open as I was told happens in real life. It was most effective.

The original three weeks' guarantee on my contract was forgotten as months slipped by. Twenty weeks for one's first movie! It was almost unbelievable. Four months were spent in actual shooting; one delay because of the director's illness caused a replacement, and for one month I had to stand by for the preview date. I continued to be asked to gay parties; Hollywood can be very gracious when word has gotten around that you are to join its constellation.

Much as I enjoyed playing the grim, bitter Mme. Defarge, she created one impression it is unlikely I shall ever overcome. Having made my first success as a "meanie" it was only natural that I would never play anything on the screen other than a sadistic harridan with dark hair, wearing drab rags and presumably drinking hot blood for breakfast. I did contribute something of my own to the character I was depicting: my conception of her as a symbol of oppressed humanity—of a creature who had been wronged and saddened as well as embittered, as she stolidly and determinedly built up her list of names in her knitted record. I had never played anything remotely like this in the theatre. I tried to counteract the effect of my screen role by taking great pains to look well-groomed and chic whenever I visited the studio. Long afterwards Mr. Colman told me that he was always a bit puzzled by the recurrent visits on the set of a tall, blonde woman whom he never associated with the relentless knitter of the French sequences. If one is to choose, I suppose there is comfort to be derived from not having to look like that in private life. But I could wish one were not so readily typed and then restricted to that type.

Colman's sensitive talent expressed on the screen a charm which characterized his actual personality to a notable degree. I never really got to know him; the inconsecutive shooting of scenes is not conducive to the camaraderie which usually develops in a theatre company. It is a little surprising when one finally sees the finished picture to find friends in the cast of whose presence one had not even been aware, actors who had finished their stint and gone on to other studios. Basil Rathbone's baleful and aristocratic Marquis d'Evrémonde had been shot in June; in September I was still "Defarging." He couldn't believe it. "I've done four pictures since then," he said.

We finally reached the Tribunal sequence, my big challenge. An entire stage which usually accommodated several sets was given over to a reproduction of the Palace of Justice in eighteenth century Paris. Over two thousand extras filled the galleries—villainous looking types for the most part, having been selected for just that reason. I sat in their midst awaiting my cue for the big scene. There was excitement in the air. Even at that early hour the visitors' stand was crowded. I spied Clark Gable playing hooky from *Mutiny on the Bounty,* director Reuben Mamoulian, even David Selznick, who very seldom appeared on our set, although he was producing the picture. My nerves were tense; I knew that this scene would make or break my performance. The first "take" earned a burst of applause from visitors and extras. This was gratifying but carried a dangerous implication. I knew that I had played to them instead of to the relentless camera, only a few feet away. So, calling silently on my guardian angel, and audibly on Jack Conway for help, I did the scene once again, keeping the intensity but contracting the range. Once again we did it. The results must have been satisfactory for my director kissed me with tears in his eyes as he helped me off the platform. And then whispered quizzically, "You've just acted yourself out of a week's work, Baby; that's how long I expected to spend on this scene." We had done the whole sequence in less than two hours.

As I was passing the stand where the "jury," most of them with cauliflower ears and beetling brows, were still munching the meat and dry bread they had been eating in the scene, one of them hailed me. "Hey, lady, you a stage actress?" "Yes," I replied, "I've acted on the stage." Turning to his neighbor he said, "See? I told you she ain't no five-dollar-a-day extra." His pal had evidently thought that one of the tattered crowd had suddenly been given a break.

Everything for the next few weeks seemed to point to a happy and prosperous future for me in this new world of make-believe. There was a customary period of waiting before "option time." I had been told, via the grapevine, that a contract was "in the bag," so, in a suitably opulent mood, I accepted an invitation to go to Palm Springs for a week's visit.

Eventually the preview took place. There was applause again, after the Tribunal scene. Everyone congratulated me. Immediately after, I left for New York on the midnight train to clear up some business matters, leaving my agent to attend to the MGM contract.

The change from California sunshine (there was no smog in those days) to the wintry blasts and slushy pavements of New York was not too pleasant. Impatiently I awaited the wire my agent had promised to send me the moment he secured the studio's signature. It never came. No satisfactory explanation was ever forthcoming, other than that MGM had "reconsidered." But I told Rose of a remark my agent quoted as coming from an important executive: "When we do another French Revolution picture we'll get her again—even if we have to pay her twice as much." They had no other French Revolution pictures scheduled. The idea of free-lancing, gambling on what parts might be left over when contract players were safely cast, did not appeal to me. I remained in the East. It was a costly decision.

CHAPTER **18**

"IF YOU THINK YOU'RE GOOD, TRY SAGINAW!"

$\mathcal{S}$ OMETIMES A MINOR incident, a fragment of experience lodges in one's mind and bears fruit many years later. It was something of this sort which was to lead to one of the most interesting and satisfying of my undertakings in the theatre.

Shortly after World War I, following the closing of *The Americans in France,* I boarded the *Aquitania* en route for Europe. Also on board was an old acquaintance, Jan Masaryk, son of Thomas Garrigue Masaryk, the president of the new Republic of Czechoslovakia. Jan and I spent many pleasant hours together, often in the company of Porter Emerson Browne, the playwright. He and Jan engaged in lengthy discussions about the political problems of the young Czech Republic, and I listened eagerly to their stimulating exchange of ideas.

One morning, as Jan and I were walking the deck, a lady whom I knew very slightly stopped me to ask if I would be willing to participate in the ship's concert. (It was to raise money for the Seamen's Fund.) I told the lady that—alas—there was nothing I could do. There we were in the middle of the Atlantic ocean and I without a parlor trick to my name! Jan, however, made short shrift of my refusal. "Of course you will appear," he said. "You will sing a group of Czech folk songs, and I will play your accompaniments."

He was an excellent pianist and musician, having in his

youth, he told me proudly, "bummed" (his word) his way across the whole of the United States, playing the piano in movie houses, in night clubs, for anyone who would pay him enough for him to live on. Overruling my objections, he led me down to the ballroom to an idle piano. We ran through the little repertory of songs that I had known from childhood, adding, at his insistence, one song which he proceeded to teach me. It had only two verses so it was not hard to catch it by ear. "Pod Tim Naśěm Okenečkem" (Underneath Our Little Window) was one of his father's favorites, he told me.

On the night of the benefit my modest effort was well received, especially the new song. When the second verse ended he said quickly over his shoulder, "Sing it again." Then he proceeded to improvise a variation on the accompaniment. Four times he repeated this performance, each improvisation more colorful, more brilliant than the last. I could have murdered him! But we had a great success, so I had to forgive him.

Rather than feeling crushed by the elder Masaryk's fame, as is so often the case with the sons of great men, Jan expressed his love and admiration of his father frankly. One day he told me that he had something in his cabin that he wished to show me. Etchings!—flashed through my mind. But I was quickly ashamed of my flippant suspicions. For what he handed to me was a beautifully framed photograph of his father, "my old man," he said with feeling and pride.

His humanitarian impulses were not confined to speeches—they were genuine, deeply felt, and expressed in a delicate sensibility in his everyday behavior. One day the group of American sophisticates with whom we were spending our evenings were being taken on a tour of steerage quarters. Jan said to me firmly, "You do not go down there; you do not stare at those poor people," he urged, "let them go without you." I understood and shared his revulsion. One does not go and stare at people as if they were animals in the zoo. Nor had I forgotten that my own parents had come to America as steerage passengers.

To know Jan Masaryk was a great privilege. He was warm, approachable, lively and full of fun. It was all the more painful, therefore, to read in Marcia Davenport's *Too Strange for Phantasy* a poignant account of the sadness which engulfed him during those last years before his tragic death. All that capacity for joy and life extinguished—what a waste, what a loss!

For me, that shipboard performance was only a beginning. In the years that followed, I was haunted by the idea that as an actress I should be able to do something on such occasions. (This was long before the "one-man show" idea had been seized upon by almost everybody who could get away with it.) I felt that it was disgraceful for an entertainer not to be able to entertain alone.

It was many years, however, before the incentive to do something about this presented itself. One day an agent called me to say that Fanny Hurst, who was under his management, was unable to fulfill a scheduled lecture appearance in Newark, New Jersey. "Would you be willing to pinch-hit for her?" he asked. I said that I would provided I could try out some material I had in mind. I had dreamed up a program of scenes, I said, selected almost entirely from plays in which I had appeared at various times. "Could I do that?" I asked. He said he didn't care what I did so long as I filled the date for him.

Concentrating like mad, I whipped up a program. In making it up I used the pattern which most singers follow: they start with early classical music, then progress through the famous lieder and eventually end up with contemporary composers. I planned a sequence of scenes (almost all of which I had played in full productions) which would start with the Titan Greeks, move on into the Elizabethan splendors of Shakespeare, then into the sophisticated comedy of Molière and Congreve, followed by Oscar Wilde and Shaw. The program would close with the final scene between Elizabeth and Essex from Maxwell Anderson's *Elizabeth the Queen*. It was, at least, in the grand style of the classic scenes. When I wrote Maxwell Anderson for permission to use the scene and inquired about the royalty payment for its use, he responded with charming modesty: "There will be no royalty charge. I am happy to be in such proud company." I was touched.

Two weeks later I walked out to face my first audience as a "One-Woman Show." I was a "seuliste" at last.

A heavy snowstorm almost obliterated the roads as my friend Muriel Hutchison drove me over to Newark. "Thank God there'll be nobody there on a night like this," I muttered to myself. But when we arrived, Muriel brought back word that the house was sold out and already packed at 8 P.M. "They are going to hate me! I simply can't face them!" I wailed. Muriel wisely said nothing. Once I had donned my beautiful Paris gown I felt a bit better, but I was still paralyzed with stage fright when I plunged into the awful emptiness of that bare stage. Over five hundred repetitions of that evening's program have not obliterated the memory of that night's hideous stage fright. In the hurried preparation for my experiment I had not had time to realize that there would be no friendly actor to whom I could send a frantic glance, nothing on that bare stage but myself, some great playwrights (most of them dead and how I envied them that) and God!

The applause after the Greek scenes, from *Electra* and *Lysistrata,* told me little. American audiences are notably polite. Shakespeare's bawdy humor in the Nurse's scene in Juliet's garden brought heart-warming laughter. (My manager in St. Augustine, much later, told me of an exchange between a mother and her daughter who were sitting in front of him. The daughter, thank God! giggled at the fat old Nurse's lines. Her mother whispered vehemently: "Don't laugh, dear! This is Shakespeare!" Portia's first dialogue with Nerissa evoked more laughter. The eighteenth-century scenes and Wilde's Lady Bracknell in *The Importance of Being Ernest* carried the mood further, and Shaw's sure-fire *Candida* worked her usual magic.

A pause gave the audience time for its inevitable indulgence in a smoke, then they returned for the tragic, powerful scene which closes the Maxwell Anderson play—and my program. This scene won heartening applause. All in all, it seemed that the program had entertainment value, and I was encouraged that it might lead to something. For once I was not disappointed.

The Newark evening proved so successful that word of it reached New York. The top agent in the lecture field (he represented Mrs. Roosevelt and Winston Churchill, whose contract called for a case of champagne to be furnished daily by the agent!) approached me. He offered me a long season with drawing rooms furnished on trains whenever these were available, as well as other minor privileges. It was a good contract (though no champagne), including a sizeable guarantee. There was one disadvantage; I would have to commit myself six months in advance and pay a large penalty if I should wish to cancel. This meant I could accept no offers in either pictures or the theatre. I could not make up my mind to accept. While I was still debating, something occurred which galvanized me into a decision.

During the run of *Romeo and Juliet* a tall, poetic-looking young author of my acquaintance came backstage one night with a play which, he said, he had written for me. Naturally it had a classical theme. I read it that same night and thought it very good indeed. Next morning I congratulated him and said that I would help him to place it. I submitted it to several producers. One or two reacted favorably, but—! Finally, one expressed great enthusiasm for it. He thanked me for bringing him the play. A few weeks later he announced its production, starring another actress. Neither he nor the author ever sent me word of any kind. The day I saw the announcement in the *Times* I really saw red.

"What is the use of my wading through dozens of manuscripts?" I wailed. "When I do find a good one, someone else gets the part! What in God's name is the matter? He said this play was written for ME! To Hell with it all!" Rose listened patiently to my diatribe. Then, although it was drizzling, I jammed on my hat, went out, and walked around the reservoir in Central Park until I was exhausted. On my return home I seized a pen and signed the contract for the one-woman tour, going out immediately to mail it lest I should change my mind. I have never regretted that decision.

The solo show offered an exciting new challenge to my acting resources, even though I had already played almost all of the scenes in full productions of the various plays. Actually that fact was very helpful, for in my mind's eye I was seeing, not a bare stage with only myself exposed in the middle of it, but was subconsciously visualizing the settings in which I had previously played the scenes; I could see my fellow actors or actresses moving about on the stage, I could even visualize the curtains which had mercifully closed every so often. In my mind's eye I saw it all—yet that first night when I walked onto the bare stage in Newark I did not realize that it was all there.

I had done relatively little "trouping" in small towns; now I made up for it with a vengeance. For four successive seasons I did tours which took me from Maine to Texas and from Palm Beach to Hawaii and which brought me in contact with new and stimulating audiences. I found a fresh, unsated public immensely responsive to "live" acting; a public made up in many instances of young people who had never seen actors except as shadows on a screen. I also found them as quick and responsive —especially to comedy—as any audiences before which the entire production of these plays had been presented. They missed no points despite the bare stage and the lack of other players. It was an experience in communication such as I had never been called upon to make. These bare stages had to be peopled by some twelve or fifteen characters and I had to be all of them!

To find the means to describe how such a performance arrests the attention and awakens the imagination of audiences is not easy, especially audiences of such varied character: young people, mature people, those who have experienced "live theatre," many who have not. I have evoked both laughter and wonderful absorbed silence from students in Hawaii and from sophisticated New Yorkers.

My first tour started in Fort Wayne, Indiana. Then I worked my way east—one night in each town—averaging four performances each week. One week I did seven. I never knew what my stage would be like. One night it would be the bare platform of a lecture hall with nothing but harsh overhead lighting; another, a raised dais in a hotel ballroom. Then, when one least expected it, I'd find a fully equipped theatre with an exquisite backdrop, colored footlights and "baby spots" galore. Under these changing circumstances, one learns to be adaptable. Finally nothing fazed me, not even when I had to perform between the choir stalls in a New England church.

In selecting my material I had naturally chosen scenes in which the character I had portrayed in the stage production dominated. Then the supporting characters were cut down to essential plot lines. The change of voice-color was sufficient to indicate who was speaking. I made almost no gestures; used no scenery; only two pieces of furniture were required: a garden bench for *Romeo and Juliet* and a formal chair for *Elizabeth the Queen*.

Before each scene I outlined the plot and commented briefly on the characters, thus meeting my audiences in my own person as well. As I grew more confident I began to enjoy interpreting such varied styles as tragical, comical, historical, pastoral and modern. It was as though I were taking a miniature repertory of my best parts to audiences I could never have reached in so many different roles. And I began to feel that I was bringing great theatre to hundreds of people who had never experienced it.

Jessie Franklin Turner designed for me a green and gold lamé gown, a straight, graceful sheath of no particular period, which lent itself to the classic as well as to the modern plays. For the Greek scenes she designed a wonderful olive-green velvet wrap to go over it and to give sweep and line to the movement of the body; its lovely flowing folds suggested classic drapery. For the more modern scenes I simply removed the wrap. One could face any audience in such a costume!

My first program and my favorite I called "The Arc of the Theatre." It included scenes from the following plays:

Lysistrata	Aristophanes
Electra	Sophocles
Romeo and Juliet	Shakespeare
The Way of the World	Congreve
The Rivals	Sheridan
Hedda Gabler	Ibsen
Elizabeth the Queen	Anderson

Later I used other material for variety, adding Molière, Wilde, and Shaw. When the Town Hall Club of New York, in my second year, invited me to perform for the third time, they asked whether I could do a program of modern scenes. I found that I would have to pay royalties for the use of even fairly old plays. By the time I paid royalties to the six or seven authors whose scenes I would use, there would be very little left for the performing artist. Perhaps that is one reason why I like dead authors best.

As the tour brought me nearer to my New York dates, stage fright crept up on me once more. I felt that sophisticated New Yorkers might not like the form of the program—that its appeal was essentially to out-of-town audiences. I was pleasantly reassured by my three New York appearances: at Town Hall, at Columbia University's McMillan Theatre, and at the Brooklyn Institute of Arts and Sciences.

John Mason Brown, distinguished critic and lecturer, re-

viewed the performance, using for his headline: ONE-WOMAN
SHOW GAINS DISTINGUISHED RECRUIT. He wrote in
part:

As a distinguished entry into the field of the "one-woman" show
. . . she achieves her aim by sympathetically communicating the
intention and mood of each of the famous scenes she essays. . . .
Amazingly enough, because one does not think of her as a comedi-
enne, she was at her best as Millamant and Portia. . . . Her aim, as
she expressed it, is to challenge the imagination . . . by presenting
a show given, as she says, "sans props, sans costumes, sans scenery,
sans everything but great playwrights" . . . each of her characterizations was received with genuine outbursts of applause.

In following seasons I experimented with fresh material, doing the Fotheringay Forest Scene from Schiller's *Maria Stuart*
and, of all things, my old friend *Magda*. Doing the denunciation
scene almost thirty years after the Belasco audition brought
home to me an interesting realization; several notes of what
Magda called "the whole scale of passions which bring us to
maturity" had been sounded in my life in the interim. Never
did I do that scene without seeing in my mind's eye that lanky
youngster with her pea-green face, without hearing a gentle-
voiced, white-haired man saying, "The timbre of the voice is
good; now let's see if you can act." It was now several years since
Mr. Belasco had died. Each time I did the *Magda* scene it was as
though I were lighting a little candle in his memory.
    One could not pass through so many small towns and meet so
many alert, well-informed people, without realizing of what fine
material the warp and woof of our American life is—for the
most part—made up. Let no one nurse the delusion that living
in "the sticks" precludes a lively and informed interest in what
goes on in the world of arts and letters. In Hiram, Ohio, I enjoyed some of the best conversation I have ever been part of
with Dr. Kenneth Brown and some members of his staff. In Den-
ton, Texas, three thousand girls made the program run fifteen
minutes overtime because of the laughs evoked by the delicate
eighteenth-century comedy scenes.
    At the University of Minnesota I gave my first real lecture to
several thousand students. The subject was "The Ever Expand-

ing Theatre"—a flexible title if ever there was one; I was free to say anything. I wrote to Rose:

Such a welcome as I got! And laughs! There was a microphone so I could be very colloquial; the lecture was broadcast in both St. Paul and Minneapolis. Naturally, in discussing the theatre as I have known it, I talked a good deal about myself, for which I apologized. They seemed to enjoy the personal note. The whole thing was a far cry from the performances of the yellow-haired youngster who used to stand on the teacher's platform in Jefferson school in St. Paul singing, for an occasional visitor, "There is a Green Hill Far Away."

The following evening my "Arc of the Theatre" program had formidable competition. On the steps of the Capitol in St. Paul, speaking "for free," was one Franklin D. Roosevelt. It cut down my attendance to only 1500 or so—a sizable audience at that.

James Gray of the St. Paul *Press* crossed the Mississippi to see the performance and had this to say:

In the Northrup Auditorium, Blanche Yurka gave her program called "The Arc of the Theatre." . . . The selections from these plays have been cleverly arranged to give variety of mood and pace and passion to the program. It gets off to an eloquent start with the at once witty and eloquent speech of Lysistrata stating woman's case against war. It reaches its first depth of emotion in the urn speech from "Electra." One of the Nurse's teasing and ribald passages from "Romeo and Juliet" provides a moment of relaxation. Miss Yurka demonstrates an unsuspected aptitude for artificial comedy as Millamant in "The Way of the World." Hedda's dalliance with Judge Brack provides a nice contrast in sophistication and makes way . . . for the passionate simplicity and . . . emotion of . . . Elizabeth's scene of parting from Essex in Maxwell Anderson's play.

It has been Miss Yurka's good fortune to appear in plays of real significance . . . she is so adaptable that she can either serve the theatre that exists, or create a theatre of her own. Resolution, imagination and a real creative vitality are in command.

It was in Minneapolis that a young university student who worked the curtain for me said, after the Congreve scene from

The Way of the World, "Gosh, Miss Yurka, I've just been studying that play and I don't remember that scene." To which I
replied, "Well, honey, you go back and read the play again because I give you my word I didn't write it." But I really did feel
it a privilege to bring to life, perhaps for the first time for some
of my listeners, dramatic values of humor and pathos which had
hitherto lain dormant on library shelves.

I drove across the High Bridge to St. Paul on a pilgrimage to
the cottage where all of us except Mila had been born. Again I
wrote to Rose:

Old Man River is impressive as ever, but oh, the little house looks
very shabby indeed, and so small! I am puzzled as to how on earth
mother and father managed to live their full, rich life in that
"baracek" (little shack). The whole neighborhood has gone to seed;
I doubt if a pot of paint has been used in the entire block for years!
So many pictures swept through my mind: the icy outside storeroom where the apple barrel was kept; the parlor with its big stove,
where Tony and I would sit, our faces burning, our backs freezing,
while I made up stories for him after supper; the kitchen where
you and I used to sing dolefully "Forsaken, forsaken, forsa-a-ken
a-a-am I" while we did the supper dishes; Mama saying, "If you'd
sing a gayer song you'd get them done quicker." The pitiful little
bathroom and our excitement when it was first installed. I stood
in our little bedroom, where Tony used to sleep on the couch on
the other side of the room. I remember how he used to creep over
into our bed and then complain "but you stop talking about interesting things when I come over" and then fall asleep and have
to be carried back into his own bed. We managed to do a lot of
living in those few little rooms.

My one-woman tour progressed eastward. In Hartford, looking across the vast stage of the Bushnell Auditorium which
could comfortably seat two symphony orchestras, panic seized
me. How was my lone figure, in that vast space, to hold the attention of that audience of three thousand people? But I was
wearing again that superb black satin, gold-flecked evening dress
from Paris; it gave me, as always, the confidence which only a
great dress by a great French couturier can give a woman.
Breathing a deep silent prayer I swept on stage with an air of

assurance which I was far from feeling. By the time I had done a scene or two I knew they liked me.

It was in Hartford, too, that I again saw the gifted Polish-American sculptor, Ziolkowski, whom I had first met during the Ann Arbor Festival. His fine busts of Paderewski and of Enesco were voted the most popular examples of American sculpture shown at the New York World's Fair in 1940. During my Hartford visit he worked on a head of me in marble. It developed into a most interesting piece of work but one which I, and others who saw it later, felt anticipated my old age to a rather disconcerting degree. Miss St. Gaudens, sister of the famous sculptor, made that comment on it when I met her next door at Paul Manship's studio. Mr. Ziolkowski was hurt, I am afraid, by my lack of enthusiasm. But one day he will be avenged—being the really gifted artist that he is his work will live and I shall enjoy a kind of anonymous immortality as the subject of "that interesting head of an old woman, done by the artist in his youth."

Alternate programs had been arranged by me for use in those delightfully appreciative communities which called me back for a return date. It was lucky I had this fresh material in reserve, for in Saginaw, Michigan, I had a unique opportunity to use it.

The Saginaw sponsors had selected my original Arc program. One of the sponsors, a pleasant gentleman, met me at the station and drove me at once to the theatre to see about lights and curtain cues. I was charmed with everything: the newly built moviehouse, intimate and richly furnished, provided me with a choice of beautiful backdrop curtains, a luxury I seldom encountered in my wanderings. I chose a silvery velvet against which my olive-green gown would be most effective, gave the curtain man his cue-sheet and instructions, and sallied forth to see the town.

Over a cup of tea my host warned me: "You know, Miss Yurka, this town has the reputation of being a very tough audience." "Really?" I asked. My inflection was noncommittal. He asked, "Have you ever been backstage at the Palace Theatre in New York?" I hadn't, though I'd often sat out front in its heyday of vaudeville. "Well," he continued, "there's a message over the keyrack, written in indelible pencil which says: 'If you think you're good, try Saginaw!'" I laughed nervously. On these tours one had to nurse one's ego a little, otherwise how could one face an audience single-handed? He left me at my hotel to rest a bit.

That evening I walked on to the beautifully lighted stage determined to give them my best. I did. I gave them not only my best, but finished by giving them my all! The program ran its usual length, about an hour and a half. The applause was polite but scarcely what would be called an ovation, even by an actor. I took a few curtain calls and the house-lights went up. Not a soul stirred to leave. "Better give 'em some more, lady; they're expectin' it," said the lean-faced, hard-bitten stage hand who was handling the curtain. So we lowered the lights, and I gave them a scene from my second program. Again, polite applause, and again they sat! Bewildered, I turned to my curtain man. "How am I going to let them know it's over?" I asked. "It's like this," he said, shifting his wad of chewing gum from one cheek to the other. "Notice that clock on the side of the wall? This is a movie-house, you know. They're used to a show that lasts until eleven, so you better just go ahead and give it to 'em, 'cause they're goin' to sit there 'till then."

Like the character in the Russian story who kept throwing children to the pursuing wolves, I trotted myself out and gave them the entire second program. It was the two-for-one system with a vengeance! Only the members of that audience who happen to read these pages will ever know what they got for their money. "If you think you're good, try Saginaw!"

En route south, I decided to stop over in New Orleans. I knew no one there but I had never seen the old city, so, depositing my bags at the hotel, I went round to dine, in true tourist fashion, at Antoine's. The "oysters Rockefeller" and the pompano were quite as delicious as they are famous; the wine, of course, was excellent. During the dinner I asked the waiter to direct me to a theatre. He mentioned one or two movie-houses. "No! No, I want theatre," I insisted, "real theatre; isn't there a famous one right around here somewhere?" He consulted a guide-book. There, sure enough, just a block or two away, was the one I was seeking, the picturesque old Theatre du Vieux Carré, built many, many years ago. Its confines now include, as a coffee room, the adjacent tavern in which Jean Lafitte and his pirates used to assemble for their grog.

It was a clear moonlit evening; the old quarter looked mellow and intriguing. I was delighted to find the theatre lighted and a performance in progress. The young man in charge was persuaded to admit me, although it was open only to members, and all seats were filled. I had to sit on the balcony steps. During intermission I wandered into the patio around which the theatre was built. A charming fountain, banked at one side with a jacaranda tree and flowers, was bathed in filtered moonbeams. As I started to return to the steps on which I had been allowed to sit, the young man stopped me. "Wouldn't you like to come back afterward and meet our director?" he suggested.

At the stage door we met him—big, burly Bernard Szold—as gentle and expansive a soul as I have ever encountered anywhere. I had known his interesting sister, Bernadine, in New York and Hollywood, which made us friends at once. After the performance, he suggested a moonlit stroll through the old quarter. We wandered about the silvered streets, he pointing out historic old houses which took on added mystery and romance in the dim light. No other city in America has such tangible charm as this! It is enveloped in the glamorous aura of another way of life.

After wandering by lacy balconies until the early hours my new-found friend had a sudden inspiration. He stopped the car in front of a wooden door in a dark wooden building. "This is Roark Bradford's house. Let's go in." I protested. "You can't barge in on a man at 3 A.M." "Oh, yes you can, on him; he never goes to bed before four," said Bernard, his hand already pulling the old-fashioned bell-pull. And he was right. The author of "John Henry" peered out and greeted me cordially. Through the long dark alley leading to the back of a quaint old house we followed him. In the comfortable book-strewn living room I was greeted with a startled, "Well, for God's sake! Blanche!" It was Sam Byrd, the actor who had played for years in *Tobacco Road*. He was in New Orleans consulting with the author about the play they were planning to do using the "John Henry" stories. Sam had scored a great personal success in Erskine Caldwell's earthy exposé of certain parts of the deep south. He was searching for further equally rewarding material.

I moved on westward to San Antonio, Corpus Christi, Oklahoma City, then to Tulsa, thriving and surprisingly modern, its skyscrapers set in the midst of vast plains which stretched in all directions. If ever a town did not need to shoot up into the air, it was that one! Yet they had to have their skyscrapers. It was dur-

ing my stay-over in Tulsa that Mr. Isley, one of the official hosts
of my engagement there, invited me to spend a day on Pawnee
Bill's Ranch where we could lunch with Buffalo Bill's "old partner." Mr. Isley asked whether he might bring along his daughter, Phyllis, and her fiancé, as both were very stage-struck and
eager to meet me. He told me he had encouraged their talents,
sending them out on tour through Texas in plays like *Smilin'
Through* and other suitable vehicles. I found them both shy
youngsters with charming manners; the boy blond and reticent,
the girl dark and glowing with a kind of hidden fire. From the
back seat she deprecated, with gracious modesty, her father's expressions of pride and faith in their futures. His faith was justified, for I was spending the day with two young people who, in a
few years, were to be known to movie fans as Jennifer Jones and
Robert Walker.

Atlantic City was my next date. Waking at daybreak I was
dazzled by a panorama of color. Sunlight flooded the sea and the
sky against which the two towers of the Traymore Hotel looked
like some fabulous dream palace in an oriental book of fairy
tales. One could grow lyrical over the green and copper of the
terraced towers outlined against the magenta of rippling water
—the strip of clear blue sky melting into delicate yellows and
mauves. But by the time the sun was up, wrapped, one might
say, in a business suit of gray clouds, the Traymore was just another huge hotel and I just a trouper with a train to catch.

CHAPTER 19

ELECTRA REBORN

THE COLSTON-LEIGH Bureau again signed me for the following season. Between tours I rested, flirting now and then with Hollywood. But no really good part was offered, and it seemed unwise to do a poor one and efface the strong impression made by Madame Defarge. This, for most actors, is a recurrent question: Whether to hold out consistently for good parts no matter how long one is idle, or to keep one's name before the public and producers by accepting whatever is offered. Too often, in my theatre career, I had resorted to the latter. I did not wish to repeat that mistake in the motion picture field.

And there was another complication. Signing up for six months in advance for my one-woman tours naturally created the impression that I had gone permanently into this branch of the entertainment field. I felt myself shut off from theatre contacts, hungering for the camaraderie of theatre-folk. Occasionally I found it in summer stock. Though playing in summer companies is seldom satisfactory, I have learned a great deal from some of these ventures. They provide contacts with a variety of directors and above all the opportunity to get away from type-casting and to play parts which a New York manager wouldn't take a chance on letting me do. In the Stuart Walker companies one even appeared occasionally in plays of high literary quality. Mostly, however, summer audiences wished to see comedies and colloquial plays, and these I have always enjoyed playing—plays like John Van Druten's *Distaff Side* and Mark Read's *Yes, My Darling Daughter*. It is unquestionably finding one's satisfaction the hard way, for the fact that a performance in stock actually emerges on Monday nights after one week's preparation is a minor miracle.

In one particular instance the difficulties to overcome were incredible. It was the production of *Lysistrata* which Bretaigne Windust staged at Suffern in the summer of 1936. I was playing for Billy Miles at the Stockbridge Playhouse in Massachusetts when I received a long distance call from Windy asking whether I could possibly open in *Lysistrata* on the following Monday in Suffern, if he were to send a car to pick me up Saturday after my performance. This would give me Sunday and Monday to rehearse with the company which would, meanwhile, rehearse with a substitute.

I agreed to do it. At midnight that Saturday Josh Logan's sister, Mary Lee (later Mary Lee Leatherbee) came for me. We arrived at Suffern at 4 A.M. on Sunday. Noon found us rehearsing on an incredibly small stage, and even this soon had to be relinquished to the crew. We rehearsed sketchily in various corners of the grounds. Josh Logan, who was to play the old magistrate, was due in from Hollywood Sunday, but didn't arrive until Monday noon.

However, miracles do occur, especially in the theatre. That Monday night we all sailed through the opening performance smoothly and with gusto; not a line muffed. José Ferrer was brilliantly funny as Kinesias, and the ballet at the end was most effective. Word swiftly circulated through the town and countryside that the show was a hit. Tickets went so rapidly that by Tuesday evening the house was sold out for the entire week. To this day I don't understand how it was all done.

That same summer Melville Burke was directing at the Lakewood Theatre in Skowhegan and asked me to come up to do *The Wild Duck*. I had not been back there since our tryout of *The Squall*. This seemed an opportune time to keep my longstanding promise to do *The Wild Duck* for him. He asked me whether I could find him someone to play Hjalmar, always a casting problem. Ideally, the actor should be tall, handsome, with a full round voice: and, according to Relling's description of him in the last act, " a shop girl's ideal of manly beauty . . . with his sympathetic voice and his talent for declaiming other people's thoughts . . . and other people's words." It takes an actor to portray the intellectual nit-wit Ibsen had created.

Suddenly I had an inspiration. Vincent Price was just finishing his personal triumph as Prince Albert to Miss Hayes' lovely Victoria Regina. I knew Vincent was ambitious as well as intelligent. I got him on the phone. Carefully omitting any mention of the length of the part, I dwelled on how "fat" it was, full of comedy, too. Then I broke it to him that we would have to leave by boat Sunday afternoon right after his Saturday night closing in *Victoria Regina.*

Sweetly and firmly he declined. His parents were coming East to join him for an oft-postponed holiday. He had disappointed them twice, he said, and simply couldn't do it again. There was his apartment to be closed up for the summer, etc. etc. Gently he reiterated, "Honey, I simply can't do it though I'd love to."

I had exhausted most of my arguments, so I took a long breath (and a long chance with his friendship) and said, "Vincent, you can't afford to pass up this great part. You've too much to learn. Having begun by playing so big a part as Albert has put you on the spot; you will have to prove a lot in your next assignment." It worked. A long silence and then—"All right, you win! When does the boat leave? God knows how I'll do it, but I'll be there" —and I heard a soft "damn you" at the end. It was only when the Fall River boat was in mid-stream next afternoon that I really believed he would come. But his face when he saw the thick five-act manuscript made me scuttle to my stateroom for safety.

The living conditions at Lakewood Colony had improved considerably since my previous visit in 1926. The owner had kept pace with his growing success, and his Colony reflected it in all the details of living quarters and working conditions. The dressing rooms were much improved; a toilet had been installed backstage; the cottages where the actors were housed, were charming; a smartly decorated tea room served excellent food.

I renewed my contact with the Cummings family, whose guest I had been in 1926 during the tryout of *The Squall.* Eleven years had intervened between my two visits to Skowhegan. Billy, the oldest son, had developed into an accomplished artist, having given up sculpture for painting in which he showed an authority far beyond his twenty-two years. There was evidence of this in the portraits exhibited in the theatre lobby. I was impressed with their vigorous handling. So when Billy, very diffidently, during *The Wild Duck* week, asked whether I would give him a few sittings for a portrait study of Gina Ekdal, I reluctantly consented. Sitting for a portrait usually bores me. These sittings, however, were anything but dull. We talked quietly, and I was frequently intrigued by the wisdom and maturity of his ideas. Occasionally Vincent joined us. He had stayed on to play *Parnell*, the next week's bill.

Sprawling his length across the couch, he would criticize Billy's work. Vincent had been an art instructor before his first lucky break into the theatre in England with *Victoria Regina*. His criticism, therefore, was of real value. Sometimes he would sit there making caricatures of me. I have always thought it important that actors have at least a bowing acquaintance with the sister arts. One's awareness of the technique back of all good work becomes more keen; invaluable impressions are stored away for future use in one's own field. Once, when I was playing *The White Sister* in stock a friend who was a Catholic asked me how I had learned to hold my hands in a certain way which, it seemed, was characteristic of "a religious." I could only think that it derived from the many paintings of sacred subjects which had left their impression on my mind.

It was while playing in the original production of *The Wild Duck*, in 1925, that I had spent a good deal of time among a group of people whose chief interest was painting and sculpture. The group included Gerald Kelly, the general manager of the old Wildenstein Galleries, and Robert McBride, the art critic. For me it was a refreshing and stimulating change of viewpoint. To them theatre was a bastard form of expression, especially on its interpretive side; they respected only creative work. Because *The Wild Duck* was a work of genius I was temporarily bathed in its glory, but as for actors and acting as a whole . . . well!

But I did gain Gerald Kelly's respect by one demonstration of perceptiveness. One evening as I sat just outside the small open showroom of the Wildenstein Galleries waiting for him to take me to dinner, I noticed in a shadowy corner an ovoid of white marble—one of the pieces in the current Brancusi show. Across the lower third of the egg-shaped mass was a simple design, unrealistic, more a suggestion of form than any actual pattern. When Gerald joined me I said, "I don't know why, but that egg-shaped thing has something Negroid about it." Said Gerald, smiling, "Why not? Brancusi has called it 'La Negresse Blanche' " (The White Negress).

Another incident occurred in the same gallery. An exhibition of highly abstract painting was being shown. Robert McBride, the critic, took me by the arm and led me to the far end of the gallery. "Now tell me," he said, "what, if anything, does that picture say to you? Tell me frankly." I studied it for a bit and then, in all honesty, replied, "Frankly, it says nothing to me. But I'm sure it's good. I feel as I might were I listening to someone who was speaking in Hindustani, for instance; I shouldn't understand what he was saying, but I should sense that he was saying it beautifully." He seemed satisfied. Next day he quoted it in his column. Painting, sculpture, music, even prize fighting —an actor can learn from all of them.

The portrait of Gina, made in Skowhegan, was a great success. Billy had caught something of the ageless earthiness of the character. A couple of years later we had proof that my enthusiasm over my young friend's work was not merely personal. A show given for charity in the Seligman Galleries featured portraits of players in character; the Gina portrait was hung along with the Speicher portrait of Katharine Cornell and paintings by Alexander Brook and George Bellows. Young Bill was excited to be in such distinguished company.

"You don't know," he confessed, "that when I was studying sculpture at Mrs. Ladd's studio that time in Boston, I made up my mind to learn to paint so that I could one day paint you as Gina." "But you were only eleven, Billy! You hadn't seen me as Gina at that time," I said. "Oh, yes, I had," he replied, "seven times." I could hardly believe my ears! Given a few million such eleven-year-olds the theatre wouldn't have a thing to worry about.

While in Skowhegan I had had a long distance telephone call from Garrett Leverton, head of the Speech Department at Northwestern University. Could I come to Evanston and do several one-woman appearances as a feature of the University's summer session? Since I had made plans to go west that summer anyway, I was delighted to accept.

A few years previously I had helped to launch the career of a gifted young friend, Muriel Hutchison. She had made swift strides, and as a result of her success on Broadway in Gilbert Miller's production of *The Amazing Dr. Clitterhouse,* starring Sir Cedric Hardwicke, Hollywood had sent for her. Rose and I decided to join Muriel in California.

There was another reason for going this particular summer. I had completed arrangements, at long last, to do a performance of *Electra* in the great open-air theatre at the University of California in Berkeley. Four years earlier, at the time of the New York production, Professor Popper, a member of the University of California faculty, had discussed with me the possibility of my doing it at the Berkeley Greek Theatre. The University was accustomed to having the visiting artists finance their own productions. Margaret Anglin had done so several years previously when her company had been playing in San Francisco, under her own management. (She made money, too!) But I was in no position to do this. Finally, after four years of persistent argument, Professor Popper's enthusiasm prevailed—the University finance committee agreed to underwrite a modest budget for a single performance to be given on September 18, 1937.

It was a quixotic adventure. We rehearsed for four weeks, although only one performance could be given. But I reminded myself that this was in the tradition of the ancient Greeks. They, too, made elaborate preparations for the single performance with which they celebrated their yearly Festivals.

When I reached Hollywood everything worked smoothly. Fortunately for me, Robert Henderson, the original producer of *Electra,* happened to be in Hollywood that summer. He was immensely helpful with the casting and the press exploitation. Mrs. Sara Teschke, a dramatic coach, assembled fifteen Los Angeles college girls for the Greek chorus and agreed to train them for rehearsals.

As part of the advance publicity, Mr. Henderson had arranged for us to be interviewed in San Francisco. In the gaily decorated Circus Bar at the Fairmount Hotel, we were met by John Hobart, drama critic of the *San Francisco Chronicle,* who was combining drinks with an interview. He was a cherubic-faced man who proved to have an engaging way of making one say things which, when immersed in the kindly ink he used, sounded quite amusing. I offer his interview as evidence of his ability to paint a pleasant pen-portrait:

The famous actress, whose production of "Electra" will take place in the Greek Theatre in Berkeley Saturday night, is a completely radiant person. She has a bubbling sense of humor, an attitude of friendliness for every one she meets and a broad, generous smile that flashes at you while she talks. She admits that she is scatter-brained, but her nonchalant disregard of time-tables and her love of doing what she wants to do on the spur of the moment are all part of her charm. Miss Yurka is one of those paradoxical women who can be serious one moment and exuberantly gay the next, and her conversation is a fantasy of changing moods. She will interrupt herself in the midst of an eloquent discussion of Sophoclean drama to recount a funny anecdote that has occurred to her or to express her passionate enthusiasm for baked Alaskan cod.

"Many people," said Miss Yurka when the subject of "Electra" was brought up, "think that Greek tragedy is too archaic, too formal, too full of antiquated theatre conversation to interest present day audiences. But that isn't true. The play is a volcano of emotions! And Electra's speech over the urn which she thinks contains her brother Orestes' ashes is one of the most moving speeches in dramatic literature."

The interview was over. Two hours later, her arms were encumbered not only with tea-baskets but with packages containing Chinese slippers, chopsticks, saucers, cups, and a long tassel. The shopping was still going on at 8:45; her train was scheduled to leave at 9. Miss Yurka caught it but only through the divine benevolence of the Gods, who must have a special affection for a woman who is as unique as she is lovely.

Back in Hollywood we plunged into rehearsals for *Electra* in earnest. As most of the actors lived there it had been arranged for us to rehearse in the small open-air theatre at Occidental College near Pasadena. Only the last three rehearsals were to take place at Berkeley. The preliminary work on the choruses had been so well done by Mrs. Sara Teschke that Morris Ankrum, who was to direct the production, could devote his attention to the principals. He had had considerable experience with open-air theatres. I asked him to be very critical of everything I did and his suggestions were helpful and inspiring.

Under the blazing August sun, that same sun that had beaten down on actors from Hellenic skies over two thousand years ago, we applied ourselves day after day to the joyous task of once more bringing the powerful old play to life. Just as everything had gone wrong in New York, so everything went well in California. Muriel Hutchison played the younger sister with an admirable mixture of weakness and defiance, her blonde beauty endowing the part with a glamour which was something new in this sort of production. In Hedviga Reicher we had a Clytemnestra who brought to the role of the queen-mother a melancholy yet baleful power which gave balance to the whole play.

And what a play it is! After two thousand years Electra lives today as vividly as when she first poured forth her hatred, her woes, under the sunlit skies of ancient Greece. In this work, Sophocles has left immortal proof of his genius. For an hour and a half the tension mounts steadily, pausing only briefly for the touching pathos of the urn speeches. I like only the Sophoclean version of the story. Euripides, in his softer romanticism misses, in my opinion, the powerful impact produced by his rival's play. In Sophocles' treatment the stark simplicity of his play-structure rises like great architecture, towering far above the lurid melodrama which the German poet Hugo von Hofmannsthal, for instance, recreated for modern audiences. The Greeks knew their craft; their legends do not, in my opinion, benefit by the revamping to which they have occasionally been subjected by modern authors. Who, for example, having seen Laurence Olivier's harrowing and superb Oedipus, could enjoy the tortured Freudianism of Jean Cocteau's *The Infernal Machine*? The Greeks need no revamping, they need only great actors in order to prove their power over audiences. They obviously had these in ancient days. And those early audiences revered their artists and their playwrights as the pride and glory of a great people.

At the Western Costume Company in Hollywood we found wonderful garments: for Clytemnestra a golden cloak and a gold-colored dress in which Hedviga, looking like some evil idol, moved with compelling majesty. Other costumes were equally right. The chorus wore wool in primitive colors which fell into sculpturesque patterns; in their midst the golden queen and the fair-haired younger sister robed in pale green stood out in telling contrast. Against this patter of color I was a drab figure in a crinkled brown cotton sheath covered with a ragged shawl of hunter's green.

At last we left for Berkeley for our final rehearsals. We were met by Professor Popper and Professor von Neumeyer, a noted authority on Greek drama; I loved his acrid humor and the dignity of his gaunt, upright figure.

We had enthusiastic cooperation from everyone, in one instance of a very practical nature. In order to get the lighting effects arranged, rehearsals had to be conducted after sundown, and we usually rehearsed until two or three in the morning. After midnight the fog rolled in cold and damp. When this was mentioned one day to some ladies who were entertaining a few of us at the San Francisco Women's City Club, they promptly organized themselves into a small committee to see to it that the tired, chilled actors should be refreshed at midnight with hot cocoa, coffee and sandwiches. As there were absolutely no facilities on the University grounds for feeding actors at that hour, the welcome which that station-wagon-commissary received was touching. The ladies drove it over from San Francisco themselves and served us at the sacrifice of their own rest and comfort. With such ministering angels the kingdom of heaven is populated, I am sure.

The final dress rehearsal lasted till almost dawn. I piled on coat after coat, scarf on scarf, as did everyone else to offset the chill dampness of the threatening fog. This fog had been our unspoken fear, our silent approaching enemy, whose appearance at that time of year was imminent.

I woke at noon next day to find the morning atmosphere warm but gray; the weather forecast discouraging. I raged inwardly; all those weeks of work directed toward this one performance! Muriel and I prayed; the fog must hold off for this one night more! At four o'clock the sun flooded through the Golden Gate, the night turned balmy and our hearts lifted. Melpomene, the muse of tragedy, must have lent an ear to our fervent prayers!

The Berkeley Greek Theatre, seating 5,000, looked eerily beautiful bathed in soft moonlight. Benches rose from the impressive first row of stone armchairs where, just as in those ancient days, the V.I.P.s were seated. The stage, some hundred and eighty feet wide, would have been frightening had it not been so inspiring. For once, I felt grateful for every inch of height with which the good Lord had blessed me. The entire cast was unusually tall, and this helped to create the effect of heroic figures which, in those wide stage spaces, was most desirable.

Sarah Bernhardt, that tiny woman who somehow managed to look nobly tall, once played Racine's *Phaedra* in this theatre.

That was a very special occasion. The Great Fire of 1906 (called by most of us the San Francisco earthquake) had swept the city the day before. Despite this fact, Madame Sarah announced that she would go through with her performance. She was prepared for an empty house. The public responded to her challenge and packed the theatre. She was inspired! Naturally, there was an ovation at the end.

Our production was of the simplest sort. Inside the tall central arch at the center of the stage we had hung two massive doors which looked as though they were made of copper. Each time Clytemnestra was to enter, there was a clanging sound—as though swords had struck on metal; then, ever so slowly, the heavy doors were pushed open for the Queen and her hand-maidens to enter. The depth of the stage, the steps leading down into the chorus arena in the foreground where the royal altar stood, made possible beautiful groupings and impressive movement throughout the play.

Unlike the previous productions by Margaret Anglin, we used almost no music. The wistful sound of shepherd piping in the distance in the early dawn at the very opening was all, and the crash of harsh percussion instruments heightened the effect of Aegisthus' return from the hunt towards the end. I was convinced that the play did not need musical trimmings. That it could do without them was gratifyingly evident in the rapt attention with which 5,000 people followed its surge and sweep through the moonlit night.

There was a wonderfully effective piece of business at the very end. We had covered Clytemnestra's bier with a royal crimson material some twenty feet in length. As Aegisthus uncovered the body of the dead Queen he cast the cloth from him in such a way that as it spilled down the steps leading to the altar below it suggested blood. While Orestes drove the guilty usurper at sword's point into the palace to kill him on the same spot where his father had been murdered, Electra was left crouching alone at the foot of the steps. Unconsciously she fingered the royal-red covering. Suddenly realizing what she was handling, she rose, placed the material across her drab shoulders and slowly ascended the steps. Behind her the crimson covering trailed its majestic length. Between the huge bronze doors, left open as Orestes backed Aegisthus in, she paused, bathed in a golden light. Then, head held high, she stepped across the threshold of her father's house—all dreams of vengeance fulfilled at last. In the utter silence, the last bit of crimson disappeared through the doors. The stage remained empty for a moment. Then the lights blacked out!

The effect of these quiet yet colorful moments, after the emotional turmoil which had preceded them, was sensational. As the stage lights blacked out there was complete silence for a minute or two, then, as the house-lights came on, pandemonium broke loose. Again and again the actors appeared. The audience swept down into the choral area, tore the garlands of flowers and the ropes of laurel apart for souvenirs; in a few minutes the altar was stripped bare.

Backstage one could scarcely reach the dressing rooms through the mob of excited visitors—hundreds of them. It was like no opening night I had ever experienced. Finally I could shut the dressing room door. Our thoughtful friends, despite the excitement of the play, had remembered to provide us with hot drinks and much needed nourishment. We blessed them.

Sleep that night was impossible: my stimulated brain went over and over the lines. At daybreak I tiptoed to Muriel's door. Instantly she whispered, "You awake, too?" "I haven't slept a wink," I said. "Let's dress and go up the hill and see the sunrise." We did. It should have been an especially fine one—instead it was definitely a class B production; God evidently felt He had done His bit in providing us with our balmy moonlit night. I couldn't complain.

CHAPTER 20

ALL CZECHS WEEP

THE NEXT DAY I left to start my one-woman tour. When that was over I went to the little country town of Carmel, New York, where Mr. Robert Goodhue had organized an ambitious summer season. In a charming medium-sized outdoor theatre, he wanted to open the season with a production of *Romeo and Juliet* on a grassy two-level stage. The lovers were to be played by Douglass Montgomery and Jane Wyatt. I was to play the nurse again and to direct the play.

We rehearsed day and night for a week, with immense enthusiasm. The simple but effective settings against the natural background of trees and bushes were charming. The stage made possible an interesting variety of movements, the lower level being used for all street scenes, the upper level for interiors and the balcony scene.

Douglass Montgomery's Romeo had a youthful vitality and grace which made some of the scenes more than usually believable. He had sent to Hollywood for the sumptuous costumes worn by Leslie Howard in the motion picture with Norma Shearer. Jane Wyatt, with her delicate beauty, made a fourteen-year-old Juliet seem plausible and poignant; her clear voice carried even in the open air. We had cause to hope for an artistic success, and the generous publicity which Mr. Goodhue launched gave us every reason to anticipate a financial success as well. But alas for even the best laid plans which depend on open-air productions!

Two days before the opening, the season was taken over by

Jupiter Pluvius! And I mean RAIN! Steadily, unrelentingly, it came down in drizzles, in sheets, in cloudbursts. Day after day it continued. The roads became impassable. Never have I seen such rains. Once or twice, towards evening, the sun would emerge for a moment or two to tantalize us with a gleam of hope. One evening the sky actually cleared long enough for a full dress rehearsal, leaving me, however, with heavy skirts soaked to the knees and a hacking cough. The next day when the rain resumed, Douglass murmured to me, "There is no pity sitting in the clouds."

There could be no question of our opening until the weather cleared. The actors, confined to the cramped quarters of the estate, grew nervous, apathetic and frantic in turn. The only really gallant soul for whom my heart bled was our manager, Robert Goodhue. He, for whom all this spelled disaster, was able somehow to conceal the despair which must have filled his heart. In our efforts to hold the performance in readiness, should the weatherman relent, we continued to rehearse on the tiny indoor stage, condensing the movement of the play as best we could in the limited space. Friday at noon the skies cleared at last, but the grass stage was hopelessly rain-soaked. There was not time to assemble audiences. We gave two indoors performances to a handful of people and sadly called it a day. Without sunshine the best open-air theatres in the world are useless.

Immediately after I was asked to come to Nantucket Island to do *Yes, My Darling Daughter* with the Morgan Farley company. It was years since I had been there. I had forgotten the softness of the air, the peacefulness of the moors and dunes, the fresh sparkle of the sea off Sankaty Lighthouse. Down at the harbor end of Nantucket several people I knew had taken houses for the season; Beatrice De Menocal, an old friend of my Institute days was installed with her delightful family on Milk street; Patricia Collinge and her husband had a charming house on the water front, and another friend had taken a similar old captain's house just across the cobbled street. Personally, I liked the more primitive living conditions at Siasconset, the other end of the island. 'Sconset's little lanes and tiny houses charmed me, and I decided to stay on after my week's engagement to enjoy the first seaside holiday I'd had in years.

As I walked along the high cliff-path to Sankaty Lighthouse every morning before breakfast, the world seemed a place of shimmering beauty. Brilliant diamonds glittered in the sea; the soft blue and mauve of giant rhododendrons and the gray of the shingled cottages softened the glare. And how good breakfast tasted afterwards! I reveled in a sense of carefree peace such as I had not known for years.

Mid-mornings I would frequently slip quietly into Bob O'Connor's barn-studio. There, curled up in one of his huge red leather chairs, one could listen without disturbing his piano practice. Music becomes peculiarly one's own when heard thus informally. He was a gay person and a generous artist—eager to share his gifts. Every Wednesday evening he kept open house for anyone on the Island who cared to come to the studio while he played a short piano recital. One saw chauffeurs, shopkeepers, garage mechanics and socialites gathered together in a real democracy of art.

Mr. O'Connor loaned me the studio to do a matinee of my one-woman show. It was a pleasant success. Most days were spent on the beach on the sands in front of Bob's house and garden. "Off-Islanders" (as the natives called the summer visitors) like Jerry Zerbi, the Roy Larsens and Patricia Collinge, occasionally gave interesting parties in their charming houses. They were still "off-islanders" to the natives despite all their years of residence. Further along the seashore, remote even from the simple social activities of 'Sconset, was Ralph Roeder, working on a book. He had earned a considerable reputation as a writer since playing Lovborg in our Ibsen season when the critic had found it "difficult to imagine him writing a book."

Lucius Humphrey gave glamorous beach parties—picnics deluxe, replete with butler, caviar, and wonderful drinks. One of these parties was given at Tom Nevers' Point. This was at the farthest tip of the Island where stood a ramshackle, abandoned wooden building which had been a rum-runner's haven during prohibition days. Its tall square tower was visible for miles around.

Interested as always in abandoned houses, I had insisted, when the party broke up, that they leave me to browse and explore, and then walk home. I prowled through the house with great curiosity and walked back along the seashore to the Inn, where I was staying.

That night at 3 A.M. the clamor of fire engines brought everyone tumbling out into the streets. The old, abandoned house at Tom Nevers' Point was aflame! But it had its one moment of beauty as it passed into limbo, when the high square tower, a flaming torch against the blackness, slowly collapsed. Next day a stone fireplace and ashes were all that remained of a building which must have seen many riotous days and nights. Friends who knew of my passion for fires all decided to pull my leg and made pointed remarks over the party-line phone next morning about my previous day's explorations. Terrified lest they seriously implicate me, I protested vigorously until I learned that practically everyone on the island was claiming credit for destroying the old eyesore. Barring this small excitement it was a month of heavenly weather and unalloyed peace.

When I returned to New York that early autumn of 1938 I experienced a sense of serenity such as I had seldom enjoyed. I had no immediate plans, but I knew I could wait patiently for the right activity. Not in many years had I faced a new season so replenished with energy, so hopeful, so confident. The early morning walks I had been taking along the high sea-road were now taken around the reservoir in Central Park. The world seemed so lovely a place in which to be a healthy, hopeful adult that I did not want to miss an hour of its freshness and light.

I called up various play-agents. I read the plays they sent, feeling sure that if I found a good one, I could get it produced. This new buoyancy could only mean that before me lay important activity—wider horizons. Those long walks beside the sun-flecked sea, looking across toward Spain and Portugal, had made my mind as well as my eyes take the far view.

But from across the sea came ominous news. Czechoslovakia, grown into so sturdy a democracy in its twenty brief years of freedom, was being menaced from without and within. Unintimidated, the people of that proud little country asked only that they be allowed to use their courage and their men to stem the threatening onslaught. For several weeks it seemed as though they might prevail. But the tension everywhere increased daily, hourly; one did little else but listen to the radio. In mid-September David once more defied Goliath; the Czechs mobilized. In my diary of September 17, 1938, I find only two words—*Slava Cechum!* (Glory to the Czechs.) Ultimatum followed ultimatum. Then came the black disgrace.

To appease Hitler, France and England negotiated with him to cede portions of Czech territory to Germany. Not only did they renege on their guarantees to protect Czechoslovakia, but they insisted that Czechoslovakia offer no resistance. When Russia offered assistance, Czechoslovakia's "ally," Poland, refused passage to Russian troops. There was no barrier now to Hitler's plans.

On September 21, 1938, came the tragic news of Czech martyrdom. A radio broadcast from Berlin brought us Hitler's hysterical voice ranting to the applause of his benighted people. I wept, and nature seemed to weep with me. That day rain and wind lashed the eastern seaboard of the United States bringing down trees and telephone poles: the physical as well as the moral universe seemed to have gone berserk.

Not long before, Blevins Davis, a radio producer, had asked me to play Hecuba in Euripides' *The Trojan Women* which was to be the first in a series of great plays to be done on NBC. The first rehearsal had been called for September 21st. Reading Hecuba's great lament over fallen Troy, I thought of Prague which might in a few hours be reduced to rubble. Hysterical, I could not go on. By the time the play was broadcast some days later, Euripides' lines had taken on a frightening timeliness. Burns Mantle, drama critic of *The Daily News,* spoke his commentaries with tears in his eyes.

But not only the actors found *The Trojan Women* deeply moving. From a complete stranger came the following letter:

> *643 South Floyd St.*
> *Louisville, Ky.*

Dear Miss Yurka:

Last Sunday morning I listened to the radio broadcast of the 'Trojan Women.' Please let me say right here that I consider yours the most magnificent, the most moving performance I have ever heard or seen. . . . After the performance was finished I looked at the friend who was listening with me . . . I saw that he, too, was weeping. One of the great marvels of your Hecuba was your ability to make her seem so real, so human. Of course it is the duty of a great actress to give life to the character she portrays. But . . . one not only felt . . . even over the radio one saw your Hecuba. My head throbbed, as when one is attempting to override some great

crisis in one's life. . . . Your apostrophe to the body of Astynax
. . . Euripides himself must have wept at that, in Heaven. . . .

Sincerely,

JOSEPH DIGNAN

No sympathizer could accept the sacrifice of Czechoslovakia as
final. Whenever two or three gathered, they protested, "But
they were ready and strong. How can 'they' make them give up
without even giving their soldiers a chance to fight?" But the
gentleman with the umbrella had his way, and "peace in our
time" was promised to a frightened, quaking world. I felt I must
do something to remind my world what manner of people these
were who were being thrown to the wolves by appeasers intent
upon saving themselves. Writing to the papers, speaking at mass
meetings was not enough. Wild plans for action whirled
through my brain. I sent cablegrams of protest to Alfred Duff
Cooper and Leon Blum. I am afraid I was a little insulting to
some of my European friends, who seemed unmoved by the behavior of their governments. But I couldn't help myself—it
seemed so terribly personal. I must do something!

The idea came to me to do a Čapek season. The Čapek brothers were dedicated nationalists whose great works, I felt, would
nobly represent their country. Karol Čapek believed, as did so
many brave Czechs, that the sacrifice demanded of his people by
their allies as well as by their enemies might save the rest of
Europe from the threatening holocaust. In such a cause, the
martyrdom of a heroic nation might be justified. His touching
prayer, written shortly after the Munich Pact was signed, shows
the spirit in which the Czech people were prepared to carry on
in the dark days ahead. It was published in Prague, on October
5, 1938:

Dear Lord, Creator of this beloved land, we need not tell you
how we feel nor how our heads are bowed. But not in shame!
We have no cause for shame, though fate has struck us with
an iron hand. . . . But not through lack of courage did we fall.
We are creatures caught within the cogs of a wheel but through
the very pain of our deep suffering . . . we know how vitally
and thoroughly alive we are . . . Dear Lord, we do not pray
that we may be avenged, but we do pray . . . that you will let no

one of us succumb to dull despair. Let each seek only to learn how he may serve the future and enduring destiny of his dear land. Never can that nation be deemed small which will not let itself be shaken from its faith—that through great effort in a common cause a better future destiny can be achieved.

I tried desperately to do the Čapek season I had in mind. It was of the prescience of his imagination that I wished to remind people. Their play about robots *R.U.R.*, produced some years before by the Theatre Guild, depicts man terrorized and destroyed by the machines which he himself has made. It was all too prophetic. Writing some twenty years earlier he had visualized the developments which changed the world—a world now capable of destroying itself by the Frankenstein of its inventions: airplanes capable of inflicting death and destruction on a scale the world had never envisioned; labor saving devices resulting in unemployment of dangerous dimensions; all these forerunners of even greater potentially destructive discoveries.

His *Insect Comedy* is a satire on greed, imperialism and war, all shown through the denizens of the insect world. Always Čapek's concern was with humanity in its everyday aspects—its courage, its laughter, its mistakes. Like most Czechs he was more interested in the men who sat in the lowly places of human experience than with those in the high. How that heart of his must have ached in those last sad months! Hitler's invasion of his beloved city in 1939 was more than he could bear: the gentle heart stopped beating.

I failed to stir up any interest in the idea of a Čapek cycle. Actually, it was a grandiose, impractical idea, but in my overwrought state of mind it had seemed possible and inactivity had seemed unbearable.

When war broke out in 1939 it permeated all our lives like an inescapable mist. The tragic fate of the village of Lidice in Czechoslovakia inspired Edna St. Vincent Millay to write her long and poignant poem, "The Murder of Lidice." When Basil Rathbone asked me to participate in making a recording of it I assembled six young actors who spoke an occasional line or hummed, in unison, Czech folksongs. The Slovak national anthem, especially, had an urgency when the tempo was accelerated, underscoring the mounting terror so tellingly expressed by the poet. I spoke the prologue. It was a moving experience, and the record has become a minor classic in its field.

The tragedy of these events left me in an overwrought state of mind. Again, seeking, as always, release in work, I hastily got involved in a production of a play by Ferdinand Bruckner, a famous German playwright. The play was called *Gloriana*—Edmund Spenser's name for Queen Elizabeth—and I found it very interesting. As one friend said about it later, "The only play about Elizabeth which made me believe that she was the daughter of Henry VIII." The critics turned it down unanimously. An overwhelming blizzard on the night of the opening may have contributed to their cold reaction. In fact, the English playwright, Sewell Stokes, said, "I knew during the first intermission that the play was doomed. Nothing was discussed except how the —— —— was anyone ever going to get home in that weather." Dr. Bruckner brought Otto Preminger backstage with him. Preminger said, and I quote him: "I have seen this play produced in every capital in Europe; I have directed it myself. Your performance tops any that I have ever seen in that part." I was gratified and hopeful. The morning notices quickly wiped out that optimism—not one good word was said about the play, the playwright or myself, nor the rest of the cast, which included Tom Powers, Harold Vermilyea, and Celeste Holm as a lady-in-waiting.

One of the people who had promised to help finance the production had "backed out" and because of my extreme faith in the play, I had taken on his share of the financial burden. The closing left what were, for me, appalling financial problems, and I readily accepted the offer to go to Philadelphia for a brief engagement in *Yes, My Darling Daughter*. It would at least take my mind off of *Gloriana*. Wee and Leventhal (amusingly enough, Mr. Wee was over six feet tall and Leventhal was very short) were sending out one of those companies which reassembled as many as possible of the original cast for short engagements in various cities. Another cast in another play would follow—a less arduous sort of stock-starring plan.

The simple domestic comedy was a great relief after the hectic efforts of *Gloriana*. Mark Reed's sane, humorous heroine tided me over what might otherwise have been a nervous collapse. But, like Maminka, I could survive almost any unhappiness through work. The two weeks in Philadelphia were made warm and pleasant by dear friends, the Maurice Speisers, whose gentle kindness was healing balm for the spirit.

After the two-week engagement I resumed my one-woman touring for the year. Again the kaleidoscope of towns, auditoriums, audiences of enthusiastic young students, of sedate elders. Again my conviction was confirmed that in those outlying cities and country towns, far from the highly centralized activity of either the East or the West coasts, there is a huge public of vast potentialities, a public which could make the American theatre a place of busy activity for authors, actors and theatre workers of all kinds.

These one-woman programs have not only kept my acting muscles exercised, my contact with audiences very much alive, but have happily solved the problem of making a living—an ever present one in the lives of all but a very few sons and daughters of Thespis. I have learned to be deeply grateful for them.

CHAPTER **21**

SMALL BEER

I WAS IN HOLLYWOOD in 1939 and considering returning to my home in New York when a telephone call from Stuart
Walker, at the Paramount Studios startled me. "Would you be
willing to play a sixty-year-old hellion?" he asked. "If she's
enough of a hellion to be a good part, I don't care how old she
is," I replied. His response was intriguing. "Oh, she's that all
right, in fact she's four good parts, and what's more she's a real
person. We got the story out of J. Edgar Hoover's Case His-
tories. She is the woman who master-minded the Barker-Karpis
gang in Minnesota. Let me send you the script."

The Woman from Hell (later changed to *Queen of the Mob*)
proved to be the story of a real-life mother who trained her sons
to be expert bank robbers and criminals. She masterminded a
powerful gang working in the Middle West. I had some qualms
when I learned that it was to be done as a B picture (this means
a small budget and limited time for shooting). The twenty luxurious weeks I had enjoyed in playing Madame Defarge (a career in itself as Hollywood gauges things) had established *A
Tale of Two Cities* as my standard for a picture. *Queen of the
Mob* was to be a three-week "quickie." But it was a part in
which I could do four completely different characterizations. Ma
Webster, as she was called in the film, changed her disguises according to the social background of whatever place she selected
for the gang to hide in between jobs. In one town she was a
gentle old-fashioned elderly woman who wore bonnets and gave
cookies to the neighbors' children. Once, she masqueraded as a
smartly dressed Texas oil-widow with money to burn, entertaining in fashionable hotel suites with her three handsome sons.
What the gang stole was regarded as "hot" money and had to be

"put on ice" for varying lengths of time until the interest of the police had subsided. Most often, however, "Ma" was shown in her basic character—ruthless, domineering, shrewd and hard as nails.

As it was a star part I felt it was worthwhile to gamble on the chance that if it should turn out exceptionally well, it just might be handled as an "A" picture and rocket me to movie stardom. The part seemed to me a kind of female Little Caesar, the character which had catapulted my former colleague of Theatre Guild days, Edward G. Robinson, to his high rank as a movie star. His talent kept him there.

There were scenes which mitigated her ruthlessness and showed her as a real human being. Of course, I did not realize that most of these would eventually end up on the cutting-room floor. An actor is incurably optimistic. For instance, there was a touching scene when the lonely old woman manages to get into her "good" son's home (he had renounced the gang, to "go straight") in an effort to steal a glimpse of her grandson whom she had never been permitted to see. There was another moving scene which showed her grieving, miserably, at the dreary mid-night burial of one of her sons in a shallow roadside grave, their flight from justice leaving no time for anything else. This scene took all day to shoot; I cried myself dry-eyed before the day was over. In the finished film the entire sequence was deleted. One particular sequence was so like a well-written stage scene that I begged the director to protect it from deletion or even from being partially cut. It couldn't have been better written.

I said, "Look, do anything you like; don't give me any billing if you think it would help; cut anything else if you must—only please—for God's sake (and mine) don't let them touch that scene!" When I finally saw the picture all but the climactic shooting-finish to the scene (about one minute on the screen) had stayed on the cutting-room floor.

Moreover, studio politics were involved. Between the time the picture was finished and the day of its release some six or eight months later, the whole executive set-up at Paramount Studios had changed. The men who might have had my interests at heart had departed; to the men who replaced them, *Queen of the Mob* was just "another gangster picture." When I saw it on the screen I could have cried. I did. Some of my most valuable scenes had been discarded. Emotion and characterization had very little place in this hit-and-run melodrama. I agreed with the critics' verdict that *Queen of the Mob* was just "another of those things," hardly worth reviewing. And a performance which the "big shots" don't bother to see, whether on the stage or screen, does the actor little good. One may have put some of his (or her) best work into it, but it furthers no interests save those of the actor's bank account. I suppose that should be enough. Somehow I never feel that it is.

With *Queen of the Mob* stowed away in cans, I went back East to start the fourth of my one-woman-show tours. By now my heart was not in it; I felt myself growing stale despite the new material I was using. The strain of constant travel, the sense of being suspended somewhere in space, alighting only for a night, of never knowing what working conditions I should have to cope with—all this grew increasingly distasteful. I began to hate the sight of a train; it became difficult to recall in what town I had been the previous night.

My agent in Hollywood insistently urged my return, saying there were many parts available if only I were on hand. He was arranging for me to be tested for the part of Emmy Ritter in *Escape;* my chances of landing it, he assured me, were good. His insistence coincided with my inclination, so, with the Lecture Bureau's consent, I canceled the balance of the tour and went West.

On my arrival after a sleepless flight my agent broke the news; Alla Nazimova had been signed for Emmy Ritter the day before. It was a blow. Still, if I had to lose out, losing to her made it easier; I had never ceased to be grateful to her for Madame Defarge. Besides, her frail figure and her tragic mask seemed perfect for Emmy; she could make the escape as a young girl believable. The studio offered me another part in *Escape,* a very unpleasant one, that of the Nazi nurse who was in charge of Emmy in the concentration camp. All my natural instincts revolted against further identification with such sadistic characters. To my protests they argued, "After all, you're an actress; the part needs one." And my agent, more realistically, pointed out that having come to Hollywood, as a matter of publicity it was wise that I be announced as having come out to do an important picture with a distinguished cast. I gulped down my pride and accepted.

Except for the privilege of watching Mervin Leroy direct and

Nazimova—a really superb artist—at work, what a dreary picture it proved to be for me! I loathed the thick ugly wool uniform, the dank surroundings, my further identification with a
"meany." But Madame Defarge had set the pattern for such casting. Few movie directors can see farther than the last picture in
which they have seen you. And having watched so altogether
delightful a person as Basil Rathbone achieve a notable career
through the brilliant playing of sadistic "heavies" I can see the
value of these parts even though only a limited facet of a talent,
as in his case, is exploited.

Again I spent my birthday in the MGM lot, but this time—
what a difference! By pure chance, it proved to be the night of
the first public showing of *Queen of the Mob,* for which I had
been impatiently waiting for six months. I had invited several
friends to go with me to the premiere and afterward to come to
my apartment to celebrate my birthday. "So what happened?"
That turned out to be my only night, in all my Hollywood experience, of really late shooting. To add to the dreariness of the
occasion, the scene took place in the bleak, snow-covered yard of
the concentration camp where I had to help carry out Emmy
Ritter's coffin!

Over and over we did the gloomy little scene; one—two—
three o'clock passed. The night grew dank and cold. Even Robert Taylor's charm faded. At 4 A.M. we were dismissed. I came
home to find the sad-looking remains of the supper party I had
arranged, with notes from all my guests wishing me a happy
birthday. I echoed Conway's message on the previous birthday:
"What a helluva way to spend it!" But work is work and cameramen and budgets take little interest in birthdays, and even
less in the premiere of another studio's picture.

If you stay in Hollywood for any length of time, sooner or
later you become infected with a disease which I call "house-
itis." It seems to seize everyone. So many beautiful homes! After
living there in a series of hotel suites and sublet apartments I,
too, succumbed. But my choice of a domicile was, my friends all
agreed, a really fantastic one.

This was the most protracted stay I ever made in Hollywood.
For a year or so I had observed, during my walks with my Scottie
Jeannie, the increasing deterioration of what seemed to origi-

nally have been a pretty, modest one-story bungalow which vandals had turned into a shambles. There was not a door nor a window intact. I couldn't resist tiptoeing in to have a look. Broken glass and rubbish covered the floors. It was a mess. Worst of all, obscenities were scrawled all over the walls. But, while wandering through the empty rooms, (the house seemed completely abandoned) I had discovered in the rear, on the lower floor, a fifty-foot studio-room which extended from one side of the house to the other. One entire side of the studio consisted of broken windows facing what had once been a large garden. It was now a mere parched grass plot.

Even in its denuded and shockingly vandalized state, the possibilities of the house enchanted me. By devious inquiries I learned that the original owners had sold the house to what turned out to be gamblers who had used the large studio-room as the gaming room. Twice the police had raided the place, the second time with axes and other very effective implements of destruction. Never have I seen a house in such condition.

I persuaded the representative of the oil company which owned the property to give me a long lease at a pittance in rent and I set out on the job of restoration. Just clearing away the broken glass, splinters of wood and other debris was a Herculean job. I was in the throes of one of those periods which most actors in Hollywood, even the successful ones, experience from time to time. No work at all! Restoring the abandoned house and furnishing it, kept me from going mad or taking to drink or to a psychiatrist's couch. Before I finished, Muriel, who knew her Walter Scott, named the place "Abbottsford, Junior."

Restoring the place with very little available cash was not easy, but it made it all the more amusing to see how far my ingenuity could carry me. I developed a taste for auction rooms and became an astute bidder. I could never have afforded to furnish the house in any other way. Mullioned windows I unearthed in a huge wrecker's warehouse; from a veteran's salvage shop I rescued a beautifully panelled door. After removing seven or eight coats of paint with my own hands, the finely grained wood I uncovered was so lovely and satiny that it made all the other doors in the foyer look horribly cheap. So the satiny wood had to be painted over again.

The fifty-foot studio presented the most serious problems.

Vandalized to a degree that seemed almost beyond repair, it showed tar paper where the paneling had been ripped out and gave me many hours' worry in deciding how those extensive spaces were to be covered. Besides, the walls adjoining the fireplace at the far end simply begged for ceiling-high bookshelves. All this, I knew, would cost a small fortune. But minor miracles never stopped happening to this house. One day, only a few blocks away, I noticed some workmen dismantling a drugstore which had just gone out of business. They were taking down shelves. I accosted their chief. "What are you going to do with all those shelves?" "Haul them away to a junk yard," he said. "Do you want to sell them?" I queried. There was a whole wall of beautiful shelves at adjustable heights. "Wait 'til I call up the boss," he said, In a few minutes he returned. "Will you get 'em hauled away yourself?" he asked. I 'lowed as how I could. "Well, then, there's a lot more of 'em piled out there in the back. He says if you'll clear out the whole lot yourself you can have the stuff for $8.oo." (Why eight, I'll never know. Why not ten?)

I nearly fainted but managed not to show it. Quickly handing him the money I hurried over to Harper Avenue where my carpenter's truck was promptly put to work. A few days later my studio was magnificently restored; a handsome wood-panelled interior, with bookshelves lining the walls on each side of the fireplace just as I had visualized them, went right up to the ceiling! And the wood was California redwood.

It became the perfect room in which to give parties, and I began to return the hospitality which so many of my friends had been extending to me. But my original intention—to use the cheery big room for a studio in which to teach acting—never materialized. Although I enjoy sharing with a really gifted young person knowledge which my experience had helped me to acquire, the organized routine which a successful "school" requires was something into which I could not settle. Hollywood at that time was full of acting classes; some of the returning veterans who had fallen in love with California sunshine were using their G.I. allowances to take these courses, hoping to crash into the movies. Somehow I couldn't see myself exploiting this situation. I have to believe in a talent before I can be helpful to it. So, except for three or four charming pupils who showed real promise, the big sunny room kept its privacy intact. Apart from the studio there was room for a surprising number of out-of-town visitors; I finally decided that "Casa Elastica" was the most appropriate name for its expansive walls. One weekend I had thirteen house guests!

But before that happy day I had many a troubled moment. As plumbers and decorators had to be paid, I did a few "bits" which were offered to me from time to time. But my sinking professional morale sustained itself on the possibility of one part which, if I landed it, would surely restore the prestige which I so sorely needed.

Ernest Hemingway's *For Whom the Bell Tolls* was to be made into a motion picture. Everyone said that Pilar was a "natural" for me after the performance I had given as Madame Defarge. Like Thérèse Defarge, Pilar was a strong, lusty peasant leader; she might have been the daughter of Dickens' fiery revolutionist. The part would require authority and power. Columnists put my name at the top of the list of the "runners-up" for the role.

For once I determined to leave nothing to chance. I undertook a campaign, sending out countless letters, I asked everyone I knew to write to the studio urging that I play it. Every chairman who had booked my one-woman show was enlisted to persuade as many as possible of his members to express their interest and write to Paramount. The response was magnificent. A casual visit to the casting director at the studio one day elicited his puzzled comment: "We've never had so many letters from all over the country about anyone except our big-name stars." I didn't explain; just hoped they would continue to come in.

Finally, I was tested for Pilar. The test director was pleased. "Honey, I think it's in the bag," he said. My agent, too, was convinced of it; but still no contract was forthcoming.

A week or two later a newspaper line leaped out at me: PAXINOU TO PLAY PILAR. When I recovered from the shock I did something which, in retrospect, I find almost unbelievable. I went down to the studio, sent my name in to Buddy de Silva, the top man, and asked him with as little emotion as I could command, if he would mind explaining what had happened to my chances. He was very kind and very frank. "We were all set on you," he said. "Suddenly we had a call from ———" (A powerful head of another studio). "He asked that Madame Paxinou be tested. Her test was good. Not better than yours, but just as good. So, partly to please him, she got the part. But she is good—make no mistake. Sorry. Better luck next time." Next time! When would there be another such part?

I went home and took to my bed for three days. Part of being an actress is learning to take such disappointments, but my courage was a long time recovering from this one.

Paxinou's performance was superb. It won the Academy Award for the gifted Greek actress and established her as an important figure in the motion picture world.

In staying on in Hollywood I was doing just what my New York agent had urged me to do. She had said: "Settle down there so they won't have to send East for you. Then there'll be dozens of parts." There were, but they were all unimportant ones. To go on refusing trivial bit-parts (even though one may be paid handsome salaries for doing them) when the alternative is idleness, becomes difficult. Idleness, too prolonged, becomes the kiss of death.

One day, after months of sunbathing and pruning of rosebushes, the call came from my Hollywood agent. He was in high spirits. There was an attractive part for me, he said, in the refilming of another famous book, *The Bridge of San Luis Rey*. There would be a three-week guarantee at what is euphemistically referred to in Hollywood as a "four-figure salary." Of course I signed. I was in no position not to. A delay in my starting date added another week to my guarantee, plus an increase in my salary. I looked forward to a period of real and interesting activity. To be sure, it wasn't an important company, but, "Who knows? They may become one," I rationalized. I was to play the Mother Superior.

Early one morning I started on my best scene, a tender, sympathetic one for a change. We worked all day. Suddenly at about six o'clock I heard the startling words, "Lock 'em up. Picture's finished." I couldn't believe my ears. "But I've only started," I protested. "What about my other scenes?" The slightly embarrassed director drew me to one side. "They're cutting all the rest," he explained, "money's given out." (I received four weeks' salary for one day's work!) I was genuinely shocked. No one could tell me this was healthy! How could one refuse any kind of a part if there were the chance of this happening? Pleasant enough economically, yes, but demoralizing, nevertheless.

The hospitality of several of my friends helped to make more bearable my relative idleness. Besides Mrs. Hutchinson's Santa Ynez ranch, I had frequent visits to the desert-home of Robert Balzer outside of Victorville. There are people who have a passion for the desert; people to whom its great open horizons, and even its heat, make a strong appeal. Bob was one of these. But to me there is always something a little menacing about the desert, even when man has met its challenge and successfully developed highly sophisticated (and highly priced!) areas such as Palm Springs with its elegant estates and countless swimming pools.

Robert's ranch house, a few miles outside the town of Victorville, was simple, comfortable and surrounded by the strange twisted joshua trees which are a special feature of the desert landscape. Weekends there were always delightful, shared by interesting friends, mostly theatre people. One evening a group of us drove out into the cool night, to a unique spot where some strange convulsions of nature had produced a group of great monolithic stones, a dozen times the height of a tall man, which loomed eerily in the moonlight. In their midst was an open oval area, almost like an amphitheatre. I was curious whether a human speaking voice would carry across that rock-surrounded space, so I suggested that they all stand at the far end of the oval; I would stand at the opposite end and recite the lines of Electra's first speech in the normal voice which I would use in a theatre. Actually, it was an interesting experiment in out-of-door acoustics. In that oval space, the sound of a normal voice carried across the wide space with complete audibility.

In Hollywood, in those days, I found relatively little interest in the other arts, painting, for instance. But I had met the curator of the Art Museum and his family and found them delightful. One day his wife invited me to go downtown to the Biltmore Hotel where, on the twentieth floor, some wealthy art patrons were giving a showing of their newly collected works of art. As we ascended in the elevator, a gentleman and his wife (very American judging by her accent) were introduced to me as Baron and Baroness Dvořak. The name naturally interested me, being that of our most famous Czech composer, so I said, casually, "Dvořak? Your husband is, then, a Czech?" With withering scorn she replied, "God! No! We're British." The elevator was speeding up to the twentieth floor. She evidently felt a little sorry for her rebuff. "You, of course," she said, "are English?" To which I let my full voice out with, "Christ, no! I'm Czech!" The elevator timed it perfectly, came to a stop and I swept out. My hostess never got over the shock! Nor, she said, did the lady!

Just as I was growing quite desperate, an opportunity came to return to Broadway in a war play called *A Barber Had Two Sons*. The director and co-author of *Woman in Hell* had collaborated on it. The mother's role was a strong one and I seized this opportunity to return to New York where one had, at least, a fighting chance for a career, and where I felt I belonged. When rehearsals for *A Barber Had Two Sons* were completed, we left for San Francisco where we were to open before coming to Broadway.

Barber had originally been written as a one-act play. The two additional acts of the final version were padding and of an inferior quality. Yet we played to fairly good business in San Francisco. The New York critics turned thumbs down, unanimously, as I feared they might. Nevertheless, the play did bring me back to Broadway. Before leaving Hollywood I had turned "Casa Elastica" over, lock, stock and barrel to my friend, Mrs. West, who had been living with me, while I once more settled into the stresses and strains of the New York theatre scene.

It was 1945 and there was war work. Just as in Hollywood, the Stage Door Canteen was enlisting the services of actresses of all ages. I also appeared in two more war plays. One of these, *The Wind is Ninety* (an aviator's phrase), was about the visit of the ghost of a flyer, just shot down, to his family which has not yet been notified of his death. He is guided back to his loved ones by another spirit-soldier, a veteran of the previous World War. The play carried a message of hope. It had been written by Captain Ralph Nelson, himself a member of the Air Force. The cast was a fine one: Bert Lytell was my husband; the ghostly veterans were played by two unknowns, Kirk Douglas and Wendell Corey. There was a startling performance by a nine-year-old child, Kevin Matthews, who played the soldier's little son and handled a big emotional scene so movingly that one wondered if there really is anything to acting other than the original gift. How do these youngsters do it? Kevin would be playing marbles or joking in the wings with one of the other children in the cast; his cue would come; he would step onstage to sob his heart out over his father's death; make an exit and resume his game as though he had never interrupted it.

A most touching incident that occurred on the opening night of *The Wind* justified my feeling that this play needed to be done. Mr. Lee Shubert assembled us all on the stage just before the curtain went up. "My friends," he said, "I want to tell you now, before there are any notices to be read, that this play is going to run in this theatre—my theatre—for at least four months. It's an important play with an important message. It is going to be kept alive for at least that long. I just wanted you all to know this before the curtain went up. Good night—and good luck!" This from one who was considered to be one of the most commercial of managers! We ran all summer in *The Wind is Ninety*.

An interim in which I toured in my solo programs preceded my next venture on Broadway. The war had ended and post-war thinking inspired the writing of *Temper the Wind,* a play about the efforts of a smooth-tongued German industrialist to re-establish his family fortunes through shrewd manipulation of the local American military personnel. It had some pertinent things to say. Brooks Atkinson declared that the play should be sent out in a dozen companies to every town in the country. My own part started out well, then dwindled to nothing in the last act. I am startled to find how often I have had to say this! The engagement was brief.

CHAPTER 22

PLAYING A HEIFER

HAVING APPEARED IN so many classical plays, I have occasionally been branded an "intellectual actress." Yet I have not deliberately sought these plays out. The *Electra* and the Ibsen plays had sought me out. Had I been given a choice I seriously suspect that what I really longed for was a chance to do plays like the ones in which Katharine Cornell and Jane Cowl had their early commercial successes: *Within the Law; The Gamblers; The Green Hat.*

But good commercial plays were never offered to me. Bad plays a-plenty seek me out, especially if they contain "a message." I once asked Howard Lindsay to read one, which had been sent to me, and tell me whether in turning it down I was completely lacking in judgment. He confirmed my worst fears by saying: "There seem to be three kinds of plays: good plays, bad plays, and the plays they send to Blanche Yurka." Only twice in my whole career have plays which later proved to be successful, both unfinished scenarios, slipped through my fingers.

Now I was steadily developing a deep distaste for the type of play and part which, with increasing frequency, was being offered me. Sadistic old women, mothers of neurotic killers, anything which stressed cruelty and bitterness, seemed to gravitate to my desk. Even going to the theatre began to be distasteful. The successful plays I saw stressed morbidity, ruthlessness, hatred and contempt for the human race. Perhaps if the manuscripts submitted had been really good plays, my revulsion at the subject matter might have been less intense. But they were not; I marveled that money could be raised to produce them.

But finally a ray of sunlight broke through. Two friends with whom I shared happy memories—T. Edward Hambleton (the young country cousin of *The Turbins* at Yale) and Norris Houghton, of Falmouth days, had launched a gallant effort to establish, on the lower East side in New York, a moderate-priced theatre where they were bravely producing plays of distinguished quality. They were having the usual difficulties which plague all such ventures: a scarcity of good scripts and limited funds for production and publicity. But actors who believed in what they were trying to do, even "stars," cut their salaries down to a mere pittance. Everyone wanted this theatre and these two men to succeed.

Norrie, since our Falmouth days and our Moscow meeting in 1934, had become not only the author of several fine books (notably *Moscow Rehearsals*) but a director as well. His stage designs, too, had attracted attention; he was becoming an all-round theatre man.

One day he called me in great excitement. At last, he said, he had a really good part for me, in a Chinese play called *The Carefree Tree*. I read the script, adapted by an American woman who lived in Hawaii. I would play a strong-willed, dictatorial Chinese Empress. I was beguiled; there was humor as well as charm in this adaptation by Aldwyth Morris of an ancient story. The original play, I was told, dated back a thousand years. Up to the entry of the present regime in China it had continued to be produced in Peking. It was the story of the fierce rivalry between the Empress of the North and the gentler Empress of the South. Their two children fall in love and are, of course, opposed in their desires by the Empress of the North, in a Chinese version of *Romeo and Juliet,* except that in the Chinese play, all ends happily. Janice Rule and Farley Granger were charming as the young lovers; Edith Meiser, most sympathetic as the other Empress.

You might easily ask why an actor of experience cannot learn to avoid appearing in "failures." You may also ask why he or she should be willing to talk about them. The wise ones don't. They hush them up as quickly as possible. Yet these so-called "failures" may have been among an artist's most beloved efforts. I know this was the case with Katharine Cornell's *Lucrece*. I know this was my own feeling about Susan Glaspell's *Coming Artist*. Both were delicately beautiful plays. We, as artists, would have been the poorer for not having done them. I agree with Joan Plowright's comment: "Actors should have the right to fail now and then. Scientists have it; why not we?"

As for talking about them—how else is one to paint any honest picture of this madly wasteful, wonderful merry-go-round which we call the American Theatre? If you succeed in snatching the prize ring a half-dozen times in a lifetime, you can count yourself lucky and enjoy a considerable sense of fulfillment. And, of course, there is always the need to make some sort of a living. The acute need of even the two weeks' salary which an Equity contract guarantees prompts many a decision. Moreover, hope springs eternal out of the ashes of previous disappointments.

When the Phoenix Theatre management invited me to appear in *The Carefree Tree* I knew that the chances of the play's being a popular success were slight. Few American actors have had the opportunity to develop the sense of style which would enable them to convey to an audience the charm and the humor of this ancient Chinese legend. Ideally speaking, only Chinese actors whose training begins in childhood could do this sort of play; to assemble a company of Occidentals capable of doing so in four weeks' time is well nigh impossible. Should it therefore not be attempted? I did not think so. It was an interesting challenge.

In Falmouth where I was visiting the John Cranes, the half-dozen friends to whom I had read the play before I agreed to do it had found it delightful and urged me to take the part. They were all highly sophisticated play-goers, well equipped to judge a manuscript. And surely, I thought, some of the charm of the original which had given pleasure to Chinese audiences for over a thousand years would come through. But apparently it didn't. Almost unanimously the critics condemned the play and the management for producing it. One critic scathingly abused the actors for "sinking so low" in their attempt to make a living and left half-way through the performance. I was not only shocked but bewildered. The cast was made up of attractive, talented and experienced people. You'd have thought they had committed a minor crime in lending themselves to the project. We closed almost immediately.

Not long after the play had opened at the Phoenix Theatre I

lunched at one of those chic side-street restaurants in the East Fifties, with a charming young friend who seemingly knew most of the soigné young men who patronized the place. On our way in we had stopped at the table of one of Judy's acquaintances, and in introducing me Judy mentioned that I was appearing in *The Carefree Tree*. Almost compulsively I said, "Have you seen it?" "Oh, God, no!" he replied. "I couldn't waste my time after that Atkinson review." Nettled, I unwisely said, "Oh, you permit Mr. A. to determine what you see? I happen to like the play very much." He made some withering remark which I have happily forgotten, and we moved on to our table, I murmuring a few epithets which cast serious doubt upon the legitimacy of his birth. In leaving, a little later, we had to pass his table again. He (perhaps a bit remorseful at the way he had crushed me) said, studying my long green gloves, "Paris, of course?" I looked down at him (he had not bothered to stand up) and said, "Paris? Good God, no! I buy all my gloves in Istanbul!" (This being my private name for Thrift Shops, it happened to be true. I had bought them for fifty cents!)

I arrived at a decision. Several seasons' reading of plays of revolting content crystallized my growing distaste for "show-bizness," as it was more and more frequently designated. Yielding to a strong impulse I announced my withdrawal from the Broadway scene.

The *New York Times* graciously printed the letter of farewell which I sent to the drama desk. Not satisfied, Mr. Atkinson sent a charming, intelligent, young man, Louis Sheaffer to interview me. His account of our meeting appeared in the *Times* on November 6, 1955.

The letter from Miss Blanche Yurka to this newspaper sounded dramatic and final. She was bidding "farewell" to her Broadway acting career.

"It is a career," she wrote, "which has given me brief periods of great joy and exultation, as well as long ones of frustration and frequent defeat. And others of comfortable affluence in utterly unimportant plays. But, I've had it, the brou-ha-ha, the name in electric lights, the occasional privilege of earning a living thanks to television, the movies, one-woman tours et al * * *.

"I am not 'renouncing' the theatre, certainly not in any moody bitterness. Au contraire, I shall very probably be busier than ever before. . . ."

Mr. Sheaffer then went on to recount some of our conversation.

Miss Yurka's career has been too long, varied and notable for her to say farewell to Broadway simply through a letter. Veteran theatregoers know her well, but for the younger generations it should be recalled here that her career has spanned David Belasco, E. H. Sothern, John Barrymore's "Hamlet," in which she played his mother; modern works, distinguished encounters with Ibsen, Sophocles, other classics, and a Hollywood record that ranges from "A Tale of Two Cities," in which she contributed a memorable Mme. DeFarge, to ephemera bearing such non-classical titles as "Queen of the Mob" and "One Body Too Many," "Sons of the Musketeers" and "Hitler's Madman."

Anyhow, a visitor at Miss Yurka's East Seventy-second Street apartment found her eager to stress that she was not feuding with or bitter toward the critics—"The Carefree Tree" took a critical shellacking—but that she was unhappy over the general state of the Broadway theatre in recent years, the direction it has taken.

"Things have taken on a coloration I dislike," she said. "I don't like the passion for ugliness that seems so much a part of our theatre today. I'd like once again to see plays in which the parents don't think their children are horrible and in which the children don't think the same of their parents, plays that aren't obsessed with the more seamy psychological aspects.

"This doesn't mean I'm against plays being deeply psychological —you can't play Ibsen for so long and be against plays of depth and honesty. Certainly Hedda Gabler isn't a pretty character. I know that when Ibsen entered the theatre people found his work ugly and nasty and said that he ate children for breakfast. But when he started writing he had to demolish the clichés of prettiness and sweet lies that filled the theatre.

"But there's so much unsavoriness and so many unsavory characters in today's plays. I can't blame the playwrights so much as the public. If they want to plunk down their $9.50 or $15 for this sort of play, well, the playwrights will write them."

Does the farewell mean that she has given up all acting? "Oh, no, that applies just to Broadway.

"None of us ever thought 'The Carefree Tree' was a great play, that it would revolutionize the theatre and cause everything to be done in Chinese style. We felt that here was a charming romance and fantasy, with humor, written in pleasant, literate English. That we don't have a theatre in which that play could run five weeks is to me appalling. It's too bad, too, too bad. . . ."

I was grateful for this opportunity to express my feelings about what had been happening in the theatre.

After the play closed I set about reorienting myself. How does one go about rechanneling energies which have been dynamic enough to hold, on occasion, the rapt attention of 5,000 people in the Berkeley open-air theatre, where we did the *Electra,* to live happily and healthily through such intensive activity as my Ibsen season had required? One must continue to live with the mental and emotional machinery which is capable of responding to such demands; it cannot, like a twelve-cylinder car, be put into storage while you comfortably use a mental Ford.

Happily, a new activity came knocking at my door. One of the editors of the publishers, Prentice-Hall, asked if I would undertake to write a book for them. They would commission it, paying a handsome advance. They wanted me to "share with teen-agers and college students" some of the impressions of "live" theatre which I had accumulated on both sides of the footlights. It was to be a sort of "How to enjoy the theatre" book.

It sounded like great fun. A contract was drawn up; several friends celebrated its signing with proper libations; we decided to call it *Dear Audience,* and lo! there I was—an author! Only I wasn't. The book had to be written! There ensued months of research, of the discipline of keeping one's anatomy firmly glued to a chair when more amusing activities beckoned; of having to overcome the ghastly feeling that none of it was any good anyway, so why finish? I became so sick of words that I finally said to the vastly helpful editor, Marjorie Thayer, who had lured me into this verbal bog: "I not only don't ever want to write another book, I don't ever want to *read* another."

Deadlines were missed. I used every possible excuse. I accepted a few one-woman engagements. When, suddenly, a part in a movie called *Thunder to the Sun* starring Susan Hayward and Jeff Chandler was offered me, I ran away to Hollywood. The picture could have been a fine character study of some

Basque villagers eager to bring their vines to this country. But when it was released it was just another "fighting Indians" melodrama, and my part, which had had possibilities, was sacri-ficed to the more melodramatic elements of the story. But I had enjoyed the respite from those blank white pages.

Finally (and again, the word expresses only faintly what lies behind it) the galleys were proof-read for the last time, and *Dear Audience* was out of my hands. I found it a bit trying to wait for the reviews to come dribbling in, accustomed as I was to the overnight verdict which one gets on a play. But gradually they did come, and the apprehension which had hung over me for many months evaporated. The reviews were uniformly ex-cellent and the book did well, though it was not a smash hit.

George Freedley in his "Of Books and Men" column in the *New York Telegraph* (December 10, 1959) called the book "a beguiling and entrancing introduction to playgoing which is not to be resisted." He praised my writing talent as "entirely persuasive and to be encouraged." *Variety* noted that "Miss Yurka's tone is lively, diverting, and of more than transient value."

As a result of *Dear Audience* I received another welcome op-portunity. Mr. Moses Asch invited me to make recordings of my "one-woman" material for his Folkways Records. I was de-lighted. He felt the book would help his sales and vice versa, and I felt that this would not only give me a kind of immortality, but would give me a chance to sit in the audience and form my own judgments—make my own comments, be my own critic. The records, too, were to be called *Dear Audience*. Infinite care was taken to make them perfect. We reworked the scenes end-lessly. And when I could finally hear Electra's moving sorrow as she mourned over her brother's ashes, as I listened to the deep guilt-haunted breathing of Lady Macbeth as she wanders in her sleep, I was grateful that the science of recording could capture the essence of one's artistry so perfectly. Who can tell what fur-ther developments lie ahead of us? My own hope is that in the process of changing media we shall not lose our hold on the treas-ures we already have. For it is these distillations of the past which nourish the present. We sometimes forget that.

In 1956 death took a step in my direction. I was in Phoenix, Arizona, playing the Empress in *Anastasia* in the charming Sombrero Theatre. Only two other parts have been so rewarding, and I was revelling in the sniffles and the applause on my exit after that marvelous second act scene. We played no midweek matinee, so Wednesday morning I had arranged to be taken out to Frank Lloyd Wright's famous house Taliesen West to see some of the minor miracles of building he was said to have wrought there. It was a very hot day. We wandered through some of the rooms; I even caught a glimpse of "the Master" himself, sitting in the distance. I did not speak to him to remind him of our having been photographed together at the dedication in Hartford of a beautiful little theatre which he had designed. During our drive back to Phoenix, I suddenly felt nauseated. I said, "Let's hurry, I feel sickish." Midway we stopped at a little shop to ask for a drink of water. As I sat on a chair waiting for it to be brought to me, I could see my friend was worried. (She told me afterwards that my face was deathly white.) We sped back to Phoenix where I found my New York friends, Mr. and Mrs. Callaghan, anxiously waiting. My friend had telephoned from the little shop and warned them to have a doctor on hand. I heard someone mention an ambulance. I protested, "Are you all crazy? Please go away and leave me to up-chuck, then I'll lie down and sleep." A moment later the ambulance drove up to the door of the bungalow. "Really," I said, "here I am with an attack of nausea and you talk about ambulances and hospitals. And who's going to play my part, pray? I won't go!"

What the doctor did, I don't know; I have no clear recollection of anything until I found myself under an oxygen mask at the hospital. There I remained for several days. When I was somewhat recovered and was able to sit up and read, I found in my mail a note from Kit Cornell; she had left the hospital the day I had moved in. Many other lovely messages were piled up (the New York papers had me at death's door! Little did they know their Yurka!) and flowers galore.

I improved steadily and refused to allow Rose or anybody to fly out to be with me—what could they do? After several weeks of hospital care I moved into a charming little room in the house of a doctor's widow, who used her home for just such recuperative visits by patients who had been in the hospital where her husband had once been a staff member.

Since I was not allowed to move about much, my chief diversion was watching television and listening to radio. One day I heard the Texaco broadcast of a matinee of *Parsifal*. I lay on my chaise longue enjoying its soaring beauties even more than usual and reliving my own years at the Opera School, when I had been so immersed in its first American production. Those years came back to me very vividly, especially Mme. Lillie and all the wonderful privileges she had made it possible for me to enjoy afterwards.

When the opera reached its end (I could see myself reverently handing the Holy Grail to Amfortas) I was so deeply moved by memory that I wrote Lillie a ten-page letter. She was living in England with her adopted daughter; I had seen her only sporadically in recent years.

When the letter reached its destination, Flora, her daughter, wrote me immediately to tell me that on the very day of my writing to Lillie—and at about the time of the *Parsifal* broadcast—her mother had passed away. Quietly, sweetly, as she would do it if she had anything to say about it. I thought it curious that I, far away in Arizona, should have been with her in thought during her last hours on earth.

I had told my doctor that I was in no hurry to return home; that only when he was prepared to say that I was as completely recovered as it was humanly possible for me to be, was I willing to leave his ministrations. I truly believe that in that decision lay the greatest wisdom I have ever exercised. I carried out his instructions to the letter. In the ensuing years there has never been the slightest recurrence of the problem, and I have been extraordinarily well ever since.

Not long after, a vast new horizon opened up for me. Our government had at long last realized the importance of letting the world know that we can produce artists as well as automobiles—that our musicians can be matched with the finest in the world. When, under the aegis of the American National Theatre and Academy, the President's International Cultural Exchange Program sent Marion Anderson around the world, the effect of her artistry and of her personal nobility transcended that of a dozen visits by political dignitaries with stereotyped speeches tucked away in their brief cases.

In 1957 Jimmy Elliott (a Greek-American friend) invited me to participate in a project on which he had been working for some time: namely, to take a group of five American players overseas to appear in Athens, Greece, at the ancient Herod Atticus Odeon (as the Greeks call their open-air theatre) in an English reading of the Edith Hamilton translation of Aeschylus' *Prometheus Bound!* To play in Greece! In Athens!

It was a thrilling project. The players chosen were a Greek-American actor—George Bourlos—who had played the title role of Prometheus in Eve Sikelianos' famous production several years previously. Clarence Derwent, the President of Actors' Equity Association, Margaret Phillips, Michael Wager, George Matthews, Robert Graves and I made up our group. We were to be the opening attraction at the August Drama Festival which was to continue for several weeks.

Our cultural safari was made more than ordinarily interesting by its starring of Miss Edith Hamilton, the enchanting nonagenarian. It was really her show. She was charming, alert, chic and full of fun for all her ninety years, and we became great friends. Despite her deafness, my voice seemed to penetrate her handicap and she would roar with laughter over some of the theatre anecdotes I dug up for her. She was especially amused, one morning, when I told her that although I had played some strange parts in the past, this was the first time I had been called upon to play a heifer.

In studying the part of Io, I was baffled. She is the pitiful creature who, raped by Zeus, is then condemned by his wife, Hera, to take the form of a heifer and roam the universe forever, never finding rest, always stung by the Gadfly, "myriad-eyed son of Argus," into further agonized searching for a haven of peace. It is one of those highly pitched bravura roles which can become mere sustained synthetic hysteria. For the life of me I could not see how I should play it.

Then a flash of illumination came to me. Io could be thought of as the Eternal Artist—cursed, one might almost say, with genius which gives no rest, no lasting peace of mind to its possessor, always driven, stung by the Gadfly of ambition, until its mission on earth is finally fulfilled. Wagner, Gauguin, Van Gogh, must all have felt this compulsion. It was, perhaps, a somewhat contrived interpretation but it did help me to shape the part. Miss Hamilton loved the idea.

In Athens, our rehearsals had to be conducted after sundown, as the August heat made daytime rehearsing unfeasible. But the evening rehearsals gave us one indescribable privilege. As we sat (or stood) before our lecterns, rehearsing, we could see above us the magical beauty of the Parthenon bathed in moonlight. Night after night the wonder was there—almost not to be believed—transforming the rehearsal into a wondrous experience.

At last we faced the first night audience—a distinguished one, come primarily to honor dear Edith Hamilton. She opened the evening by accepting honorary citizenship of the city of Athens. It was a most impressive ceremony. Ambassador Allen spoke a few words of introduction. In a charming speech of acceptance Edith Hamilton enchanted us all:

It is a deep pleasure to be able to express my gratitude for the high privilege that has been bestowed upon me . . . by the Government of Greece in inviting me to Athens for the performance of the *Prometheus Bound* of Aeschylus. They are making it possible for me to see this masterpiece come to life, one of the greatest tragedies ever written and peculiarly fitted to express the conditions which confront us today in one country after another. Prometheus stands forever as the rebel against tyranny. He speaks wherever there is courage to stand up against wrong.

She looked so marvelous standing there in her pretty evening gown and cloak—facing the spot-lights and the admiring audience. Her voice carried perfectly in that open-air theatre, as clearly as a violin. She received a standing ovation in which we, on the stage, joined heartily.

In the beautiful printed program which our hosts had prepared, Jimmy Elliott wrote:

This present effort of ours is, we hope, only a prelude to an annual exchange between the Greek and American theatres. In this way, we can learn from one another and deeply enrich our theatre skills and appreciation.

Later, after the last of the audience had dispersed, I crept up to the hilltop by myself. Here, I mused, Lysistrata had kept vigil in the early dawn, waiting for the tardy Athenian women to come to hear her plan to save Greece. Thespis, I thought, must abide among those exquisite warmly-pale columns, looking down on the stage where so many of his children had poured out their tribute to him—the Father of the Theatre.

I stayed on in Greece for three weeks, spending two of them on a cruise which included all too brief visits to Mykonos, Kos, Rhodes, and Patmos. It left me eager to see many more of those islands so drenched in history and beauty.

CHAPTER 23

CHRISTMAS IN ANOTHER ATHENS

I BELIEVE IT WAS the late George Jean Nathan—that most caustic as well as brilliant of critics—who said that the autobiographies of most actresses gave him the impression that they all lived in a nunnery. I have no desire to create any such impression.

The failure of my marriage left me reluctant to repeat the experience. It has not been my good fortune to attract the type of man who might have made it seem worth while for me to turn my back on the theatre. Even had this happened, I doubt I should have made a success of domestic life—domesticity is not one of my talents. There have, of course, been successful marriages among professionals, but these were usually possible because there were related interests—either the combining of professional work, or a pattern of living which made allowances for the unconventional time-schedules, the frequent prolonged separations which theatre careers are apt to impose. One actress of my acquaintance—a famous and beautiful star, explained her impending divorce from her charming banker-husband thus: "He leaves the house before I am awake; when he returns I have already had an early dinner and am getting ready for my performance. By the time that is over and I'm free and ready for some fun, he is through for the day. It just doesn't work."

Twice since my own divorce there were love affairs which bore promise of developing into permanent attachments. One of these filled my life for many years with warmth and devotion and the sense of shared happiness. But time and long periods of separation finally attenuated the bond between us, and he found his happiness elsewhere.

The other relationship was shorter-lived. The high-powered charm which first attracted me became a solo performance to which I was expected to play the accompaniment. I soon realized that I would not be able to do this for very long—certainly not for a lifetime. But it was exciting enough while it lasted; I've never regretted the episode.

No, it is not easy for an actress to find the right answer to her emotional needs. Yet these are very real. There are few people who need so intensely to love and to feel themselves desired; it feeds the life-giving stream of the imagination which must draw upon the heart for its understanding and its sustenance. The heart must be kept warm.

One experience I went through was revealing in its intensity. It involved a married man of exceptionally powerful sex appeal. He was very famous. He had been married twice, and he was known to have had a great many extra-curricular love affairs. Women threw themselves at him. Actually, I think some deep-seated Yurka pride in my make-up helped me to resist the physical as well as mental magnetism which he exerted over me; I was reluctant to see my scalp dangling among so many others. But even more important was my awareness of his lack of tenderness, a lack from which I knew that a liaison with him would suffer. Without it there could be no fulfillment for me.

Fortunately, at the hour of decision, my touring separated us. I lived through weeks—months—of passionate regret for what I had not done. But I knew him to be ruthless and self-centered, that his desire for me was only another incident in his life and that the final outcome would bring me even more misery than I was now enduring. But it was a long time before I could pass through the city where he lived without being deeply disturbed for days afterwards. Yet I did what I had to do. Like the heroine in Hubert H. Davies' comedy *Cousin Kate:* "The men I love and the men who love me . . . they're never the same."

Perhaps the human interests, emotionally, of theatre people, were better served when actors were less respectable—less the Solid Citizens that they have become. The disappearance of glamour among the denizens of the theatre is not altogether conducive to illusions of romance, either for the participants or for the public which watches them. The movies, of course, see to it that love affairs are widely publicized. The heroine of *Camille* today, instead of being able to hide away in a rose-trellised cottage with her Armand, the world shut out, now finds herself listed in a daily gossip-column as "carrying a torch for Armand"; small candid cameras lurk everywhere. A love affair in which a celebrity is involved is public business, and few participants are allowed to forget it.

Friendships, however, have enriched my life immeasurably. Among those who have opened their hearts to me and given me a place in their lives have been an infinite number of men and women whose devotion has heightened my buoyant hours and sustained me when disappointment and tragedy took over. Less exacting in its demands than love, friendship can be a richly satisfying element in one's life. It calls for giving as well as receiving and helps to make life endurable.

In the spring of 1958, I was engaged to play the part of Mrs. Fairfax in the Broadway production of Huntington Hartford's dramatization of *Jane Eyre*. Mr. Hartford gave it a sumptuous production, and after an out-of-town try-out period of much tribulation, the right star was found for Mr. Rochester—Eric Portman. He was perfect for the part and the New York critics gave him rave notices. I was good enough as Mrs. Fairfax—nothing could have made it a good part.

But the real thrill for me was to walk once more through 44th Street to the Belasco Theatre, and this time to see my name in lights on the marquee of that playhouse. When the play closed, some twenty weeks later, I left for Palm Beach where I played in John van Druten's *I Remember Mama* again—co-starring Margaret O'Brien as Christine. More "solo" dates followed the Palm Beach engagement, dates which took me to Texas, Alaska and even to heavenly Hawaii.

Always there has been, in my veins, the need for more or less continuous activity. If it did not present itself in the form of a Broadway engagement, I would nevertheless find it outside that somewhat overrated perimeter. The decade between the Herod Atticus milestone in 1957, and 1967, was filled with a variety of engagements of one kind or another; some highly enjoyable, even if and when the financial reward was nil, as was the case when I played *The Corn Is Green* for the Equity Library Theatre. Seldom have I enjoyed a part more.

This producing organization, sponsored by the Actors' Equity Association, was originally brought into being in the spring of 1944 when actors were desperate. They realized that they must have a way to practice their craft—and to interest agents and managers by being seen (a perpetual and crying need!) in roles other than those available to them in our restrictive type-casting system. Or perhaps to just remind these agents and managers that they were still alive. Plays were to be produced on a minuscule budget, which gradually grew to be a little more generous. But never were the actors or crew paid any salaries.

After some years of producing on small, incredibly ill-equipped stages of various public libraries (hence its name), Actors' Equity Association took a long lease on a real theatre. It was the charming little Master Theatre at 103rd Street and Riverside Drive, in New York, part of what had originally been built as the Roerich Museum to honor the famous Russian painter, Nicholas Roerich. After Roerich's death it was turned into an hotel, the auditorium being rented from time to time.

Equity decided that having a star on the opening bill would attract attention to the new location, and invited me to open the new house with Emlyn Williams' play, *The Corn Is Green*. (I was on the verge of joining a friend on a trip to Japan. I'm always on the verge of going to Japan! I never go.)

The play and the part of Miss Moffat, the English school teacher, had attracted me long before it arrived on Broadway. After reading the London reviews, I even made an unsuccessful attempt to secure the American rights (I was told they were not available), as I felt sure that it was the play and the part I had always hoped to find. So I canceled my plans for the holiday in Japan and settled into rehearsals for what proved to be the best performance of a modern play I have ever given. I felt that my Miss Moffat stood right beside my Gina Ekdal in acting value. The director, Fred Rolfe, was exceptionally good; the cast couldn't have been better. They were all first-rate actors. And none of us was paid a cent, not even our bus or taxi fares, nor our lunches.

Yet I've never been happier in a part in my whole career. The theme of Emlyn Williams' play seemed to me to be even more timely than when it was first produced with Miss Barrymore giving her superb performance. The theme—emphasizing the need of training for leadership, the responsibility imposed by the gift of intelligence, regardless of class origins, seemed to me (and still does) something which needs to be emphasized and dramatized in the moral climate in which we live.

So entranced was I with the job we were all doing that I approached a Broadway management to see if we could be transferred to one of their theatres, the company intact. He said the cost would be prohibitive, and that, although he admired what I was doing with the part, I should probably only succeed in getting a lovely new set of notices for Miss Barrymore. I thought it rather touching that he believed that such loyalty existed. But perhaps he was right. Perhaps one *must* die before one earns such loyalty.

Later I gave an Equity Library Benefit Performance of my "one-woman" program to raise money for the Equity Theatre's production fund. The theatre was ideal in size for such a performance—and they realized a tidy little sum.

Somewhat later I did a series of these performances at another small "off-Broadway" theatre called Stage 73, located on East 73rd Street. Romney Brent did a re-staging of the presentation which brought fresh life into it after so many performances through the years. I really was a little proud of this feat of memory and concentration in portraying some sixteen different characters, alone, and without a prompter, for two solid hours, especially as a famous rival of mine was circulating a rumor that I no longer could retain lines!

There were also two interesting guest-star engagements at the Brattle Street Playhouse in Cambridge, Massachusetts. This company, started by a group of Harvard garduates, produced over the years a series of plays of such high quality as has, to my knowledge, never been equaled anywhere in America. It also developed the talents of several important people: Albert Marre, the director whom we have to thank, among other things, for his superb direction of *Man of La Mancha;* Jerome Kilty, actor and author of *Dear Liar* which has become an international success; Robert O'Hearn, designer whose sets at the Metropolitan have been hailed as wonderful—and several others who achieved distinction.

I did Mrs. Malaprop in *The Rivals* for them, playing her as somewhat younger than is customary; I felt that she need not necessarily be the formidable old harridan most productions made her seem. She lost none of her humor by being played less broadly.

Betty Field came up to co-star with me in *The Wild Duck*. She was very worried about not being young enough to play the fourteen year old Hedvig. She need not have been; her performance grew in youthfulness and pathos so convincingly that I said to her, "If you get any younger in this part, you'll have the Gerry Society (organized to prevent the exploitation of children) closing us up."

How odd that the artistic elite of Cambridge and Boston would fail to rally to the support of this hard-working and dedicated group when financial problems and the lack of a proper auditorium forced it to close shop and disperse!

Then there was a delightful interlude spent in another Athens; this time, Athens, Ohio, as a guest player in *I Remember Mama*. I spent two weeks there at Christmas time. Never have I been so immersed in the Christmas spirit. Every home, every sorority and fraternity house was beautifully decorated and, at dusk, illuminated with candle light. We did *Mama* for a week. The play lent itself well to the talents of the youthful cast. Most touching was the farewell ("farvel"—as Uncle Chris would say) tendered me; the whole cast, director Chris Lane and his family, as well as several of the faculty, came to see me off at the station. They sang Christmas carols and presented me with a beautifully inscribed evening bag—my Christmas present from the cast. I boarded the train with tears in my eyes.

CHAPTER 24

WISH ME WELL

SEVERAL YEARS AGO, when the papers announced that Tyrone Guthrie was organizing, in Minneapolis, Minnesota, the theatre which carries his name, and that he was to direct the repertory of plays to be done the first season, I was excited. I wrote him at once, hoping to be invited to join him. It seemed only logical that I, a native daughter, should be in the first repertory company to be established in my home state.

Actually, Minnesota itself did not especially attract me. I had memories of those November-to-May winters. Snow galore and for endless weeks. Besides, St. Paul (where I was born) had shown a marked indifference to my one-woman celebrity, although Minneapolis (St. Paul's "twin city") had had me out there three different times. I was not in love with my birthplace.

But the real motive for my application was Tyrone Guthrie himself. I had met Dr. Guthrie and his warmly sympathetic wife, Judith, several years before he emerged as the white hope of the English speaking theatre, and I prized their friendliness. To have the privilege of watching him put on a play, of working under so exceptional a director, was something for which I longed . . . something I had all too seldom enjoyed.

His replies to my letters were, of course, disarming—and kindly. But there were, it appeared, no parts suitable for me in the repertory of plays planned for the first season. Nor for the second. I gave up. (So much for "knowing the right people!") I have learned, at long last, to take such things philosophically. It did not change my feelings of warm affection for the Guthries.

Imagine my pleasure, therefore, when, one sunny day in New York, in the early spring of 1966, Dr. Guthrie's voice on the phone invited me to come down to see him to discuss a play he was to direct for Broadway—a revival of Kaufman and Ferber's

Dinner at Eight. He stressed that he wanted it to be an "all-star" cast and wanted me to be a part of it.

Excitement blazed in my breast. I remembered the play only vaguely, but I did remember that there was the part of an aging actress—a composite of Maxine Elliott and Mrs. Patrick Campbell. Having known them both, I knew it would be my meat— that I could do the part beautifully.

Imagine my feelings when Tony Guthrie handed me a copy of the play and said: "I want you to play the Swedish cook." A moment of dreadful silence ensued. I managed to keep my face immobile and my eyes down, letting no trace of my feelings show. I searched for the part in the play, meanwhile thinking very fast: "You've always wanted to watch Guthrie work; that is the important thing to remember. This is your chance to do it; you can watch him direct even better, if you are not worrying yourself stiff over that long, wordy part of the gabby actress." One rationalizes. One has to!

Finally, I found the place in the script where Mrs. Wendel's few lines were buried. She had two brief scenes. She could be played with a Swedish accent—and I could sense that there were two or three good laugh-lines if I were very, very clever. I made up my mind I would be.

Rising cheerily to my feet, I went in to talk "bizness" with the producer. I agreed to an infinitesimal salary, assuming this would be a necessary concession by every one of the eight or nine stars involved, especially since the play called for seven changes of sets and two revolving stages, making it a very expensive project for the management.

Only when I reached the street did I begin to laugh; at myself, at the theatre in which I worked, even a little at God! (I'm sure He didn't mind!)

Contracts were signed. It was nice to have settled plans. Rehearsals were to begin in August. There was, however, the New York summer ahead; the horrible heat, the customary breakdown of one's apartment air-conditioning, the breathless nights —all of which can make you wish that Peter Stuyvesant had never put through that little business deal with the Indians.

I have lived through many of these summers. So with my theatre plans all set for rehearsals on August 22, I began to look at travel folders. I remember, in my childhood, a friend of Mila's

who spent most of her leisure examining these folders and planning trips to far-distant places. She never went to any of them;
she had no money. When someone said to her, "But, Anna, you
never take these trips!" she answered, "It doesn't cost me anything to dream, does it?"

A travel agent with whom I had tentatively negotiated earlier
called me suddenly: "That stateroom I talked to you about several weeks ago, on the *Bergensfjord,* is still available. It's a good
buy. The cruise goes to Iceland; you hate the heat. Why don't
you grab it?" "When does it sail?" I asked. "Tomorrow afternoon! I'll meet you at the gangplank You can pay me by check
then." Iceland!—instead of our muggy New York heat! I said,
"O.K. See you on the dock." Next afternoon I sailed.

Unlike many of my friends, I like cruises—"floating hotels" as
one of the staff on the *Bergensfjord* called them. I know it is
considered more chic to go off by yourself when traveling, or
with perhaps one or two companions although this, too, has its
risks. But on a cruise, if you happen not to like your companions, you can always hie away to your stateroom, or to a remote
corner of a deck and catch up on your reading, leaving the bulk
of your fellow-travelers to their cocktails and their endless
bridge games. For some people these cruises are a whole way of
life. My estate is the more gracious in that I love to retire early
and get up early, so I escape the endless bingo games, jitter-
bugging and other forms of diversion which the attractive "entertainment personnel" plan so assiduously for the cruise guests.

When the word that I was a "celebrity" leaked out (owing to
my late departure, my name was not on the passenger list)
people beamed at me—I found myself using my smiling muscles
far more than was my habit in daily life. But that was good for
me—a painless face-lift which has seemingly had lasting effect,
for my friends have been saying ever since, "How well you are
looking!"

As the great ship headed northward I realized that there is,
unquestionably, some kinship between me and those Northern
countries. It had made me fall in love with Ibsen—it drew me to
Norway years ago when Stalheim and Gudvangen revealed their
beauty to me. Now I was to go much farther North, up past
glaciers with their great expanses of blue ice which made you
think that an unbelievable amount of "blueing" must have
been expended to achieve that effect; the fantastic midnight sun,

and fjords of indescribable beauty. How could one wish for more?

I made a half-dozen new friends, whose kindness and charm added immeasurably to my enjoyment of those few weeks and, I hope and trust, to the rest of my life. I refused the rather pressing request that I do "an evening" of my scenes for the entertainment of the guests, not feeling inclined to give up my relaxed mental state. I've always felt a little ashamed of that persistent refusal; the entertainment-captain was such a charming fellow! I was delighted with the "coolth" (as a youngster I know calls it) of the climate; never a day without a sweater, never a night without a blanket.

One night I suddenly became conscious of the very slow speed at which the huge ship was moving. Frequently it would stop altogether. Later I learned that we had passed through a very narrow fjord, in the waters of which several mines had been laid during the German occupation; because of the great expense involved in removing them they had never been detonated. The *Bergensfjord* was the first large steamer (18,750 tons) to pass through those waters since the war. The superb seamanship of our distinguished captain (Capt. Odd Aspelund) was our only protection from possible disaster.

Finally I had to leave the cruise at a certain place on the itinerary and fly back to the States in order to report at the first rehearsal of *Dinner at Eight* at 10 A.M., on August 22. Several important cities in Europe had to be skipped, but they were cities I had already seen, so I was not too disconsolate. On Sunday night of August 21, I was back in my New York apartment; on Monday at 10 A.M. I was at the Alvin Theatre ready for work. Dr. Guthrie beamed. Someone had bet him that I wouldn't be there. He had won.

Everything went well from the start. Miniature settings had been set up on the tables; the costume designs (period of 1932) were displayed for us to study, and a group of really charming and talented people were assembled to begin work under ideal circumstances. I was delighted to see the familiar faces of old friends: Walter Pidgeon, Darren McGavin, and June Havoc. The production was too heavy to be traveled, so a week of previews led us right into the opening night on September 22, 1966 at the Alvin Theatre.

There was excitement in the air. The first night floral tributes were overwhelming; the passageway to our dressing rooms was almost impassable. I was deeply touched by the reception which greeted my first entrance. I had not had a Broadway opening for some years, and I was not prepared for the burst of applause which came when Mrs. Wendel lumbered across the stage mixing a batter, impervious to the chaos existing throughout that crazy household. Perhaps her down-to-earth quality, after all the disturbed or flighty characters which the authors had presented in their social satire, made my part a welcome diversion. The characterization took hold of the audience's imagination immediately. In Act II, the lobster aspic calamity drew huge and heartening laughs, a sound as welcome as manna from heaven to an actor. Only a dozen lines or so—but that second scene was worth anyone's playing. (I recalled Stanislavski's quoting of Dantchenkov's remark: "There are no small parts; only small actors.") And the applause on my exit after that aspic-scene was even greater than that which greeted my entrance. In the dimness backstage, Walter Pidgeon embraced me and whispered ecstatically, "I heard them in my dressing room. I had to come down . . . it was thrilling . . . honey, they love you!" These are moments that make up for the many heartaches the dear old theatre can deal out to its adherents. I was a very happy woman.

And happy I continued to be throughout the run of *Dinner at Eight*. Because of the "all-star" cast, a constant stream of celebrities came backstage to congratulate us. Among those who came to see me was one who left an indelible impression: Tallulah swept down the corridor, opened her arms, embraced me and said, in a voice charged with emotion: "Dahling, you were simply wonderful! where's the john?" "Right behind you," I answered. She disappeared and I saw her no more.

Yet, after she had left I found myself thinking, as I so often had, of the superb talent which she had wasted. She to whom had been given the immense vitality which is the bedrock of all great talent; rare physical beauty which she had not bothered to preserve; above all, real acting talent of which she gave us occasional glimpses with long stretches of absence or frivolous radio appearances.

Had she only had the dedication and the respect for the *art* of the theatre which, for instance, we find in the lives of a Bernhardt or a Chaliapin, Tallu could have out-acted all her American contemporaries.

The manuscript of this book, which I had begun some years before, had languished for a long time in a suitcase in the back of my closet—unopened—a piece of unfinished business which I could neither tackle nor throw into the incinerator as I had often been sorely tempted to do.

Suddenly a fresh access of energy animated me. I pulled out the battered old suitcase where the manuscript lay and got to work. A Herculean job! At 6 P.M., I would quickly make up as Mrs. Wendel—then settle down to examine what I had written the previous night. Often I worked until one o'clock in the deserted theatre until the night watchman came to tell me he had to lock up. How glad I was that my part (so short, so rewarding!) was tidily placed in the middle of the play so that I could go on stage, play it, and then concentrate on this other task in my dressing room.

Presently another interest developed. I had many times been asked if I would teach, and actually, in two instances, my pupils became professionals. I felt impelled to use some of my boundless energy in the coaching field because it is clear that those of us who have solved some of these acting problems have a responsibility to share our knowledge. Leonard Lyons heard of it and mentioned it in his column. People began to call me.

My sister, Rose, having passed away, I converted her room into an exciting little studio and took on a few young pupils. One or two show great promise, and I have found working with them very stimulating.

Whenever actors foregather—in drugstores, at Sardi's, or in small groups anywhere—endless discussions ensue on "the alien question." They comment bitterly, if they are in the neighborhood of Broadway and 45th Street, on the fact that in the entire block, some five or six theatres are housing English companies, playing almost invariably, English plays.

There is much bitterness in the ranks of Equity, whose council has been trying for years to find some equitable way to cope with this take-over. But there is one indubitable fact to be faced: British actors are better trained in most instances than are ours.

One day after discussing the alien situation with some young actor friends, I felt impelled to write the following letter to my fellow-councilors of the Actors' Equity Association:

. . . I have read carefully all the "explosion" re the alien situation and I must say I admire the determined attack being made by some of our younger members upon the shocking proportion of English players now dominating our Broadway theatre scene.

I say this despite my very warm appreciation of the fine performances being currently exhibited on Broadway by our visitors from abroad. Being on the "Tony" awards committee, I have seen practically every hit play in town and have watched some superb British acting talent. . . .

But—when I hear quoted in our papers scathing remarks by certain American managers whose pro-British policy is supported by some of our critics—I feel prompted to point out certain facts of theatre practice as I have known them these past twenty years or so on Broadway.

"They" speak a good deal about the "impossibility" of finding American actors who are capable of acting (according to them) with any knowledge of style. How much effort is put forth by them, I wonder, to locate such "rara avis" in our membership? I will, lest I embarrass certain of my colleagues, take only myself as an example.

Being fortunate enough to have been exposed to "good English" at an early age, and never having had any reason to discard its use, I was equipped from the start of my acting career to play to English-speaking roles from almost any walk of life. Add to this my passionate interest in well-spoken words and you have the explanation of my being able to play roles such as the Queen to Barrymore's Hamlet—the "Electra" of Sophocles—Aristophanes' "Lysistrata"—the Nurse in "Romeo and Juliet"—and a dozen or so of modern scripts which are not important enough to mention (even though one of them did run a full year on Broadway). Yet, for the past ten years— and possibly a little more—I have seen one good part after another being cast with imported (usually English) actresses, while I sat at home twiddling my thumbs and asking, "Why?" In several instances the characters were American women—which didn't make the situation any clearer.

One concrete instance comes to mind—though I am perhaps foolish to tell it—since it points up the fact that actresses (even those who have achieved stellar status) must at times not only eat but pay the rent. A few years of idleness can wipe out anyone's bank account.

A management, which shall be nameless, asked me if I would be willing to stand-by for a famous English star, who was seemingly not feeling quite well even though she was playing in a hit! Both the part and the play interested me and I thought it would be better for my morale to be rehearsing than to be sitting biting my nails in idleness. Besides, I could use the money.

When the manager and I came to discussing that subject, I mentioned what seemed reasonable to me—half of my customary salary (never a monumental one). We finally settled on terms far from satisfactory to me, and I did "cover" the part for about six weeks.

But that's not my chief point. One day after an understudy rehearsal, he said, "You should have played this part in the first place." To which I replied, "What a pity you didn't think of that when you were first casting." He looked embarrassed. I meant that he should. I'm telling you this lengthy tale merely because it is not only the small-part people who suffer from this virus of pro-British snobbism which so sorely affects our theatre. British Equity wouldn't tolerate such a condition for one week. We all know that.

Enclosed is a brochure which indicates the range of "style" which my one-woman program requires me to draw upon. I think it tells its own story. I have actually played almost all those parts—most of them on Broadway.

I call attention, finally, to the fact that a few years ago, Diana Wynyard (a lovely Britisher) was imported to play the American mother of John Kerr in Elmer Rice's "Cue for Passion." Why? Had the manager never heard of Peggy Wood, Aline MacMahon, Geraldine Page, Cornelia Otis Skinner, Violet Heming, Eva LeGallienne —even Blanche Yurka? We must find some final solution to this most embarrassing and unsatisfactory situation.

Our American stage has a fine tradition. American players have from time to time over many decades given performances comparable to the best to be seen on any stage. I feel that I can say this with authority; I have seen acting in five different languages.

If the lowered standards of our present theatre have resulted in a deterioration of the equipment, vocal, physical and even mental, which our players and directors bring to their work, then the place to cope with these limited techniques is in the studio.

One story illustrates this: Gilbert Miller once told a friend of mine that when he went to Paris one year he wanted to talk to Gabrielle Dorziat about presenting her in a play in New York. She was, and is, one of the shining stars of the French Theatre. She spoke English beautifully and had appeared here some fifty years previously on Broadway in *The Hawk* produced by William Faversham. When Mr. Miller telephoned her he suggested a certain hour the next day for an interview. "Impossible, Monsieur," she replied, "that is the hour when I take my acting lesson!" He was enormously impressed.

We must learn to do as well—even better than our visiting players from abroad if this problem is to be intelligently and permanently resolved. We must have the courage to face facts. One must continue to study. Relatively few American actors do.

The year 1966–67 was a wonderful one for me. It was the year in which I finally worked with Tyrone Guthrie and when I learned again that no part is too small to be worth playing well. It was a notable year for several other reasons as well.

My fellow players awarded me the highest honor they could bestow: an honorary life membership on the Actors' Equity Council. At the March 31 meeting of Actors' Equity, Angus Duncan presented the award with the following citation:

It has been Council's intention to grant future life memberships only as an honor or award to such Equity members who have distinguished themselves, or who have rendered great service to Equity. No such awards have been given until now.

The Council has now found someone who is deserving of the honor and who, in turn, honors Equity by being the first recipient since the change in its status. The recipient who has had a long and distinguished career in the theatre and who has served on the Council, from which she is now retiring after serving 17 out of the past 32 years.

Equity has many members with long and distinguished careers and many of them have served on the Council. So, there is an additional ingredient present which caused the Council to unanimously and unerringly choose this first recipient, which need not be further explained, when I say that I am happy to present on behalf of the Council and the entire membership this life membership card, with a gold star, to Miss Blanche Yurka. As I moved forward to make my response, Mr. Duncan offered me the microphone. "No thank you," I said. "If I need that thing, I don't deserve this." I got my laugh.

ANTA too paid me tribute when Colonel Lawton Campbell, its chairman, presented me with a gold medal which is only awarded once every five years.

It was a year distinguished by the publication, to my utter astonishment, of a little poem which I had tossed off some years ago:

FRIENDS

There's a little black doorway and not any door,
And you go down a passage with stones on the floor,
And it's ever so dark, and the wall's rough and hard,
And you turn round a corner, then into a yard,
And there's steps that go down to the water.

And out in the yard there's a very old man
Who's painting a boat; and he says if he can—
And the boat's ever finished—we'll go out to sea
And bring back a big fish—bigger'n me!
So I sit on the steps to the water.

I'd like to be old and be painting a boat
And have some white whiskers, and not wear a coat
And live in a shack; 'cause then I could play
And paddle, an' climb up an' down all the day
On steps that go down to the water.

Another delightful honor descended upon my surprised shoulders when I received the following telegram:

"Very happy inform you Board of Trustees voted Doctor of Humane Letters Honoris Causa Unanimously. We need list of friends to be informed or invited.

Congratulations
David E. Delo Pres
University of Tampa"

Of course I was thrilled. And as I sat on the platform, listening to the presentation eulogy, I couldn't believe it was me Dr. Delo was describing. I had an amusing vision of my sister Rose sitting somewhere on a rose-colored cloud, saying, "That brat! She never even finished high school—had no education, really. And I, a schoolteacher for fifty years—and nobody ever made me a 'Doctor of Humane Letters, Honoris Causa.' She was always lucky!"

And I'm sure le bon Dieu, or whichever of his representatives was nearby smiled and said, "Aren't you glad she was?"

When some years ago I threw a party to celebrate my sixty years on Broadway I am sure that some of my friends thought I had finally decided to retire from acting. Nothing could be further from my thoughts. After all, I shall be celebrating my eighty-third birthday as this book is published.

But my friends were wrong. This vitality with which I have been blessed continues to sweep me on to all sorts of exciting activities. In May, 1969, I did another one-woman show at the University of Tampa in Florida where Dr. Hugh Fellows is building a superb speech department.

And I recently packed my bags once more. I was invited to star in London in Giraudoux' *The Madwoman of Chaillot,* a part which Walter Huston once said to me "was written for you." And so it might have been. Indeed, the manager who first bought the rights to the play for Broadway called me to say, "I've just bought a play with a wonderful part for you. Only you must play it." But, alas, she failed to raise all the necessary backing and then her rights expired and someone else did it. But the part has haunted me ever since and here, ten years later, came the fulfillment of my desire to play it. Miracles do happen, and this was one of them.

Since my purest joy has always been in what some people call work, I count myself most fortunate to be able to continue in my profession. I hope I shall be able to do so until my last breath. Meanwhile, dear audience, wish me well.

AFTERWORD

BEFORE BLANCHE YURKA played the crucial part of Gina, Ibsen's *The Wild Duck* was generally looked upon as a trifling play. But the beautifully modulated performance by the Actors' Theatre and Miss Yurka's measured acting of the inarticulate, patient heroine reversed the public attitude. Since her memorable performance, *The Wild Duck* has been recognized in America as a penetrating and compassionate play—a devastating attack on the mischief of self-righteousness. When she read the text of *The Wild Duck,* Blanche Yurka noted some essential points that had always escaped my notice. She saw that Gina had three of the five curtain speeches and one especially dramatic scene towards the end when Gina learns that her child has committed suicide. Being a professional actress she read *The Wild Duck* in terms of the scenes in which she could best use her skills. It is because of such thoughtful interpretations and sensitive performances that Blanche Yurka is and always has been a total actress.

Blanche Yurka's autobiography is invaluable for many reasons—including her fond description of her life as a girl in St. Paul and her account of the life of an impecunious family in New York. Nothing in her girlhood prepared her for a stage career. Her mother thought, with good reason, that a career as a teacher would be more secure. Miss Yurka did not decide to become an actress: everything that interested her pushed her in that direction. Her cousin acted in Richard Mansfield's company and sustained the bruises of his temperament. As a girl Miss Yurka thought that her cousin's repeated disappointments and setbacks were dramatic and well worth enduring. In school she loved languages and history but loathed mathematics—a proper scale of values for any actress. And she has never learned to cook—which may also indicate a sound theatrical temperament.

She forced the theatre to accept her. When Miss Yurka was a member of the chorus at the Metropolitan, she schemed a way to emerge from the ensemble. She persuaded the director to let her play the wordless part of the bearer of the grail in *Parsifal,* and Henry Krehbiel, critic for the *New York Tribune,* mentioned her in his notice. He complimented the "little lady who carried the grail with such a reverent and touching consecration to her sacred duties"—a heady experience for an adolescent.

When Miss Yurka realized that she could never be a great singer, she persevered until, after a long, weary interlude, David Belasco offered her a walk-on part that paid one dollar a week. After she had become an actress, and in due time a star, her commitment to the theatre remained total and is best revealed by her in a comment about rehearsals for *The Wild Duck:* "I find it difficult, distasteful even, to revert to the routine of daily living. This explains why some theatre people lead a life of isolation with few outside contacts." Theatre people refer to members of the public as "private persons." Although Miss Yurka has a privtae life she is a "public person." In her scale of values acting on the stage has first priority. Giving the public a good performance takes precedence over everything. "Consecration" is a word Henry Krehbiel used about her silent acting as the grail bearer. It describes every moment of her career.

Did the theatre return her devotion? She played Gertrude in the illustrious Barrymore production of *Hamlet.* She had a long and entertaining interlude in *The Squall* which ran forever. She played Electra. She played Hedda Gabler. Even if there had been nothing more, this would be enough reward for a lifetime of devotion. Blanche Yurka is not a civilian. She is an actress; her values are theatrical.

Brooks Atkinson

INDEX

Actors' Equity Association, 76–77, 295; Equity Library Theatre, 287; and pro-English problem, 295–97

Actors' Fidelity League, 76

Actors' Theatre (Equity Players), 83, 85, 86; production of *The Wild Duck,* 86, 90–93

Aherne, Brian, 169, 172, 215, 218

Americans in France, The, 82

Anderson, Dallas, 139

ANTA (American National Theatre and Academy), 213–14

Archer, William, 86, 147. See also *The Wild Duck;* review of

Arden, Elizabeth, 181

Athens, Ohio, 289

Atkinson, Brooks, 271. *See also* "Afterword," 301–02

Bankhead, Tallulah, 294

Barrymore, John, 98–102, 210

Beckhard, Arthur, 154–55, 167, 169, 170, 173

Beebe, Elswyth Thane (Mrs. William), 135, 181–82

Beebe, William, 182–83; *Half a Mile Down,* 183

Belasco, David, 37–40, 53–55, 107, 114, 234

Bel Geddes, Norman, 151–53

Ben-Ami, Jacob, 84

Benchley, Robert: *The Squall,* review of, 116; *Spring in Autumn,* review of, 175

Berkeley Greek Theatre, 246, 249

Bernhardt, Sarah, 115, 249–50

Birthplace (St. Paul, Minn.), 3, 290

Bradford, Roark, 239

Brady, William A., 94

Brent, Romney, 115, 122, 210, 219, 288

Brown, John Mason: *Romeo and Juliet,* review of, 218; one-woman show, review of, 234

Burleigh, Harry, 12

Byrd, Sam, 239

Campbell, Mrs. Patrick, 16, 158–60, 162–63

Čapek, Karol, 257–58

Carry Nation (Frank McGrath), 166, 168

Caubet, Suzanne, 115

Chandler, Helen, 87. See also *The Wild Duck;* review of

Charlie (brother), 7, 48, 130; death of, 154

Chevalier, Maurice, 53

Clayton, Ethel, 112

Collinge, Patricia, 58, 95, 109

Colman, Ronald, 223, 225

Comic Artist, The (Susan Gaspell), 173, 174

Conried, Heinrich, 14, 17

Conway, Jack, 220, 222, 225

Cornell, Katharine, 158, 164; in *Candida,* 83, 86; in *Lucrece,* 169, 170, 171, 172; in *Romeo and Juliet,* 215–16

Cowl, Jane, 54, 75–76, 83; and *Lilac Time,* 68–69; and *Daybreak,* 69–72; and *Enter Madame,* 79, 80

Cummings, William, 243–44

Dale, Esther (Mrs. Arthur Beckhard), 154, 166, 167, 168, 175
Damrosch, Dr. Frank, 32
Davis, Bette, 148, 149, 221
Dietrichstein, Leo, 82
Diggs, Dudley, 87, 88
Dunn, Emma, 63; and influence on Blanche Yurka, 49–50

Eames, Clare (Mrs. Dudley Diggs), 86–88
Electra, 44, 185, 248
Elizabeth the Queen (Maxwell Anderson), 229, 230
Elliott, Maxine, 78–79
Enter Madame (Gilda Varsi), 79, 80, 81
Evans, Edith, 215

Falkenburg, Jinks, 223
Fogarty, Dame Elsie, 180, 183–84
Fontanne, Lynn, 83, 102–04, 157
Freedley, George: *Dear Audience*, review of, 278
Fremstad (singer), 16, 18–19
Friebus, Florida, 147
Fuchs, Anton, 17
Fuller, Rosalinde, 97
Furness, Dr. Howard Horace, 151, 152–153

Garland, Robert: *The Comic Artist*, review of, 174
Gielgud, John, 210
Girl of the Golden West, The (La Fanciulla del West), 59
Goat Song (Franz Werfel), 102–03
Gould, Jay, 183
Gray, James: one-woman show, review of, 235
Greenacre Fellowship, 22–23
Gulbranson, Ellen, 47
Guthrie, Tyrone, 35, 290–91

Hamilton, Edith, 281–82
Hammond, Percy: *The Wild Duck*, review of, 90–91; *Lady from the Sea*, review of, 146
Harkness Theatre, Yale, 178

Hartley, Marsden, 23
Henderson, Robert: director, Detroit Civic Theatre, 164; producer of *Electra*, 155–58, 246
Hepburn, Katharine, 44
Hobart, John: interview with Blanche Yurka by, 246
Hope, Anthony, 210–11
Hopkins, Arthur, 63, 65; and production of *Hamlet*, 96, 97, 98
Horton, Edward Everett, 57
Houghton, Norris, 273
Hughes, Betty, 23
Hutchison, Muriel, 245, 247

Jones, Jennifer, 240
Jones, Robert Edmond, 97, 99, 145, 169
Julius Caesar, 13

Kalich, Bertha (Mrs. Leopold Spachner), 48–49
Kauffman, George, 66
Keith, Ian: marriage of, 95–97, 111–113; and John Barrymore, 101; and *As You Like It*, 105–10
Khan, Mirza Ali Kuli, 23
Krehbiel, Henry Edward: *Parsifal*, review of, 18

Lady from the Sea, 146
Last Days of the Turbins (Michael Bulgakov): Moscow Art Theatre production of, 177–78, 195–96; Yale production of, 178–79
Lindsay, Howard, 160
Logan, Josh, 155, 167–68, 242
Loraine, Robert, 169, 170
Lord Dundreary, 65
Lucrece (The Rape of Lucrece, Andre Obey), 169, 170, 172
Lunt, Alfred, 102–04
Lydia Mendelsohn Theatre, 157
Lysistrata, 151, 212

McClintic, Guthrie, 169–70, 215, 216
McLaughlin, Russell: *The Merchant of Venice*, review of, 164
McMein, Neysa, 66

Magda, 39, 40, 234
Malone, Dudley Field, 85, 109
Malvern Festival, 184
Maminka (mother), 3–4, 6, 11, 24, 67; previous marriage of, 25–26; influence on Blanche's role in *The Wild Duck*, 89; death of, 104
Man and the Masses (Ernst Toller), 84, 185
Mantle, Burns: *Electra*, review of, 162; *Romeo and Juliet*, review of, 217–18
March, Fredric (Bickel), 94–95, 221
Marlowe, Julia, 64–65
Masaryk, Jan, 227–28
Mathis, June, 123–24
Metropolitan Opera School, 15–16
Mila (half-sister), 7, 25, 27, 75; death of, 116–18
Mizerovska (maid), 122–23
Montgomery, Douglass, 252
Murfin, Jane, 68, 69, 70
My Ántonia (Willa Cather), 3

Nazimova, Alla, 90, 219, 263, 264
Nordica (singer), 16, 19
Nowak, Adelaide (cousin), 12–13, 33

Oliver, Edna May, 224

Parker, H. T.: *Electra*, review of, 156
Parsifal, 17
Paxinou, Katina, 267–68
Perley, Miss, (grammar school teacher), 10–11
Pickford, Mary, 50–52
Power, Tyrone, Sr., 97
Powers, Tom, 87, 89. See also *The Wild Duck;* review of
Preminger, Otto, 259
Price, Vincent, 243–44

Rathbone, Basil, 215, 218, 221
Ratoff, Gregory, 124
Revolt of the Actors (Alfred Harding), 77
Reynolds, James, 158, 160
Robinson, Edward G., 103
Roeder, Ralph, 145, 254

Rölvaag, O. E., 137
Romeo and Juliet, 230
Romero, Cesar, 222
Rose (sister), 7

Saginaw, Michigan, 237–38
Sang-Collins, Lillie, 21, 24, 28, 31; death of, 280
Schirmer, Rudolph, 21–22, 45
Selznick, David O., 220, 225
Sesso, Mlle. (French teacher), 13
Shaw, George Bernard, 211
Sheaffer, Louis, 275
Sheppard, John Tresidder, 155
Shubert, Lee, 64, 139, 140, 271
Sikelianos, Eva (Palmer), 166–67
Simonson, Lee, 84, 102, 185
Skinner, Otis, 135–36
Skinner, Richard Dana: *The Wild Duck*, review of, 92–93; *Hedda Gabler,* review of, 142
Sokol, 6
Sothern, E. H., 64, 65, 66
Spring in Autumn (Marlenez Sierra), 134, 174–76
The Squall (Jean Bart [pseud.]) 114–116, 125, 132, 133
Stage Women's War Relief, 61
Stanislavski, Constantin, 35, 100, 103, 202–05
Starr, Frances, 42
Stefansson, Vilhjalmur, 92
Stokowski, Leopold, 28–31, 41–44
Szold, Bernard, 239

A Tale of Two Cities (movie), 219
Tatinek (father), 4, 6; teaching career of, 4–5; interest in theater of, 5–6; and Czech Benevolent Society, 8; temperament of, 7, 27; marriage of, 26–27; blindness of, 66; death of, 73
Taylor, Loretta, 83
Tellegen, Lou, 62–63
Ternina, Milka, 16
Thomas, Augustus, 106
Thomas, Joe, 126–27
Toller, Ernst, 84–85, 201

Tony (brother), 8, 166; death of, 128
Traubel, Horace, 23

Wadleigh High School, 12, 13
Wagner Music Festival (Bayreuth), 45, 47
Wagner, Robert F., 213
Walker, Charlotte, 64
Walker, Robert, 240
Walker, Stuart, 109–11, 149–50, 221, 261
Warrens of Virginia, The, 49
Welles, Halstead, 177–78
Welles, Orson, 165, 215
Wild Duck, The: reviews of, 90–93
WPA (Works Project Administration), 165
Wright, Frank Lloyd, 279
Wyatt, Jane, 252

Yersin *système*, 22
Yurka, Blanche: childhood, 3–10; East 68th Street Grammar School, 10; *The Bohemian Girl*, 11–12; high school education, 12–13; introduction to opera, 13; and Metropolitan Opera School, 14–20; *Parsifal*, 17–18, 280; review of, in *Parsifal*, 18; *Il Trovatore*, 20; interview with Rudolph Schirmer, 21, 32; Greenacre Fellowship, 22–23; theatrical tryouts, 33–36; and St. Bartholomew's Choir, 28–31, 42–43; auditions for David Belasco, 36–40; contract with David Belasco, 41–42; trip to Wagner Music Festival, 45–47; *The Warrens of Virginia*, 49–52; *Is Matrimony a Failure?*, 54; *An Old New Yorker*, 56; summer stock, 56–57; "name in lights," 57; *Don*, 57; *Everywoman*, 58; *Secret Strings*, 62; *The House of Bondage*, 63; *The Two Virtues*, 64; *Lord Dundreary*, 65; *Daybreak*, 70–75; production of *The Wayfarer*, 80–82; *The Americans in France*, 82; and yoga, 83, 127, 175; *Man and the Masses*, 84; *The Wild Duck*, 86–93, 138–39, 242; *The Lawbreaker*, 94; *Hamlet*, 96–100;

Goat Song, 102–03; marriage to Ian Keith, 95, 105–11; *The Squall*, 114–125; *A Doll's House*, 137–38; *Hedda Gabler*, 141–44; reviews of, in *Hedda Gabler*, 142, 144–45, 149; *Lady from the Sea*, 145–47; review of, in *Lady from the Sea*, 149; *L'Arlesienne*, 150; *Lysistrata*, 150–54, 242; *Electra*, 156–62, 246–51; reviews of, in *Electra*, 156–57, 162–63; *The Way of the World*, 157–58; *The Merchant of Venice*, 164–65; review of, in *The Merchant of Venice*, 165; *Carry Nation*, 167–68; review of, in *Carry Nation*, 168–69; *Lucrece*, 169–72; review of, in *Lucrece*, 171; *Comic Artist*, 173–74; review of, in *Comic Artist*, 174; *Spring in Autumn*, 175–76; review of, in *Spring in Autumn*, 175; *Last Days of the Turbins*, 178–79; visit with Stanislavski, 202–05; *Romeo and Juliet*, 216–17; review of, in *Romeo and Juliet*, 217–18; *A Tale of Two Cities*, 219–26; development of one-woman show (The Arc of the Theatre), 229–38, 288; reviews of, in one-woman show, 234–35; *Yes My Darling Daughter*, 259; recording of "The Murder of Lidice," 258–259; radio performance of *The Trojan Women*, 256; *Gloriana*, 259; *Queen of the Mob*, 261–63; auditions for *For Whom the Bell Tolls*, 267; *A Barber Had Two Sons*, 270; *The Wind is Ninety*, 270–71; *Temper the Wind*, 271; *The Carefree Tree*, 273–275; retirement, 275–77; *Dear Audience*, 277–78; review of *Dear Audience*, 278; *Thunder to the Sun*, 277–278; *Prometheus Bound*, 286; *Jane Eyre*, 286, *I Remember Mama*, 286, 289; *The Corn Is Green*, 287–88; *Dinner at Eight*, 291–93; election to Actors' Equity Council, 298–99; awarded ANTA gold medal, 299; *Madwoman of Chaillot*, 300

Ziolkowski (sculptor), 237

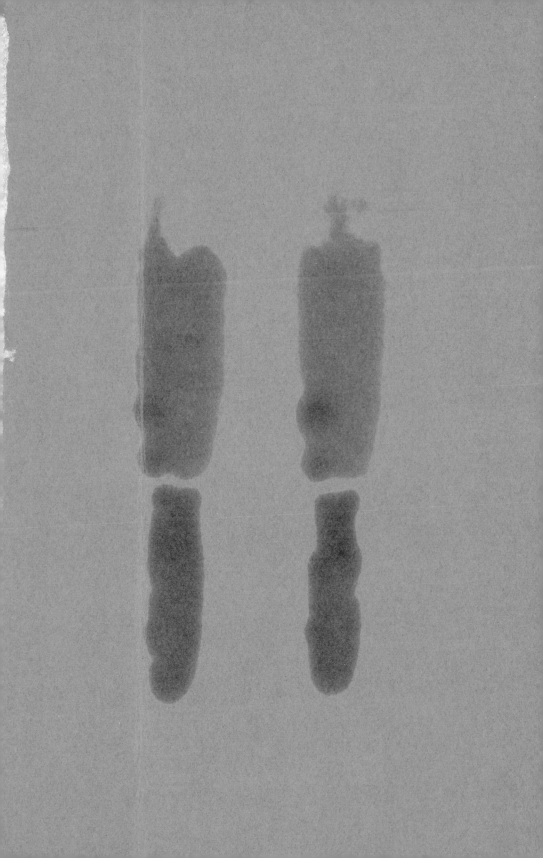

DATE DUE

GAYLORD   PRINTED IN U.S.A.